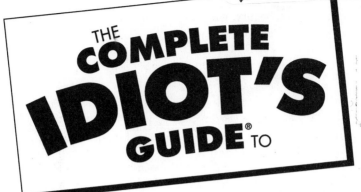

THE
COMPLETE
IDIOT'S
GUIDE® TO

Sexual Health and Fitness

by Kate Bracy, R.N., M.S., N.P.
with Kathyrn Arendt, M.D. and
David Winchester, M.D., F.A.C.S.

ALPHA

A member of Penuin Group (USA) Inc.

To my parents, who smooched in the kitchen

ALPHA BOOKS

Published by the Penguin Group

Penguin Group (USA) Inc., 375 Hudson Street, New York, New York 10014, USA

Penguin Group (Canada), 90 Eglinton Avenue East, Suite 700, Toronto, Ontario M4P 2Y3, Canada (a division of Pearson Penguin Canada Inc.)

Penguin Books Ltd., 80 Strand, London WC2R 0RL, England

Penguin Ireland, 25 St. Stephen's Green, Dublin 2, Ireland (a division of Penguin Books Ltd.)

Penguin Group (Australia), 250 Camberwell Road, Camberwell, Victoria 3124, Australia (a division of Pearson Australia Group Pty. Ltd.)

Penguin Books India Pvt. Ltd., 11 Community Centre, Panchsheel Park, New Delhi—110 017, India

Penguin Group (NZ), 67 Apollo Drive, Rosedale, North Shore, Auckland 1311, New Zealand (a division of Pearson New Zealand Ltd.)

Penguin Books (South Africa) (Pty.) Ltd., 24 Sturdee Avenue, Rosebank, Johannesburg 2196, South Africa

Penguin Books Ltd., Registered Offices: 80 Strand, London WC2R 0RL, England

Copyright © 2008 by Kate Bracy

International Standard Book Number: 978-1-59257-766-8
Library of Congress Catalog Card Number: 2008920998

10   09   08   8   7   6   5   4   3   2   1

Interpretation of the printing code: The rightmost number of the first series of numbers is the year of the book's printing; the rightmost number of the second series of numbers is the number of the book's printing. For example, a printing code of 08-1 shows that the first printing occurred in 2008.

Printed in the United States of America

Note: This publication contains the opinions and ideas of its author. It is intended to provide helpful and informative material on the subject matter covered. It is sold with the understanding that the author and publisher are not engaged in rendering professional services in the book. If the reader requires personal assistance or advice, a competent professional should be consulted.

The author and publisher specifically disclaim any responsibility for any liability, loss, or risk, personal or otherwise, which is incurred as a consequence, directly or indirectly, of the use and application of any of the contents of this book.

Most Alpha books are available at special quantity discounts for bulk purchases for sales promotions, premiums, fund-raising, or educational use. Special books, or book excerpts, can also be created to fit specific needs.

For details, write: Special Markets, Alpha Books, 375 Hudson Street, New York, NY 10014.

Publisher: *Marie Butler-Knight*
Editorial Director: *Mike Sanders*
Senior Managing Editor: *Billy Fields*
Senior Acquisitions Editor: *Paul Dinas*
Development Editor: *Michael Thomas*
Senior Production Editor: *Janette Lynn*

Copy Editor: *Amy Lepore*
Cartoonist: *Steve Barr*
Cover Designer: *Bill Thomas*
Book Designer: *Trina Wurst*
Indexer: *Tonya Heard*
Layout: *Chad Dressler*
Proofreader: *Mary Hunt*

Contents at a Glance

Contents

Introduction

Sex is a topic that everyone seems to know about. Or thinks they do. Or at least pretends to. There are manuals telling you how to do it in every imaginable position and every room in the house. There are books to help you understand how it works, why it doesn't, and where to get help when you can't figure it out. There are relationship books, health books, and books about sexy diets or magic pills that make you the perfect lover. This book is not any of these things.

This is a book about your sexual health and your sexual fitness. It explores how to take care of your body and mind so that you can enjoy sex for your whole life, in your favorite ways. It will give you hints and information for getting and staying healthy enough to participate fully in the sex life you want.

What You'll Find in This Book

The Complete Idiot's Guide to Sexual Health and Fitness is divided into five parts:

Part 1, "Understanding Sexual Health and Fitness," is an overview of what we mean by those terms. Everyone wants to be healthy and fit, but what does it mean to be *sexually* healthy and fit? See how you can connect the dots between a healthy body and a satisfying sex life. Check out some of the myths that might still have you fooled, and discover why emotional balance is essential to your sexual health.

Part 2, "Your Body and Sex," reminds you that tending to your body's needs is the foundation for sexual health.

It's true that advice on diet and exercise is not news, but have you considered the effect that these everyday good habits might have on your sexual health and fitness? Sometimes it isn't until you start noticing the effects of *bad* habits that you begin to take an interest in undoing some of the damage.

Understanding this early can help you prevent sexual problems altogether or can intervene while there is still time. Here's how to build a sexually healthy body and how to maintain that sexual fitness through the years.

Part 3, "It's All in Your Mind," explores the ways in which your mind can affect your sexual health. Learn how to use it to your advantage in the search for a healthy, balanced sex life. No doubt about it, your mind is the most powerful tool you have to keep yourself sexually healthy and fit.

Part 4, "Protecting Yourself," is the caution light at your sexual intersection. As much fun as sex is, it also carries some responsibility and risk. Having the facts about sexually transmitted disease, contraception, and risky sex will help you protect yourself and your sexual health so that you can stay well, play fair, and stay in the game for a long, long time.

Part 5, "Challenges and Solutions," helps you understand sexual problems that arise. The road to sexual health and fitness is not without its detours and rough patches. There are plenty of challenges and barriers that interfere with healthy sexuality—maybe you are facing one now. Some challenges you will take in stride, but some require your full attention and maybe even professional help. Whether the problems are medical, hormonal, or emotional, there are ways to manage them that will improve your sex life and put you on a healthier path.

Along the Way

The Complete Idiot's Guide to Sexual Health and Fitness includes additional details, information, advice, and suggestions for being sexually healthy and fit. They are highlighted in sidebar boxes like these:

def•i•ni•tion
> This sidebar is where you'll find definitions of words and terms that may not be explained in the text.

Try This!
> When you are trying to stay sexually healthy, sometimes the devil is in the details. Here is where you will find ideas and suggestions for putting information into action.

Beyond the Basics
> Sometimes additional facts, statistics, and informational tidbits can really make you think. Find them here.

Proceed with Caution
> Look in these sidebars for warnings and advice about things that could put your sexual health at risk.

Acknowledgments

No book ever comes to life without the efforts of many. I want to thank Andrea Hurst, my diligent, compassionate agent, for connecting me to this project. I am grateful to editor Paul Dinas for his patient and steady vision for the book. A special appreciation for my tech reviewers Kathy Arendt and Dave Winchester—not only clinically sound medical professionals, but wonderful, generous people to boot. Thanks to my writing friends in Minnesota and on Whidbey Island, all of whom know what it is to type a manuscript until you can't see straight.

Special thanks to my family. To Dad, who fixed his own dinner and took care of the pets. Thanks to daughters Lynne and Micah, whose independence and cheerleading gave me freedom and energy. And to Anne, who is my first, best, and most unwavering supporter. I love you all.

Special Thanks to the Technical Reviewers

The Complete Idiot's Guide to Sexual Health and Fitness was reviewed by two experts who double-checked the accuracy of what you'll learn here, to help us ensure that this book gives you everything you need to know about sexual health and fitness. Special thanks are extended to Kathyrn Arendt, M.D., and David Winchester, M.D., F.A.C.S.

Kathryn Arendt is an urogynecologist and pelvic reconstructive surgeon. She specializes in vaginal reconstruction and minimally invasive surgery. Kathryn is passionate about empowering women to lead healthier and more active lives through education and a holistic approach to women's health and wellness. She is in private practice in the Seattle area where she lives with her husband and three sons.

David Winchester is a genito-urinary surgeon specializing in minimally invasive surgery and male health and wellness. He is a native of Portland, where he is in private practice. He leads a quiet life with his wife, four children, and a very peculiar dog.

Trademarks

All terms mentioned in this book that are known to be or are suspected of being trademarks or service marks have been appropriately capitalized. Alpha Books and Penguin Group (USA) Inc. cannot attest to the accuracy of this information. Use of a term in this book should not be regarded as affecting the validity of any trademark or service mark.

Part 1

Understanding Sexual Health and Fitness

Sexual health is a combination of ingredients that adds up to satisfying and positive sexual experiences—for you *and* your partner. Sexual fitness is about having the ongoing ability to enjoy sex the way you want, for as long as you like, with the person(s) you are attracted to.

You may be operating with some bad information or wrong ideas about what is sexually healthy. There are sexual myths that can sidetrack and distract you from finding the balance in your sex life. And speaking of balance, don't underestimate the role of emotions in your sexual health and fitness. Being sexually healthy includes being *emotionally* healthy about sex and sexuality.

YOU'VE GOT TO ADMIRE SALLY. SHE CERTAINLY SEEMS TO HAVE A HEALTHY SEXUAL APPETITE!

BARR

What Is Sexual Health and Fitness?

In This Chapter

♦ The meaning of "sexual health" and "sexual fitness"

♦ The first steps toward being sexually healthy

♦ Keeping yourself motivated

♦ Rewarding yourself for becoming sexually fit

If you browse the self-help section of any bookstore, you will find plenty of books to help you out with your sex life. There are books on technique, on choosing the right partner, on spicing up the bedroom, and on when you should, when you shouldn't, and how to tell the difference. But seldom do they spend much time on how to stay healthy while you pursue sexual connections or how to be fit enough to thoroughly enjoy those connections. You don't have to be a "world-class" athlete to be sexually fit, and even small improvements will have very tangible rewards.

This book takes a closer look at both of these aspects of your sexuality—how to stay sexually healthy and how to be sexually fit. It's not focused on "how to," or "with whom," or even "why" you have the sexual relationships you do, but on becoming well enough to participate fully in the sex life you want.

As you read through this book, or parts of this book, give some thought to what "the sex life you want" means to you. Some people have very little sexual activity in their lives, and that is fine and comfortable for them. Some have a great deal of sexual activity, and that suits them, too. It's when you are feeling out of balance—frustrated, disconnected, or pressured by your sex life—that you might want to rethink whether you are having the kind of sex you want, with the person(s) you want, as often as you want. Deciding where you are on that continuum will help you determine how *you* can stay sexually healthy and what it takes to be fit enough to engage in the sexual activities that you enjoy.

Sexual Health

When you hear the term *sexual health*, what do you think of? Healthy, strong erections? Being able to lubricate enough to enjoy sex? Do you think of avoiding sexually transmitted diseases? Or would you be puzzled and wonder what it means?

def•i•ni•tion

> **Sexual health** refers to your body and body tissues being in good physical shape and functioning as they are designed and intended to, particularly those areas of the body involved in sexual activity.

Sexual health includes everything it takes to keep you vigorous enough to desire and benefit from sex. And as you might guess, it is closely linked with general physical health. For some people sexual health is a motivator for general physical health, and for some it is a side benefit of being healthy. But it will be a little different for each person, depending on what level of health is possible, what sort of sex life he or she wants, and what the particular barriers are for that person.

Is Everything in Working Order?

The term "sexual health," as we use it in this book, implies that all your sexual parts are functional and ready for action. This includes your genitals, of course, but also other parts of your physical body through which you experience sexual pleasure. When you think about it, what doesn't that include? Sexual activity is a full-body experience, and it requires that your body is tuned up and ready to roll.

For women, being sexually healthy means that your vagina is healthy, lubricates well, responds to sexual stimuli, expands readily, and registers pleasure. It also means that your skin, breasts, and nipples react to touch and that this touch triggers secretion of oxytocin and other neurochemicals that cue the rest of your body to relax and respond.

But beyond the areas of the body that women usually associate with sexual activity, you also want your skin to register every touch that it receives. If you have areas that are particularly sensitive or arousing—your ears? your feet? your abdomen?—you want all the connections in place for them to join in the game.

For men, sexual health goes well beyond having a working penis. While that is, of course, important, there is so much more to having a healthy body, ready for sexual enjoyment. Your circulation has to be top notch for achieving a good erection; your level of testosterone needs to be high enough to sustain sexual desire; your emotional state has to be relaxed enough that you are really present to your partner. These things combined let you ride the wave of desire.

For both men and women, sexual health also depends on your own personal "chemistry" being in balance. Invisible to you, your body is constantly using a complicated mixture of biochemical processes. Many of these require the right hormone balance, adequate production of the right *neurotransmitters*, and a metabolism that makes it all run smoothly. Feeling sexually aroused and acting on it requires all these elements being in order, and *that* requires a healthy body to work with.

When the biochemistry of your body is out of whack, you can't move as well, perceive as well, or feel emotionally stable. Being sexually healthy includes tending to your body in a way that helps it stay in chemical balance.

def•i•ni•tion

A **neurotransmitter** is a chemical that carries a message from a nerve cell to another cell. Neurotransmitters help your brain tell your body what to do and help you interpret sensory messages like pleasure and pain.

More Than Just "STD Free"

When you think of being sexually healthy, you probably first think about sexually transmitted diseases (STDs), also called sexually transmitted infections (STIs). Or more accurately, you think about the lack of these. But being healthy is much more than just not having infections.

Sexual health means making choices that help your body have the best function possible and that are healthy for you, with your own unique needs and limitations. For example, is it possible for someone with a herpes infection (which cannot be cured but can be treated) to be sexually healthy? The answer is "yes and no." That person will always have the herpes virus in his or her body, but he or she can make good choices that keep the infection as quiet as possible, prevent spreading it to partners, and allow the person to explore and enjoy his or her sex life.

As you learn about sexual health, think about what that term means to you. Do you have a chronic sexually transmitted infection? Do you have limitations or disabilities that rule out certain sexual activities? Do you take medications that interfere with your sexual response? If so, then sexual health will be different for you than for someone who does not have these challenges.

Body-Mind-Feelings: It All Adds Up

It would be impossible to separate sexual health from emotional health or from your state of mind. Your body responds to what you think, what your mood is, and how you perceive your situation. What one person considers exciting and arousing, another may consider frightening or distasteful. Sexual health takes into account how you feel, what you think, and what sex means to you.

In later chapters, we will explore how you can adjust your state of mind, your emotions, and your thoughts in order to be and feel sexually healthy. Sexual pleasure is not a simple or universal experience. It will be unique to your personal desires, values, understanding, and experience. Sexual health is unique to each person, and you will have the chance to discover exactly what it means to you.

Beyond the Basics _____

The World Health Organization takes a very broad view of sexual health. According to that group, sexual health is "a state of physical, emotional, mental, and social well-being in relation to sexuality; it is not merely the absence of disease, dysfunction, or infirmity. Sexual health requires a positive and respectful approach to sexuality and sexual relationships, as well as the possibility of having pleasurable and safe sexual experiences, free of coercion, discrimination, and violence. For sexual health to be attained and maintained, the sexual rights of all persons must be respected, protected, and fulfilled."

You can't separate sexual health from your general well-being. If your lungs are congested and you are thrown into a coughing fit at a critical moment, it can be a definite mood breaker. If you are too tired to enjoy your partner's overtures, it can be a negative experience for both of you. So sexual health encompasses, or at least depends on, your general health. With that said, this book will look at specific ways of tending to your general well-being that contribute to your sexual health.

Sexual Fitness

Sexual fitness is a matter of your body being in good condition for sexual activity. You may have heard it in the context of men's health because it involves training and conditioning your body so that it is ready for sex. But it is not just a man's issue. Women want to be sexually fit, too, and there are some approaches to sexual fitness that will work better for women, and some that will work better for men.

def•i•ni•tion _____
Sexual fitness is the state of being physically and emotionally sound, adapted, and ready for sexual activity. A sexually fit person is prepared and in condition to enjoy the types of sexual activity that he or she finds satisfying.

Healthy Enough to Do What You Like

Sexual fitness is about being ready and in good condition. The next question to ask yourself is: Ready to do what?

What sexual activity is important to you? Is *any* sexual activity important to you? Maybe you are already fit for the sex that matters to you. Or maybe you want to have more sexual fun, but you tire easily or can't seem to make love without having pain or hurting yourself. It's time to do a little sexual fitness inventory and discover what might help.

Try This! _____

Ask yourself these five questions when making your plan for sexual fitness: What sexual activities do I most enjoy?

- Which of these activities am I *not* in shape for?
- How much do I want to be able to enjoy these activities?
- What three changes could I make to get ready for these activities?
- What do I need to get started with these three changes?

Take a look at your answers and decide what your next step is for becoming sexually fit. Whether you decided you need running shoes or an attitude adjustment, make a date with yourself to get started.

What in your life keeps you from becoming sexually fit? Are you embarrassed to think about fitness as it relates to sexual activity? Do you resist getting fit in general? Or have you just never thought about how being fit could affect your sex life?

Whatever your reasons, this book will invite you to think about not only why you would want to be sexually fit, but whether and how it would enhance your life. If you have a partner, talk to him or her about getting sexually fit together as a way of getting closer and enjoying each other.

Does Your Lifestyle Support Sexual Fitness?

Do you live a life that supports you in staying sexually fit? If you make a choice to improve your sexual fitness, will any changes be easily sustained with your current lifestyle? For starters, ask yourself these questions:

- Do I *want* to be sexually fit?
- Am I willing to change the way I take care of my body?

◆ Am I willing to eat differently to improve my health and sex life?

◆ Will I move more if it improves my ability to enjoy sexual activity?

◆ Am I willing to look at the stressors in my life to understand their impact on my sexual enjoyment?

If your answer to these questions is "yes," then you are in a great place to start your plan to be sexually healthy and fit.

When you are busy living your hectic life, it is easy for bad health habits to sneak up on you. Stress and too little time usually add up to forgetting about your body and health until one day you realize you are not enjoying your sexual self as much as you used to.

You can turn that around. Some attention to health basics and a conscious decision to improve your sexual health can make a big difference in your sexual capacity and your outlook in general. If inertia and inattention have put your love life on the back burner, now is a great time to start cooking again.

Proceed with Caution _____

This book offers many suggestions and opportunities that you can use for improving your overall sexual health and fitness. It is intended as a guide for adults and should not be interpreted in any way as permission to engage in sexual activities that exploit vulnerable persons. It assumes consenting adults in every sexual situation and should not be used to explore criminal or manipulative sexual activities.

Sexual fitness implies a well-functioning body and an emotionally healthy attitude toward your sexuality. It's up to you to decide how fit is "fit enough" to enjoy sex as you'd like to, and it's your decision whether this is important enough in your life to make the effort.

Staying Fit Once You Get There

It's one thing to tone up your muscles and build your aerobic capacity to the point where you have good stamina in bed. It's quite another to maintain a level of fitness that supports an ongoing enjoyment of your sex life. And while losing a few pounds may be an effort, keeping them off requires ongoing vigilance.

Rather than thinking of sexual fitness as a destination, it works a lot better to see it as a lifelong journey to your best sexual self. Making changes to become fit is best seen as making permanent changes that ensure your pleasure for years to come. Once you fold exercise and good diet habits into your daily routine, why not consider them decisions for lifelong sexual health?

It's important as you make changes to support your sexual well-being that you keep yourself motivated. Since changes are usually incremental, you will need to be your own best cheerleader from the sidelines. Think ahead of time about what rewards and incentives you want to build into your plan. While getting sexually fit is a reward itself, it helps during those discouraged moments if you are working toward something tangible. Set up little "congratulatory markers" along the way to keep you upbeat and interested in your own progress.

Here are some ideas for rewarding yourself for making sexually healthy decisions:

- Tell your partner that you are trying to become sexually fit so you can enjoy him or her more and ask him or her to join you in a specific activity.

- Women, take yourself (or go with your partner) to a nice lingerie store and buy one item that makes you feel attractive.

- Men, get tickets to a sports event, concert, or cultural event at least three weeks away and do something good for your sexual health every day between now and then.

- Treat yourself to a class in something you've wanted to explore or get better at.

- Invite your partner or a new date to do something that is both physical and fun: bike riding, bowling, dancing, a charity walk, or something else that you can enjoy together while getting fit.

- When you reach a fitness goal, treat your body to a sensual experience like a facial (yes, men and women), a pedicure, a long bath with no interruptions, a spa day, or a massage.

- Get clothing or equipment that supports your ongoing sexual fitness: running shoes, a yoga mat, or a sports bra.

- Plan a weekend with your partner that combines activity in and out of bed.

After you've made a list of possible rewards for your progress, create a chart listing your personal sexual fitness goals on the left and the appropriate reward on the right. If you are doing this sexual fitness plan for and with a partner, ask him or her to make a similar plan and share them with one another.

Remember to make your goals in tiny increments and after reading some of the chapters that describe what you can do to achieve sexual fitness. The rewards should be appropriate to the effort it takes to achieve those goals.

Recognize your victories as you reach them. If you haven't been walking more than from the car to the house, and you get to the point where you are walking a quarter of a mile on your lunch hour, remind yourself that this is progress. Give yourself a star in your journal or your calendar and tell yourself that you are building stamina for your next date.

Do what you can to "disappointment proof" your plan. Build in flexibility, and if you can't get out one day to walk, then take the stairs at work. Anything that takes you even a tiny step closer to fitness is another block in your sexual fitness foundation. After a while, you will notice that you are moving more and liking it. This will translate into your self-image and into your sexual self-image as well.

Notice as you go along which things are in your control and which ones aren't, and put your attention on the things that are. You can't control the weather, but you can dress for it. You may not be able to afford a gym membership, but you can probably spring for some dumbbells that will fit under the bed. Focus on what you can do, and don't be discouraged by what you aren't able to control.

With the right attitude and some persistence, you will be able to make progress toward your sexual fitness goals. Read through the chapters in this book that apply to the areas you need most to improve your sexual health. Success breeds success, so don't be surprised when your effort gets you noticed by just the person with whom you'd like to explore your sexual fitness!

The Least You Need to Know

◆ Even if all your "sexual parts" are in working order, being more sexually healthy and fit can lead to more satisfying sex.

◆ Your emotional makeup has a big impact on your sexual health.

◆ Finding unique ways to motivate yourself and then rewarding those efforts will pay off in and out of the bedroom.

◆ Attitude and persistence are your best buddies when you are on the road to sexual fitness.

Sexual Myths

In This Chapter

- ◆ Beauty myths you can let go
- ◆ Is the myth of "in love" worth chasing?
- ◆ Are there *any* real aphrodisiacs?
- ◆ Sexual myths that are dangerous
- ◆ At what age do you have to give up on sex?

Your sexual health and fitness are too important to put at the mercy of sexual myths. Your self-perception and your ideas about what enhances sexual health—and what doesn't—all influence your sexual well-being in both obvious and subtle ways. This chapter examines some of the myths by which you may be living your sexual life so that you can let go of the mythology and enjoy the reality.

If I'm Not Gorgeous, I'm Not Sexy

We are a culture that worships physical beauty. We are not alone in history for that, but it is an obsession that blinds us to qualities that are attractive in a much more far-reaching way. And despite the media norms of impossible beauty, there is good news about what we truly consider to be attractive and "sexy."

Billboards and Centerfolds

As much as we tout the long-legged, trim-bodied models that we see in billboards and magazines, that sort of beauty is not the final decider of our preferences. There have been numerous studies to determine what men and women find initially attractive. Very few, however, have looked at what we find attractive over time or in addition to physical looks.

In fact, our ideas about a person's attractiveness are profoundly influenced by that person's personality and character traits. Being attracted to someone is a complicated combination of conscious and unconscious observations.

One study demonstrated this by showing high school pictures to people who did, and people who did not, know the people in the pictures. There was a high correlation between certain traits—like cooperation, dependability, courage, diligence, and intelligence—and finding the person to be attractive. Those who were familiar with the subject of the photograph were strongly influenced by their opinions of the person's behavior when rating them as attractive or sexy. If they knew and liked the person, they were much more likely to rate them as attractive. Those who did not know the photo subjects, and had a more "objective" rating of their attractiveness, tended to rate very highly some who were rated much lower by people who knew them. The overall assessment of beauty is, in the end, in the mind of the beholder.

Confidence Is Sexy

Another quality that both men and women find sexy is confidence. Not overconfidence, but that quality of being comfortable with one's sexual desirability. One study demonstrated that "attractiveness ratings" increased by 50 percent when women walked with a confident hip sway and when men walked with a swagger in their shoulders. Another study noted that decisions about attractiveness take into account numerous cues, including how the individual moves. People who move easily leave a youthful impression and are more attractive to others.

The "Right" Way to Look

While there is no "right" way to look—despite the stereotypes of being thin, blond, and well endowed—the best look for you is one that emphasizes your most attractive qualities. If those qualities are physical, they will attract a certain sort of attention. If they are qualities of character and personality, they will attract a deeper, more longstanding interest.

Try This!

Physical symmetry, youthful skin, hair, and body type are attractive initially, but they are trumped by kindness and generosity of spirit in the long run. Rather than copying a standard that doesn't suit your own strengths, do an inventory of what you think are your most appealing characteristics and then dress and behave to highlight them. You can't go wrong being yourself since you will attract people interested in exactly that.

Size Matters

The age-old debate about whether "size matters" is partly myth and partly based in truth. The bottom line to the question of whether size matters is: It depends. It depends on who is doing the sizing up, how far from the average the measurement is, and what other factors the "measurer" is allowed to consider.

In general, when considering only physical factors, women are seen as most attractive if they have a waist/hip ratio of about .7—small waist, larger hips. Men are attractive if they have a "V-shaped" torso and a waist/hip ratio of .9—small waist and hips. Considering physical attributes alone, men tend to like women to have larger breasts, and women tend to prefer muscular men. Both of those preferences, though, seem more likely to hold true for a sexual hook-up than for a long-term, committed relationship.

What the Women Say

Of course, the "size matters" myth is discussed most often with regard to penis size. Only about half of men are satisfied with their penis size.

Beyond the Basics _____

Average penis size is hard to pin down. Various studies use different measures and describe penises in various stages of arousal. Probably the most reliable information is that the average penis size for American men is 5.5 inches when erect. (Studies that rely on self-reporting tend to average erect penis size at about 6.2 inches. Draw your own conclusions.)

And if half of men are dissatisfied with their penis size, women have no such dilemma. Eighty-five percent of women report being satisfied with their partner's penis size. In most studies that query women about their partner's penis size, women do not seem to care about length in the least, but they do state a preference for larger circumference, if given the choice. Most women say that other characteristics, such as how their partners treat them and how their partners try to please them during sex, are far more important than any measurement.

What the Men Say

While men are busy worrying needlessly about how long their penises are, women are obsessing about their breasts. Too small, too large, too saggy. They buy bras and creams and surgery to remedy their "inadequate" breasts. Add to that women's conviction that they need to be extremely slim to be attractive, and you have a recipe for angst.

Men are not as interested in thinness as women think they are. In studies, women choose slimmer than average as the body build they think men would prefer. But in fact, men chose average body builds and not the slimmest ones. Other studies have shown that men prefer slim women with large breasts if they are thinking only of a sexual liaison, but when choosing someone as a wife or committed partner, men tend to choose a more average build and take many other factors into consideration.

How to Measure Up

In many studies, the results point to being "average" as the road to attractiveness. Not above average, not below average, but average. Both men and women prefer symmetrical features and sexual stereotypes ("feminine" body type for women, "masculine" body type for men) when speaking strictly of physical, sexual attractiveness. But sexual health encompasses long-term connection as well as initial attraction, and long-term attractiveness is enormously dependent on personality and character traits.

Measuring up, for the vast majority of people, is not a matter of reaching a certain number of inches. It includes a combination of the following:

◆ Being yourself

◆ Staying within a moderate body range

◆ Having symmetrical features

◆ Moving well

◆ Standing tall

◆ Showing confidence

Stop measuring yourself against some arbitrary standard. If you work toward a moderate body appearance and put energy into your good *internal* qualities, you will discover how unimportant the size of any one thing (or two things) is in the big picture.

Unless I'm in Love, Sex Is Out

As Americans, we are in love with being in love. We see it as a prerequisite for marriage, commitment, and often for sex. The "love" factor is explored in later chapters, but the myth that "in love" is the marker for any sort of physical connection will probably limit you to a single partner in your lifetime. If that partner turns out to be the one you truly want to spend your life with, waiting for love to hit can be a sexually healthy choice.

But for most people, being "in love" may or may not ever happen. And holding it as the standard will make you unavailable to many satisfying and enriching relationships along the way. Love and caring are not always the equivalent of being "in love," and you can have a fulfilling sex life with and without experiencing romantic versions of being "in love."

Love, Lust, or Both

Men and women do seem to differ on the necessity of deep caring as a prerequisite for a sexual connection. Research confirms common beliefs about these differences. Men are more likely to agree to a sexual encounter with a woman they have never met before. Women are more likely to connect sexually only after they have a sense of whether they "like" a man, and many want to "love" him before agreeing to sex. These are generalities, of course, and there are men and women on both sides of this equation, but studies do seem to point to male and female differences.

Mr. Right, or Mr. Right Now?

The most sexually healthy behavior for you is the one that is in sync with your values, your goals, and your long-term health. If you have a high libido and you have safe, honest sexual relationships, you can learn a lot about what you want in a life partner while enjoying your sexual side.

If genuine caring and real bonding are your biggest turn-ons, then you will want to wait until you find a partner to whom you feel that attraction before heading for the bedroom. There are many right ways to have healthy sexual connections, and being "in love" is only one of the ways to create them.

What Your Body Can Tell You

If you are in a state of indecision or anxiety about your sex life, it may help to tune in to what your body tells you. There are many sensual ways to experience the world without having a sexual relationship with someone else. If you are trying to sort out whether you want or need a love relationship before you have a sexual one, pay attention to your body. Notice what seems to provoke your desires, and notice how you respond to that. Use a journal or make daily notes on your computer to keep track of what you are feeling and thinking.

Are you generally healthy? Do you feel pain in your body? Are you getting every virus and bacteria that comes along? These are messages from your body about your current choices. Do you feel uncomfortable when you are with a partner? How about when you are not with a partner?

How do you feel after sex? Satisfied? Guilty? In pain? Only you can sort through all the sexual choices and decide which one suits your values and temperament. Hearing your body's signals on this matter can be very educational. If you notice physical discomforts of any kind related to sexual activity, talk it over with your medical provider and then with a counselor if there are no physical causes. Let your body have a word with you, and listen to what it is saying.

There Should Be Fireworks Every Time

If you watch popular movies, read novels, or see pornography, you may be under the impression that every orgasm has to be earth shattering. We have idealized notions about what sex is and should be. Since we aren't usually privy to others' everyday sexual realities, and since we don't usually ask other people about this, we go along with our outsized expectations, thinking we are missing the boat.

This isn't to say that you shouldn't expect to have a satisfying sex life or that you shouldn't want it to feel really good. But every sexual encounter is its own event, and they won't all be mountaintop experiences.

What Is "Good" Sex?

"Good sex" is, of course, subjective. But defining it for yourself is one of the tasks of creating a satisfying sex life and assuring your sexual health. And what you consider "good" changes over your lifetime. Men and women sometimes have different criteria for "good" in the bedroom, but not as different as you might think. Men look forward to cuddling and women appreciate orgasm, but not always in the same proportions.

Are You Setting the Bar Too High?

You and your partner can set the standard by defining "good sex" for yourselves. Sex that leaves you satisfied, feeling emotionally good about yourself, and with no damage to your body is a place to start the discussion. How to get there, and finding the specific details, is part of the fun. Knowing what the other person likes and considers exciting lets you create your own type of fireworks, and you can ignore the movie versions in favor of your own.

Aphrodisiacs

Are there any true aphrodisiacs? If you are looking for a magic potion that will make your dream date fall instantly in love with you, you'll probably find that the research doesn't support it. But it's hard to shake the hope that there might be some magic that will turn you—or your partner—into the perfect lover.

What qualifies as an aphrodisiac? For the purposes of this book, an aphrodisiac is any substance used to enhance or improve sexual desire or performance. The choices fall roughly into two categories: sensory enhancers that arouse and intensify sexual desire, and ingestible substances that one can consume to increase sexual desire or performance. Most so-called aphrodisiacs fall into one of these two categories.

Magic or Science?

Increasing your sexual arousal or potency (or your partner's) has been a dream for centuries. As with the diet industry, people are willing to pay to get a "magic" pill/drink/supplement/food that will painlessly grant their wish—in this case, to turn themselves (or their partner) into the best lover in the world. Even smart people fall for this—we love to dream.

There are lots of choices to pursue this dream. One line of purported aphrodisiacs is those that suggest sexual intention or that appeal to a person's associations with sex. These sensory triggers are sometimes strategically (or hilariously) used to evoke a sexual response. Foods that resemble human anatomy (think bananas, oysters, eggplant, avocado, figs, raspberries, and chocolate chips) can be prepared, served, or eaten to suggest the much hoped for event. A banana split can be a preview to the perfect evening's end. A carefully prepared and sensuously served mushroom dish can evoke the musky smells of sex.

Other types of sensory enhancers are perfumes, body lotions, photographs, music, and candy. Anything that arouses the senses while promoting relaxation can arouse sexual interest. These "aphrodisiacs" work at a subconscious level to remind, suggest, evoke, and encourage a person to turn his or her mind and body toward a sexual theme.

Beyond the Basics _____

One study seems to confirm that smells can actually heighten arousal—and it's not the smells you might expect. The Smell and Taste Treatment and Research Foundation tested many smells for their effect on penile blood flow. Combination smells were most powerful, with the combinations of lavender and pumpkin pie, and licorice and doughnuts having the two strongest impacts on male arousal. Next time you are having your guy over for a romantic evening, dab a little lavender behind your ears and toss a pumpkin pie in the oven. Couldn't hurt. Might help!

Then there are the ingestibles—food, drink, drugs, and supplements that claim to arouse desire or enhance performance.

You have many choices for what you can ingest to chase your "perfect lover" dream. There are, for starters, the foods. Among the foods suggested through the centuries for increasing sexual arousal and performance are the following:

◆ Spices and flavorings like ginger, vanilla, garlic, nutmeg, basil, coriander, fennel, and mustard

◆ Fruits such as bananas, figs, raspberries, strawberries, and pineapple

◆ Many vegetables, including asparagus, arugula, avocado, broccoli rabe (a broccoli-like plant with more pungent taste), and carrots

◆ Stimulant foods such as coffee and chocolate

◆ Pine nuts, walnuts, almonds

◆ Honey and truffles

Although many of these foods do have physiologic effects such as improving circulation or acting as plant estrogens, none have actually shown the capacity to improve either libido or sexual performance.

Proceed with Caution _____

Cantharides are also called blister beetles and Spanish flies and can be ground to a fine powder, then mixed with other substances to make medicines. This Spanish Fly has long been a famous aphrodisiac, and a dangerous one. Even tiny doses of this powder can cause stomach upset, nausea, vomiting, bloody stools, severe pain with urination, swelling of the genitals, seizures, kidney damage and death. It works by irritating the urinary tract, and is illegal in the United States for human ingestion.

Herbs promising amorous excitement have been used for centuries. You may see ads for ginseng, horny goat weed, Yohimbe, and other herbs that guarantee sexual arousal or stamina. And while many herbs may act as stimulants, urinary irritants, or erectile aids, they are also known to be toxic to your kidney or liver. Herbs are strong medicine and being "natural" does not make them harmless.

Many drugs, legal and illegal, have a reputation for enhancing sexual function. Alcohol and marijuana in small doses foster relaxation and reduce inhibitions. But in larger doses, these drugs can impair your sexual function.

Illegal stimulants, such as cocaine and methamphetamine, are well known as agents that make you hypersexual. The problem is that, while they may initially cause sexual excitement and arousal, they create a quick tolerance, and higher and higher doses are required to get the same euphoric effect. These high doses, in turn, can cause sexual dysfunction and problems with arousal and erection. Add to that a high risk of heart attack and stroke, and it is not the desirable sexual high you had in mind.

Finally, there are the legal prescription drugs for sexual arousal. Testosterone replacement is often a successful treatment for low libido and may be prescribed for people who have lowered testosterone due to age, menopause, or other causes. When low libido is the side effect of other medications, sometimes a dopamine agonist called pramipexole is prescribed to raise sexual response. (It is not approved for this purpose but may be prescribed for it.)

If you meet certain criteria, your medical provider may also prescribe a class of drugs called PDE-5 inhibitors to improve blood flow to the penis. These drugs (Viagra, Levitra, and Cialis) are about 70 percent effective for men. They are sometimes prescribed for women as well but have not had similar good results for women. This family of drugs has been very effective in improving erectile function, but there are serious side effects when they are taken with certain other medications, and not everyone is a good candidate. Although they do not directly raise sexual desire, they do improve sexual function in many men and therefore reduce anxiety, helping men relax and enjoy sexual activity more. These are such popular drugs that many questionable entrepreneurs are taking advantage of men's eagerness to have them. Beware of promises of cheap, generic, herbal, or mail-order versions of these medications. The knock-offs are not FDA approved and can be dangerous.

Ingested substances may or may not help increase your sexual desire and pleasure. Before you take *anything* that promises better sex, be sure that it is safe and that you are physically able to engage in the sexual activity you have in mind.

The Power of Suggestion

The most powerful aphrodisiac is your mind. After exploring and/or treating any physical problems you might have, the aphrodisiac effect of a good relationship and lowered stress can go miles toward increasing sexual desire. If you want your partner to be full of desire, then listen to what he or she finds desirable. Soft music and a backrub may go almost as far as Viagra in raising sexual enthusiasm.

Try This!

Plan an "aphrodisiac afternoon" with your partner. Set aside an afternoon when you can both be completely uninterrupted. Have a "planning meeting" a week or two before and describe for each other what is *really* sexy to you. Include foods, music, places, clothing, perfumes, sexual acts, erotic literature, or anything else that you want to name. Plan an afternoon of playful, sexy surprises where you both cater to each other's sexual desires. An afternoon of eating sexy foods, wearing sexy clothes, and doing things you find arousing will be a "pleasure memory" that all by itself may be an aphrodisiac in the future. Enjoy!

Just as "placebo effect" can be healing when you take a medication or treatment, there is a placebo effect from anything you perceive as an aphrodisiac: If you think it will make you sexy/desirous/aroused, it probably will. Your mind leads your body, and it can lead you in any direction you really want to go.

Your Own Recipe

Aphrodisiac foods, pills, lotions, and potions are, to a large extent, more psychology than magic. You can create your own glamour around sex and make it magical for you and your partner. And if you are part of a couple, it's a delightful way to maximize your enjoyment of each other. Dream up your own aphrodisiacs and make them sexy little "inside jokes" that only the two of you know and understand. If you have a code word like "vanilla" to remind you of one of your aphrodisiacs, you might find that just the casual mention of "vanilla pudding" during a conversation sends you both to the bedroom at the first opportunity. Find your own recipe for sensual play, and it will hold an aphrodisiac quality for you and your partner every time.

The Dangerous Myths

There are some sexual myths that we persistently believe, even against lots of evidence to the contrary. Sometimes it is because we want to believe them or because we don't want to think we are vulnerable. But believing these myths can make you take chances that will damage your sexual health and fitness.

STDs Happen to Other People

Sexually transmitted infections and diseases happen to every sort of person. They happen to law-abiding people and to criminals, to church-going types and to atheists. They happen to gay people, straight people, young people, old people, male people, and female people. If you are human and you have sexual relationships, you can get an STD.

Proceed with Caution _____

The fastest growing number of new *human immunodeficiency virus* (HIV) diagnoses is in people over the age of 50. If you think that being older makes you *less* likely to get HIV, think again. Women in particular are at risk because vaginal tissue may be dry and easily injured, allowing the virus to enter. Protect yourself at any age, and learn everything you can about your partners and their sexual history *before* you have sex with them. Get tested together—and protect each other.

When you hear about someone with a sexually transmitted infection, the first thing you probably do is find all the ways that person is not like you. You tell yourself, "I would never have sex with a stranger, or without a condom, or when I'm drinking," or whatever you think would protect you from the same fate. But unless you are abstaining completely from sexual contact, you are vulnerable to STDs. If you accept that there is a risk, you are more likely to protect yourself from that risk. If you don't accept that there is a risk, you may find yourself with a viral STD that will remind you forever. You only have to be wrong about it once to pay the price.

Once Is Okay

Somehow we think that if we only do something once, it isn't taking a risk. Just go home with a stranger this once, only have sex without a condom this one time, drink too much with someone I don't know well just for tonight. If something is dangerous for your sexual health, it is dangerous every time. And believing that just because you beat the odds once you will beat them every time is probably the most dangerous myth of all.

In adolescence, people begin to experience a sort of cognitive distortion called "magical thinking." As a teenager, you think that rules don't really apply to you and that you will magically escape the problems that others have. You build a little fairy tale about your own infallibility. Usually life straightens you out on this score, but sometimes people carry some version of this forward into adult life. (For example, "I don't have to wear a seatbelt because *I* won't get into an accident." Or "My house doesn't need insurance even though it's on a flood plain because this river hasn't flooded since I've lived here.") Staying in this magical thinking mode into adulthood, and in areas of sexual behavior, is the equivalent of believing that the tooth fairy will reward you for your lost teeth. One day you are going to wake up a really disappointed person with no quarter under your pillow and a new case of herpes.

Are Condoms Enough?

Condoms are a great start on protecting your sexual health, but they don't protect you from everything. You can still get pregnant or get a sexually transmitted infection from your partner if you use a condom. It reduces your chances of these things, but it doesn't eliminate your risk completely. If you think that using condoms is enough to protect you from every possible sexual bad outcome, you are headed for trouble.

In addition, you need to protect your sexual health by using condoms correctly and using them every time. Next you need to be familiar with your partner and with his or her sexual history. You must understand what types of sex are the highest risk and how to minimize your chances of getting into situations that will damage your sexual health. Condoms are good, but they don't replace common sense and caution when it comes to playing it safe.

How Safe Is "Safe Sex"?

"Safe sex" is a term often used to describe sex using barriers to prevent the spread of infection and disease. Most medical professionals and health educators, however, do not use the term "safe sex." There are very few sexual activities that don't have some downside, up to and including STDs and injury. Probably better terms are "safer sex," "cautious sex," "protected sex," or "risk-reduction sex." Calling it "safe" gives you a false sense that nothing bad can happen.

Germs Rule

People are tough, but germs are tougher. Microorganisms that cause disease, including the ones that cause sexually transmitted disease, adapt and spread more readily than we can devise ways to stop them. It's a mistake to think that because you are healthy, or because you have a great immune system, or because you are strong that you are impervious to these little guys. Germs are very good at their job, and no amount of healthy living on your part, no daily vitamins or muscle workout can equip your body to keep them from invading if you are sufficiently exposed. Your body will do a good job of fighting infection, but give it a break and protect yourself in every way you know how.

Balancing Caution and Spontaneity

Being careful with your body does not mean you have to be bored with your sex life. Of course, you want to have fun, enjoy sex with your partner, and pursue sex in ways that are satisfying. But keeping your body healthy enough to keep enjoying sex for the long run is also part of the deal. Be careful about how and with whom you have sex, and you will be enjoying it for your entire life, not just for one wild, careless night.

Sex Stops at 60

That we have to stop being sexual as we age is a myth worth leaving behind. As a culture that insists on youth, we seem to think that satisfying sex disappears when we start getting the senior discount. Not so. Luckily, satisfying sex continues past 60 and well into our later years.

Age and Your Sexual Health

As people live longer, healthier lives, it is clear that sex remains part of the picture. But there are some differences in your sexual health as you move past 40 and into middle age. It doesn't mean "sex is over," but it does mean that "sex is changing."

Beyond the Basics

People tend to become more satisfied with life in general as they age. The majority of people over the age of 40 rate sex as important to their quality of life—and men rate it more highly than women. The majority also say they are satisfied with their sex lives. Not too surprisingly, people who have a regular partner are more satisfied than those who are alone.

The first thing you may notice is that as levels of testosterone decline, both men and women have lower overall libido, and both take longer to arouse. Women are usually more philosophical about this shift since they have weathered so many hormone cycles and changes that they understand the waxing and waning of desire. Men, though, can be very distressed about the changes and might worry that it signals the end of their virility.

Pay attention to the levels of desire and arousability that you are experiencing. If you are finding that it takes more physical stimulation than it used to or that you are not so preoccupied with sex, these are normal changes that occur when testosterone levels drop naturally. If you are in a couple, you can see it as the opportunity to slow down your sexual pace and enjoy each other in new, sensual, relaxed ways.

Older women reported more satisfaction with their sex life once their partner was treated for erectile dysfunction. Their partner's enthusiasm and pleasure improved their own. When you are part of a couple, your partner's pleasure is part of *your* pleasure.

How Old Is Too Old?

There is no age at which a person is "too old" to have and enjoy sex. A better marker for sexual capacity is health. As long as your health supports having sex, you will probably want and enjoy it.

Try This!
Take the "two finger test." It's very simple and easy to do—take the first two fingers of your left hand and place them on the inside of your right wrist on the side of the thumb. If you can feel something wiggling around in there you're still young enough to be sexy.

Your biological age is a more important sexual marker than your chronological age. Your habits, lifestyle, genetic makeup, stress level, and diet all help to make you younger (or older) than your age in years. Here are a couple of websites where you can calculate your biological age and/or your life expectancy:

www.growyouthful.com/quiz.php

www.realage.com/index.aspx

moneycentral.msn.com/investor/calcs/n_expect/main.asp

preventdisease.com/healthtools/articles/health_age.html

As long as you are enjoying life, you can express your sexual side. At 40 or 70, sex is as good as you make it, or let it, be. Even if some of your function decreases, there are ways to play at any age.

Something to Look Forward To

If you have a positive and open outlook toward your sexual health and toward life in general, you can look forward to many years of satisfying sex. There are things you can do right now to extend your health and sexual well-being. Many couples report that sex gets better after 40, as stress about children, financial issues, and their relationship decreases.

People who seem to age into a healthy and satisfying sex life are those who ...

♦ Have a partner they love and respect.

♦ Take care of their health along the way (and deal with problems early).

♦ Adapt to their changing bodies with a calm, accepting attitude.

Knowing this, you can take steps today to prepare for a lifetime of enjoying your sexual self. Sort the myths from the realities, and base your sexual future on solid information.

The Least You Need to Know

♦ What people find attractive is based partly on physical characteristics but also on less tangible traits.

♦ Sexual attraction is part of the picture, but not as much so when choosing a steady mate.

♦ Listening to your body can help you make sexual decisions.

♦ There are things you can take to boost libido and sexual performance, but your mind is the strongest aphrodisiac.

♦ Believing only what you want to about sexual risks can ruin your sexual health and even your life.

♦ Your state of health is more important than your chronological age in determining how long you will enjoy sex.

Chapter 3

Emotional Balance and Sexual Health

In This Chapter

- ◆ How emotional and sexual health are connected
- ◆ The role of trust in sexual desire
- ◆ Anger and anxiety's impact on your sexual health
- ◆ How sadness and grief can sidetrack your sex life
- ◆ Managing feelings to protect your sexual health

Sexual health is more than a body that works plus being fit enough to enjoy it. It is also having enough emotional comfort to be truly present to sexual experiences. Sexual expression is a topic that brings up all kinds of emotional issues and responses. Your childhood ideas about what sex means, your adult desires and experiences, and cultural influences all add up to some emotionally charged reactions to becoming sexually fit.

Add to that your emotional state at any given time, as well as its impact on your sexual activity, and you can see that emotions are vital to a healthy sex life. If you can be consciously aware of these emotional responses, it will help you use that awareness to reach an emotionally healthy sexual outlook.

Emotional balance is a combination of your feelings, your beliefs, your state of mind, and your desires. Pulling these forces together can be an ongoing effort that brings you to a comfortable understanding of your sexual self.

Positive Feelings and Sexual Fitness

Your feelings have a tremendous impact on your sexual fitness. Once you have prepared your body for sexual activity by becoming healthy and physically equipped, your feelings come into play—literally. In order to enjoy sexual activities, your feelings have to be in a balanced place.

> **Beyond the Basics**
>
> People who tend to be ruled by emotional states are more likely to be carried away with their sexual relationships, sometimes to an unhealthy extent. Emotional balance for some may mean not letting your feelings overrule your judgment about what sex is right for you, with whom to have sex, and whether this sexual activity is in your best interest.

If you are a person who hides your feelings—even from yourself—then you may want to learn ways to check in with yourself with questions like, "What am I feeling right now?" or "How do I feel when I'm around this person?" The answers to these questions will help you decide whether sexual activity is good for you or bad for you in a given situation.

Good Feelings

Obviously sex feels good. The motto from the 1960s, "If it feels good, do it!" was connected to the sexual revolution going on at the time. But if it feels good physically, does that mean it feels good emotionally? Sometimes yes, sometimes no.

Sex and feelings are interconnected. Having sex can release dopamine and other neurotransmitters that affect your mood, and being in the right mood can make sex better. Your level of desire can depend on your feelings, and your feelings can be improved with satisfying sexual activity. In other words, when you feel good you want sex, and when you get sex you feel good.

Love, Trust, and Libido

Emotional states such as love and trust have a strong impact on desire. Caring for another person enough to trust them is the entrée into a satisfying sexual relationship and greater sexual fitness.

Sexual fitness includes a healthy libido, and your sexual desire is affected by your feelings when you are with a sexual partner. Not too surprisingly, this experience is different for men and women.

Although no statement is always true for one gender or the other, men and women do seem to take different roads to trusting and feeling emotionally intimate. This is not to say that one way or the other is better, but understanding the differences can make trust possible sooner.

For men, trust seems to come more strongly once they are sexually involved. Perhaps it is the "trust hormone" oxytocin that is released during orgasm. Or perhaps it is that it takes men a bit longer to put words to their feelings, and they do feel trust early but aren't as likely to verbalize it.

For women, trust is usually the prerequisite for sex, not the result. Women tend to feel more comfortable once they can trust that they won't be abandoned or dismissed after an intimate interlude. They often want some reassurance that the relationship is more than a one-time event, and this in turn makes them comfortable enough to relax and enjoy the experience rather than spending their time and energy trying to figure out if he "means it."

Trust and the resulting commitment can give both partners permission to be themselves. This in turn makes it possible to explore fantasies, check out compatibility, and generally enjoy the heck out of each other.

Desire and arousal require muscle relaxation, after all. Your penis doesn't get hard until the muscles relax and allow the blood vessels to fill it up, and because clitoral engorgement follows the same basic pathway on a smaller scale, women won't achieve an orgasm until they are comfortable enough to relax into it. Trust and intimacy are more than idealized notions of relationship—they are the yellow brick road to better sex if you let yourself follow it. For more detail on love and attraction and its impact on your sexual fitness, see Chapter 9.

"Bad" or Destructive Feelings and Sexual Health

There are some feelings that drain you of your positive energy and erode your ability to enjoy sex. It's important that you be familiar with your own thresholds for these feelings and that you learn to manage them in ways that don't ruin your health or relationships.

Any thought or feeling that carries you away from the present moment will keep you from experiencing what is happening *right now*. Since sexual activities are very much in the "right now," it is important to be present to them in order to appreciate and benefit from them.

Anxiety, anger, grief, and sadness can whittle away at your sense of well-being and eventually bring your sex life to a halt. If you are in a negative frame of mind most of the time, it will begin to diminish your enjoyment of all activities, including sex, and your sexual health will suffer. While no one escapes these emotional states completely, being aware of negative feelings can actually help you to understand how to respond to them.

Anxiety

Anxiety is an underlying emotional state based on fear, and it can be obvious and immediate or subtle and ongoing. It could be either helpful or destructive, depending on how long it lasts and what you do with it.

def•i•ni•tion

Anxiety is a state of apprehension, dread, or worry. It is different from fear in that it involves what *might* happen or *is likely to* happen and therefore requires thought and memory. Being anxious triggers an autonomic response from your body, including an increase in heart rate and blood pressure and the secretion of the hormones adrenaline, noradrenaline, and cortisol.

Anxiety, contrary to what you might think, is not always bad. Men and women tend to respond differently to anxiety, and its impact on sexual function varies. Managing your anxiety so that it doesn't overwhelm your body's response to sexual stimuli is an important tool in your sexual fitness toolbox.

Men are not as likely to let anxiety throw them for a loop when it comes to sexual activity. For the most part, men seem to be better at setting aside their anxiety during a sexual encounter. The exception to this is if the anxiety is about sexual performance. Men who worry about their performance tend to focus on that worry when in a sexual situation, which creates *more* anxiety and more performance problems.

Women, on the other hand, report that when they are anxious it usually keeps them from enjoying sex. One exception to this is when women experience an anxiety-provoking activity unrelated to their own lives, such as watching a high-stress movie or a daredevil performance. Such an experience serves to rev up their sexual engines without interfering with the sexual encounter itself.

The bottom line seems to lie with distractibility. If anxiety distracts you from paying attention to sexual stimuli, or if it is related to your sexual ability, it will negatively affect your sexual experience and performance. But if it is make-believe stress or unrelated to your life, it can actually increase your arousal and make you more tuned in to your sexual response. You be the judge of whether anxiety is a plus or minus, depending on your own threshold and "operating system." For suggestions on how to manage anxiety, see the section "Managing Overly Negative Feelings" later in this chapter.

Beyond the Basics

According to one study, about 10 percent of men and 20 percent of women are actually *more* sexually aroused when they are anxious than when they are not. This may account for people who seek higher risk sexual situations or activities. The anxiety of the situation makes the sex more exciting to them but also more likely to result in negative outcomes. In fact, it is the *possibility* of the negative outcome that makes them feel aroused. If your partner is the sort of person who likes risk as a way of feeling aroused, find ways to edge up the anxiety without actually harming or putting yourself at risk for disease, injury, or unwanted pregnancy.

Anger

Anger damages your sexual fitness from more than one angle. Being angry can distract you at the very least and can hurt your relationship if you bring it into the bedroom. But beyond its mood-spoiling qualities, anger can physically injure your body—particularly your heart.

First, there is the emotional impact of anger. If you allow yourself to be angry when you engage in sexual activity, you are introducing hostility into that sexual experience. Whether your anger is directed at your partner or at something outside your relationship, if it invades your bedroom it is not sexually healthy. Angry energy, while sometimes useful and important for responding to a perceived threat, can only damage or traumatize your connection to a partner.

Second, anger is literally heart breaking. The rise in blood pressure and release of stress hormones that occur when you are angry are damaging to your cardiovascular system. People who are often or continuously angry are at much greater risk for heart disease and stroke. Since your sexual fitness depends on a healthy heart, you can only damage your sexual health by remaining in an angry state.

Proceed with Caution

Most of the research on anger has been done on men, and it consistently reveals that anger is dangerous. In one Harvard study, the men reporting the highest anger were three times more likely to develop heart disease than their nonangry counterparts. In another Harvard study, which included both men and women, an episode of intense anger more than doubled the risk of heart attack if it occurred in the two hours preceding the attack. And if that doesn't persuade you to curb your anger, how about research from Israel showing that intense anger increased the risk of stroke within the two-hour period following the angry event by *14 times*. Anger is an invitation to serious cardiovascular problems—what could be more dangerous to your sexual health?

Although not as much research has been done on women and anger, we know some things. Women who report being more angry also report being less sexually satisfied. Anger also seems to decrease sexual arousal more for women than for men. Both men and women claim to be less angry as they age, suggesting that we do learn to manage angry feelings over time.

Are you an angry person? If you have found yourself losing control, have a reputation for being "hot headed," have been told by a partner that you are too angry, or have a history of being physically or emotionally violent, then you are risking your health with your anger.

If you think that anger is damaging your life or relationships, make an appointment with a counselor or health-care provider. At the very least, he or she may advise that you begin taking one low-dose aspirin a day to help prevent heart attacks. If you agree that some anger-management skills are in order, then you can find resources for that as well. You owe it to yourself to reduce your risk of heart disease, and managing your anger is an important step.

Sadness, Grief, and Loss

Sadness is an emotional fact of life; everyone feels sad sometimes. And everyone deals with *grief* and loss at some point in his or her life. When you feel sad or suffer a loss, your sexual health may or may not suffer as a result. People respond differently to grief and loss, and depending on your coping skills, you may find that grief is a time when you can maintain sexual health as you work your way through the feelings of sorrow.

The older you are, the more losses you will probably have dealt with. But loss can come at any age, and your emotional maturity at the time of a loss will affect how you grieve. If you are young or haven't had much practice with grief, you may be less able to cope. Or if you are the sort of person who has avoided discussing emotional issues, you may be ill equipped to deal with the strong feelings that emerge with grief. The main road out of sadness and emotional pain is communication.

def•i•ni•tion

Grief is the normal, usually sorrowful reaction to a major loss. It is different from *depression*, which is a mental state in which sadness, loss, or frustration interferes with a person's everyday life for an extended period of time. Most people experience grief following a loss but are not considered depressed.

If you are part of an established couple, grief involves you both. If a loss is mutual, you will both be sad and distraught, which may make the road back to each other more difficult. If only one of you is suffering the loss, it may be an isolating time. The important thing during a time of loss is that you talk to each other—without anger or blaming—and help each other understand what grief is like for *you*. Even if your partner doesn't seem to "get" what you are feeling right away, continuing to talk keeps the door open for being close.

If you are single, grief can be a terribly lonely experience. You may have trouble with anger or sadness and feel cut off from the outside world, including people who might help you. Almost any emotion can accompany grief, and you will be unpredictable to yourself at times. If you do not have close friends or a partner to talk to during a time of grief, consider seeing a counselor. Just saying out loud what you are feeling can go a long way toward getting you to a place of feeling "normal" again, and it can help you feel less crazy along the way.

People relate to sadness in many different ways, and sex can be a gift or a point of conflict during such a time. Again, talk to your partner about what sex means to you during the period of loss and let him or her do the same. At the very least, you want to someday resume your sexual connection, and if you talk to each other now you will make that possible. Emotional intimacy is often enhanced by shared sadness, even if physical intimacy is lessened for a time.

Sex may be the farthest thing from your mind when you have suffered a major loss, but that may not be true for your partner. Some people find sexual contact to be comforting or a great relief during a stressful time. Others are hypersensitive and do not want to be touched. Tell each other what sort of touch feels soothing and what things are just too much for now. Listen carefully to each other about how to nurture each other, and cut each other some slack if one of you needs physical space. Continue to do thoughtful things for each other and remind yourself and your partner that you love each other and still find the other attractive, even if your sex life is on hold. Reassure each other that this is a temporary blip in your life together and that you are there to support each other as you heal.

Beyond the Basics _____

If your grief lasts more than a year or keeps you from rejoining your life, it could be something more serious. Pay attention to any of these symptoms if they are present after a year has passed:

- ◆ Overwhelming anxiety
- ◆ Ongoing emotional numbness
- ◆ Frequent insomnia
- ◆ Intense longing for whom or what was lost
- ◆ Bitterness, irritability, or agitation
- ◆ A feeling of "meaninglessness"
- ◆ Thoughts of hurting yourself or dying
- ◆ Inability to trust people

If you or someone you know has these persistent symptoms, it's time to seek professional help.

There are also some gender differences with respect to grieving and sex. Women often just want to be held and cuddled as they recover from a loss. They may be angry or repulsed if their partner turns a soothing touch into a sexual one. It's important to respect the need for nonsexual touch if that is what is helpful to a grieving partner. Male partners may be at a loss as to how to offer this touch and may need some guidance about what feels good and what should wait until you are feeling more available.

Men, on the other hand, may seek sex as a way to get some relief from the sadness they are experiencing. Sex and orgasm release dopamine and oxytocin, which are chemical messengers that increase the endorphins in your system. Sex can be not only relieving but a great comfort if it is offered sensitively and in the context of other consoling measures. If your male partner seems to be pushing for sex as a response to grief, ask him to talk about that. It's not a wrong way to deal with sadness and loss, but it should occur in a larger context of support and reassurance.

Dealing with the pain of a loss is a very individual and subjective process. Everyone has to do it on his or her own timetable and in his or her own way. The main objective, as far as maintaining your sexual health is concerned, is to keep the lines of communication open. This will make it possible to stay close or regain closeness as you and/or your partner heal from the loss.

Managing Overly Negative Feelings

Now that we've established that everyone has feelings and that those feelings affect your sexual health, what do you do about feelings that seem to be overly negative or out of control?

Managing feelings is not a simple matter, and if you experience feelings like anger or anxiety that overwhelm you and interfere with your life, you will probably need professional support in learning new ways to manage them. Still, there are some principles that can be applied to many situations and many types of feelings.

Proceed with Caution

If you notice that there is a pattern of anger ruining your relationships, ranting and raving will only make it worse. Contrary to popular belief, venting your anger is not a healthy way to manage it. In fact, venting and aggressive expression can be just an excuse to hurt someone. If you know just one way to get mad, find a program or therapist who can help you learn new ways to deal with angry feelings. You will find yourself infinitely more "datable."

Here are three approaches that can help you manage feelings that cause problems for you in your life:

◆ Cognitive restructuring

◆ Relaxation

◆ Communication

Cognitive Restructuring

Cognitive restructuring means changing the way you think. Since your thoughts determine what you feel and how you respond, they are the key to changing your behavior. If your thoughts about yourself or your situation lead you to be anxious ("She doesn't find me attractive") or angry ("I think he is cheating on me") or sad ("I think she wants to break up"), they affect how you respond. Cognitive restructuring can teach you to think different thoughts, which in turn can lead you to have more effective responses to situations in your life. Cognitive restructuring is useful with feelings of anxiety, anger, insecurity, fear, and sadness.

Relaxation

Relaxation exercises help you learn to give yourself space during emotional events so that you can choose a response rather than letting the response overwhelm you. Relaxation can be learned, and you can teach yourself to act calmly in situations that used to send you over the edge. Usually a combination of muscle relaxation and controlled breathing, relaxation exercises can ease you through many tense and *in*tense feelings and situations.

Try This!

Next time you are feeling anxious before or during a date, try a relaxation technique. Find a place to be alone, like the elevator or the restroom. Breathe in deeply from your diaphragm, filling your abdomen first and then your chest. Close your eyes and say a kind word or phrase to yourself over and over as you breathe. Try something like "I am okay" or "Hon, you can do this." Picture yourself in a quiet, placid place—either one you make up or one you know about. As you say your phrase, feel the tension leaving your body, first from your feet, then your torso, then your neck and shoulders. Do this for about a minute or two. Open your eyes, smile, and tell yourself that you are going to be fine. If you practice this in calm moments, it will be easier to use during emotional or stressful situations.

Communication

It's not by accident that preschool teachers tell children to "use your words." People who are taught from a very early age to talk about their feelings are better at managing them. Men have more trouble than women at this, and brain-imaging studies show that women's brains light up in more places when they are having a feeling than men's do.

This is probably evidence that women's language centers are more connected to their emotional centers, making it easier for them to identify feelings and respond. But everyone can get better at talking about feelings, and when you do you make it possible to change direction, even in tense or emotional situations.

Here are some other tips to help you manage your feelings:

- **Make a plan.** If women are better at labeling their feelings, men are great at logical planning. If a situation consistently raises strong emotional responses for you, make a plan about how you are going to address it. Set some goals and track your progress as you try to overcome your tendency to be anxious or angry or negative. Dating relationships, marriages, and even work relationships can improve if you take small steps toward being more effective with your feelings.

- **Keep your sense of humor.** Try to keep your perspective on emotional situations. Using humor to put things into perspective or to defuse the tension is a great way to manage your feelings. But keep in mind that using humor in a sarcastic or hurtful way can make things worse, so be aware of how your humor is coming across. Don't take yourself too seriously—you want to ease your negative feelings, not feed them.

- **Change your environment.** This could be anything from stepping into the next room to leaving your job. If your external world is provoking such a negative response from you, ask yourself why. Are you this way when you are in other places? Is there something about this place (home, work, the gym, etc.) that persistently puts you in an anxious or angry mood? Once you have analyzed the reason why you feel the way you do, you may want to get away from that environment. While a "geographic cure" won't work if your problem lies within your personality, some environments *are* toxic, and it can be a healthy move to get away from them. Talk to your partner, a friend, or a counselor if you are trying to find a way out of a destructive environment.

- **Exercise.** Exercise is an excellent way to deal with strong emotions. Not only does it release endorphins that improve your coping ability, but it gives you time to think about what you want to do. Sexual fitness depends on a healthy body, and exercising to deal with strong emotions can offer the added benefit of a stronger body as a side benefit. Next time you feel like you are going to burst with an emotion, take a break and go for a rigorous walk. Chances are very good that you will feel differently by the time you return.

♦ **Consider a medication.** There are many medications that can help with chronic emotional problems, but they are not without risks and side effects—including sexual side effects. Anxiety, irritability associated with depression, and aggressive behavior associated with *intermittent explosive disorder* are all emotional conditions that can be helped dramatically by the right medications. If you think you might be helped by medication, check with your healthcare provider to see whether you are a good candidate.

Managing your feelings is a lifelong effort. Even people who are very good at managing their feelings can improve. If you are having trouble with strong feelings of any sort that get in the way of your life or your sex life, then it's time to find a counselor or therapist to help you. There are many skilled people who can help you increase your repertoire of options so that you will behave the way you *want* to behave, not just how you've

def•i•ni•tion

Intermittent Explosive Disorder is a condition wherein a person has outbursts of uncontrolled violent and aggressive behavior, harming people or property, and where the response is out of proportion to the precipitating event. It is classified by mental health clinicians as an "impulse control disorder."

always behaved. Taking charge of your emotions will make all of your relationships—personal, professional, *and* sexual—stronger and more rewarding.

The Least You Need to Know

♦ Positive feelings release chemicals that make sex not only more enjoyable but more possible.

♦ A feeling of trust enhances sexual experience. For men, trust often comes after sex; for women, trust usually comes before sex.

◆ Anxiety damages sexual experience if it distracts you from the moment. However, in some cases, anxiety can actually raise desire and improve your sexual experience.

◆ Anger not only ruins a romantic moment, it can damage your body's ability to perform sexually.

◆ Managing negative emotions may take a combination of learning new ways to think, learning how to relax, and learning better communication skills.

2

Your Body and Sex

It's not much of a stretch to make the connection between bodily health and sexual health. But specifically, how do you prepare your healthy body to lead a satisfying sex life? Are there certain things you should focus on to maximize your sexual health and fitness? If diet and exercise are so important, which diet and what exercises will be worth your while when you want to improve your sexual fitness?

These are all worthy questions to ask yourself when you want a body that responds well to sex and one that will perform—in bed and out.

Chapter 4

Healthy Body, Healthy Sex

In This Chapter

- ◆ Why a healthy body is a sexy body
- ◆ Why both organic and dynamic fitness are important
- ◆ What circulation has to do with sexual fitness
- ◆ How hormones affect your sexual health

To be sexually healthy and fit, you need a healthy body to work with. You can find the sexiest lingerie or read about the hottest sexual techniques, but if you don't have a healthy body to back up your sexual ambitions, you will find yourself disappointed again and again.

On the other hand, you don't have to be the guy with the most rippling abs or the gal with the Barbie doll figure to be healthy enough to be sexually fit. Small changes in your routine and life-style can reap big results, and you will find that your body will take you anywhere you (sexually) want to go.

There are many ways in which improving your overall health will spark your sex life and turn you into the sexual tiger or love kitten that you long to be. But before you jump into a new workout or a dramatic diet, it helps to understand the connection between your body and your sexual health.

A Strong Body Is a Sexy Body

It's easy to look through a magazine and choose the bodies that you think are sexy. Media images have taught us to see certain body types as ideal, and sometimes we think that this ideal is what we should aim for in order to be considered "sexy." But most research supports the fact that while we are hard on ourselves and hold ourselves up to these unrealistic standards, our mates and potential mates are much easier on us and find us more attractive when we just relax and enjoy our bodies, whatever shape they happen to be.

There is a difference, however, between accepting your body and letting yourself become a body slob. There *are* some common physical characteristics that contribute to your sexual attractiveness, and it shouldn't surprise you that they are directly linked to your state of health.

Posture and Strength—Muscle Up

When you walk across a room, what will people notice about you? Although you may hope it is your outfit or your startling green eyes, they will probably first notice how you hold yourself when you walk. Whether you are looking for a sexual partner or are already in a steady relationship, you want your body to reflect your sexual fitness.

Your body posture says volumes about you. It implies your age, your mental state, your confidence level, your level of comfort, and your general health. You may not even be aware of it when you make these judgments about another person because they happen at a subconscious level, but we all make assumptions about people based on how they stand and carry themselves. Your comfort with your sexual self is evident from the first moment, so you want to portray yourself as confident about your body since you know how difficult it is to undo a first impression!

And what do you suppose it is that holds your body up easily and comfortably? In a word, muscles. If the muscle tone in your torso is poor, you will slump and slouch. Your back muscles as well as your abdominals hold you erect and available. Your leg, thigh, and butt muscles carry you gracefully through your day—or they don't! And your shoulder, arm, and hand muscles allow you to hug and shake hands, which convey warmth and connection to the people you meet.

Try This!

Next time you go to a movie, study the characters for the way they move and how they stand. If one character is what you consider "sexy," pay attention to exactly what it is that gives you that impression— and not just the size of body parts! Chances are that you will notice how easily the person moves his or her body, how comfortable and seemingly unaware he or she is of this ability. This unselfconscious ease of movement implies youth and vitality at any age, and the basis of it is good muscle strength.

Your body is the structure that you present to the world—your bones are the beams in that structure, your muscles the joists and girders that hold the beams in place so that your edifice doesn't sag or come tumbling down. This is the structure you use to express your sexuality. It is the home to your fantasies and the "place" that you invite partners to share.

Naturally, you want everything "up to code" in your structure so that it will continue to look as though it was built to last. When you invite someone to share your body in sexual activity, you want him or her to see how structurally sound it is, not just the great paint job you chose. When you work to build muscular strength in your body, you naturally assume a more confident posture, which in turn expresses a certain eagerness for life and sexual connection that others will find appealing.

Besides helping you stand straighter, muscles are responsible for your general strength. Women begin to lose their muscle mass as early as age 20, but both men and women begin to lose muscle at an increased rate after age 50—probably due to waning *hormones* for both. To sustain your youthful appearance and your ability to enjoy sexual activity, it is important to find activities that preserve your muscles and maintain your strength.

def•i•ni•tion

A **hormone** is a molecule produced in one cell that acts as a messenger to particular "target" cells and whose purpose is to change the growth, function, or metabolism of those target cells.

Energy and Sex

Energy is the capacity of acting or being active. It is a dynamic quality that implies you are ready for whatever comes next. When people have "sexual energy," you get the impression that they have the ability and capacity for sexual activity, even if they are not being overtly sexual at the time.

To be energetic does not mean you have to jog in place or be restless or constantly moving. In fact, when you have lots of energy for life, and therefore for sex, you may be rather quiet but with a certain "readiness" and enthusiasm for whatever you are doing. Energetic people *seem* young, whether they are or not.

"Sexual energy" is not the same as "sexiness," which you might express though your dress, posture, or appearance. Sexual energy is a certain poised eagerness, a comfort with your sexual self and a confidence that you are sexually able. Sexual energy is hard to quantify, but others know it when they see it. And you usually know it when you have it, although others can probably point it out to you if you don't see it in yourself. Having good energy and great sexual energy depends on a number of things, most of which are under your control.

How can you get more energy for sexual expression than you have now? And how do you keep your energy at high levels? The answers are not simple but are definitely worth exploring.

Your sexual energy level depends on many factors. At the purely physical level, it depends on the following:

- What you are eating
- How much sleep you get
- Whether you exercise
- Your age
- What sort of work you do
- Whether you drink or smoke

On the psychological level, these elements affect your level of sexual energy:

- Your mood

- Your everyday stress level

- Your general outlook

Most of these factors, both physical and psychological, are matters of choice. *You* have the power to improve your sexual energy level if you decide to do it. People with higher energy tend to have a passion for life, a healthy libido, and are lively enough to make it all happen.

Flexibility Stretches Your Options

Physical flexibility is a characteristic that can open up your sexual world. As you get older, you lose the flexibility that was characteristic of your youthful body. Like posture, it is something that subtly tells the world that you are physically able and ready for life. The longer you stay flexible, the longer you can move in a young, graceful way that signals others that "you've still got it."

Losing flexibility happens slowly, probably unnoticed, until one day you can't seem to touch your toes or wrap your legs around your partner during sex. Many of us lead lives that encourage a loss of this flexibility, and sitting at a desk is a great recipe for becoming a stiff.

Proceed with Caution

If you want to be more limber in order to be more comfortable and creative during sex, go about it slowly and regularly. You didn't lose your flexibility in a day, and it will take more than a day to get it back. Take some stretching classes or get a good book on stretching. Warm up before you begin and do a little each day rather than a sudden panicked session the afternoon of a big date. No one wants an injured hamstring, and your date may not find an icepack on your bottom particularly desirable.

Besides being able to just plain do more, a flexible body is a comfortable body. If you want to combat the pain associated with long hours in front of the computer monitor, getting limber is a great place to start. Later you can add to those office exercises so that you will be comfortable all through your day, including your time in bed with your partner!

When you improve your flexibility, you will notice a certain gracefulness and sensuality to your body, no matter what age or shape you are in. The more flexible you are, the more freedom of movement you have, which makes you capable of more (and more interesting) sexual positions.

Types of Sexual Fitness

To be in great sexual shape, you need to be fit in a couple of different ways. Your body tissues and structures need to be sturdy and made of "the right stuff." Just as you wouldn't choose to build a house out of inferior materials or make a suit out of flimsy fabric, you don't want inferior materials to be the foundation of your sexual health.

If your body is sturdily made with good materials, you then want it to move readily and easily. Being able to enjoy your sexual life requires a little attention to what you're made of and how well you can move. If you are fit in both of these ways, you will experience pleasure from your body throughout your life.

Organic Fitness

Organic fitness refers to the condition of the tissues that make up your body. It is your baseline physical state and ideally is one in which your body organs are free of disease and well nourished, ready for whatever activities—sexual or otherwise—you may want to engage in.

You want your muscle tissue to be able to maintain physical strength, you want bones to be solid enough to support you, and you want skin to be intact and protecting you from the elements. If each type of tissue is doing its job and can maintain itself, you are organically fit.

Organic fitness depends on several factors. Take your heart, for example. You may have a very healthy heart, with good heart muscle fibers that will beat faithfully—including under stress or rigorous physical activity—until you are 100 years old. Or you may have a fragile heart, one that is, at any moment, in danger of stopping altogether. What makes the difference between a healthy body organ or system and one that is not? It is a combination of the genetic cards you are dealt and how you play them.

First, you have a certain genetic map that makes your body tend toward certain characteristics. If your family history is full of heart disease, diabetes, or osteoporosis, you know that you will have to be on the lookout for those conditions. Knowing your family health history can give you a heads up on how to make your own sexual fitness plan. Did your dad have diabetes or prostate cancer? Was your mom going through menopause at 40, or did she develop osteoporosis at 70? These are clues about what conditions may affect your own sexual health.

Another ingredient in your organic fitness is your collection of lifestyle habits. If your habits include regular exercise and good nutrition, your body tissues will reflect that. If, on the other hand, you are a smoker who eats a high-fat diet, then your body will show wear and tear at an earlier age. What you do day after day to and for your body eventually becomes what you are made of. Your baseline health reaps the rewards or consequences of your everyday habits.

Organic fitness suffers if you are injured or have a chronic disease. Some injuries keep you from being able to take proper care of yourself, which takes a toll over time. And chronic diseases are very hard on your organs and systems. For example, diabetes can cause poor circulation and high blood-sugar levels that can mean the beginning of erectile dysfunction or more vaginal infections. Your body will find it harder to fight the effects of aging. You literally aren't made of the same stuff that you were when you were younger.

Hormones, too, can have a dramatic effect on your organic fitness. Hormones regulate many processes in your body. With normal fluctuations and the eventual waning of hormone levels, these functions can be slowed or interrupted, changing the condition of your body tissues. For example, the protective role of estrogen on your bones is well known. As estrogen declines, your bones may become more porous and be less able to hold you upright.

Proceed with Caution

Most chronic diseases have early warning signs that you can pick up with minimal attention to your body. If you are short of breath, more tired than you used to be, subject to headaches, thirsty, gaining or losing weight, or having any unusual pain, have a physical exam to see if you are beginning to suffer from something that could seriously damage your body.

Eventually, they can even crack or break, making even daily activities impossible. And the testosterone that maintained your muscles when you were young may decrease and cause a loss of your muscle mass. Not only will you be weaker, you will be more likely to gain weight.

When you do things to minimize the impact of these forces on your organic fitness, it makes it easier to maintain your general health and sexual fitness. Maintaining your baseline organic fitness is the first step in staying sexually well and rigorous.

When you are organically fit, each organ is in shape to perform as it was designed. Organic fitness assures that your reproductive organs are all functioning well, making the hormones your body needs and responding easily to sexual stimulation. Sexual organic fitness includes not only your genital organs but also your muscles, brain tissue, bones, heart, and lungs.

Dynamic Fitness

If you are organically fit—you have all your parts in working order—the next question is: What can you do with that equipment? This is where dynamic fitness comes in.

Dynamic fitness means being able to move vigorously and with little effort. It is a combination of general strength, cardiovascular fitness, endurance, suppleness, balance, and speed. If you can move your body easily, your dynamic sexual fitness will enable you to perform sexually and get the maximum enjoyment. Being able to move well and comfortably allows you to take advantage of sexual options and opportunities.

Your dynamic fitness typically begins to decline in your mid-30s. Although this is a normal aging phenomenon, you can have an enormous impact on the rate of that decline. Anyone who wants to remain sexually fit can take steps early—or at any age—to slow age-related changes and maintain the ability to move your body easily.

Stamina

Stamina is the ability to sustain a prolonged stressful effort or activity. It requires a combination of dynamic and organic fitness, and it allows you to sustain physical activity—sexual activity—for as long as you need and/or desire. Usually it's mentioned in relation to male sexual fitness, but women need stamina, too. The more able you are to stay active for longer periods of time, the more you can maintain your everyday activities and have energy left for sexual activity.

Stamina requires a certain amount of "training" in order to build your capacity. If you start with a healthy body and get enough rest, you can slowly build your endurance to the point where you are doing as much as you like for as long as you like, whether it is sexual activity or running marathons.

Ask yourself how long you have good energy before you have to slow down and recharge. Can you go through your day and still have energy for romance in the evening? Do you have the stamina you want for the life you want to lead?

It Starts in Those Tiny Cells

Cells are the building blocks of every part of your body. They are the foundation of everything you want to be able to do, and they all depend on each other. You want your nerve cells to fire properly, your heart cells to push blood out to the rest of you, your liver cells to screen out toxic substances, your taste sensors to register sweet and savory foods, and your white blood cells to kill invading infections. Every minute of every day your experience depends on each cell functioning exactly as it was designed to do.

When it comes to sexual activity, you especially want the cells in your smooth muscle and blood vessels to make the erectile tissue in your penis or clitoris respond. You want the nerve endings in your skin to register touch and your olfactory receptors to pick up your partner's scent. When you are in tip-top shape at the cellular level, it all works together to create an exciting and satisfying sexual experience.

While every cell has a specific job, they all have certain things in common. Cells need to have nutrients brought to them, be able to rid themselves of toxins, produce substances that they were designed to produce, communicate with each other, and replicate themselves.

> **Beyond the Basics** _____
> One example of specialized cells is the smooth muscle cells in both female and male erectile tissue. These cells are contracted most of the time, but they respond to sexual stimulation by relaxing and letting blood fill the spaces to create an erection in the penis or clitoris. Medications like Viagra work at the cellular level to relax these muscle cells so that the tissue can fill and become available for sexual pleasure and orgasm.

Circulation Is the Key

The circulatory system is made up of your heart, blood vessels, and the blood that flows through the system. Everything depends on circulation. It brings oxygen, nutrients, proteins, enzymes, and other chemical compounds to the cells to enable them to operate smoothly.

Good circulation also makes you more responsive to sexual arousal. In men, it opens and closes blood vessels at the critical times to assure that the hydraulics of your penis are operating smoothly. In women, it brings blood to not only your clitoris but to your nipples and other erogenous zones where you will welcome your partner's touch.

At the cellular level, good circulation takes away waste products and carries cell byproducts off to other cells that need those byproducts— like nitric oxide to your erectile tissue so that the muscle cells relax. Cells have a complex communication system and use chemical messengers, carried by the circulatory system, to cooperate.

Whatever interferes with this transport system interferes with your body's ability to perform—whether it's cholesterol in the vessels, low oxygen levels in the blood, lack of exercise, or poor heart function. Interrupting this system is like a major transportation strike—nothing gets in and nothing gets out. After a while it's a messy scene. Think of a disaster that stops the flow of materials into and out of an area— hurricane, earthquake, and so on. It takes a long time for things to function properly even once the flow is restored.

Good blood flow determines sexual function and pleasure and your capacity for orgasm. Keeping circulation healthy is critical to sexual health and fitness.

A Little Oxygen, Please

Oxygen helps cells to turn sugar into energy, and this energy is then used by cells to perform their many specific functions. Everything from healthy skin to functioning ovaries depends on oxygen getting to the cells—your cells need to breathe.

When your *hemoglobin* is at a normal level, your cells get all the oxygen they need. But when you don't have enough hemoglobin to carry oxygen, or if your oxygen supply is low for some reason, every tissue in the body suffers. This can be devastating to your sex life if you frequently become too tired or short of breath to enjoy sex or if there is damage to sensitive cells like the ones in your genitals.

There are several things you can do to be sure you are giving yourself enough oxygen for good cell health:

def•i•ni•tion

Hemoglobin is a protein molecule in red blood cells that is used to carry oxygen to each cell.

♦ Do deep breathing exercises. (You can find them online under "yoga breathing" or "relaxation.")

♦ If you have asthma or another respiratory illness, get it treated.

♦ Wear a mask if you are doing activities where you might be breathing in particles of paint, dust, or other pollutants.

Don't underestimate the role of oxygen in your sexual health. If you are counting on the erectile tissue in your penis or clitoris to be functioning at peak levels, you need to give those cells what they require, including a steady blood flow of oxygen.

Beyond the Basics

Smokers have a falsely high hemoglobin and poor oxygen transfer to the cells. Cigarette smoke contains carbon monoxide, which uses up the available hemoglobin so that your body is forced to make *extra* hemoglobin molecules to carry the oxygen you need. Therefore, smokers with a normal hemoglobin value may actually be robbing their bodies of the necessary oxygen to perform well.

Blood Flow and Nutrients

To repair, rebuild, and strengthen body tissues, cells need the nutrients that come from the food you eat. Your bloodstream carries these nutrients to the cells, and as each cell is nourished with proper blood flow, it can process nutrients and get rid of waste and toxins, which are in turn carried away by the blood.

If you want to see this process in action, pay attention to a healing cut or keep a diary as you recover from surgery. The better the blood flow, the faster the healing. That's why people who walk every day recover faster, as do people who eat properly.

Sexually, this constant rebuilding and recovery process is observable when you see how long it takes to bounce back from one orgasm and be ready for the next—or how quickly your libido returns after an illness or injury.

Providing your cells with important nutrients requires two basic things: eating the right foods and keeping your circulatory system in running order so that nutrients can be delivered. You have a lot of control over what you eat, and you can keep your circulatory system healthy as well, so "feeding your cells" is a responsibility you can handle.

Hormones and Sexual Health

Hormones are major players in sexual health and fitness. While there are many types of hormones, the ones we think of most when thinking about sexual health are the so-called "sex hormones" or steroid hormones. The main categories of these sex hormones are androgens and estrogens, which are produced in the gonads—the testes in men and the ovaries in women.

Sex hormones have a dramatic impact on your sexual fitness and are responsible for your sexual appearance, your sexual appetite, and your sexual capacity. These hormones are designed to affect your reproductive systems and are responsible for the growth and condition of these systems.

Androgens are the "male" steroid hormones and are responsible for the development and maintenance of masculine sex characteristics. In males, androgens are responsible for the following:

- ◆ Growth of the penis and testes

- ◆ Typical male pattern body hair

- ◆ Muscular body makeup

- ◆ Sperm production

- ◆ Influence on behavior including healthy sex drive

In women, androgens are produced in the ovaries and are needed to make estrogen. Androgen levels that are too high or too low in women can cause problems with libido and fertility.

Estrogen is usually considered the female sex hormone. In women, it is responsible for the following:

- ◆ Development of the uterus, ovaries, vagina, and breasts

- ◆ Distribution of pubic hair (combined with androgens)

- ◆ Establishment of the menstrual cycle

- ◆ Curvy female body type, including a wide pelvis and fat distribution on the breasts and hips.

Men also create estrogen in small amounts as a byproduct of testosterone production. In these tiny amounts, estrogen seems to balance out testosterone's powerful cell stimulating qualities and helps with brain function. But in larger amounts, estrogen can make testosterone production drop, causing low sex drive. As with women, research is mixed as to whether higher estrogen protects men from heart disease or is actually a risk factor.

Testosterone and Desire

Testosterone is the androgen you've probably heard the most about. Besides being important for male sexual development, it is the hormone most closely linked to libido, or sexual desire.

When sexual desire wanes, it can be for many reasons. In some women and men, it is because their normal levels of testosterone are sliding. Treating low libido with testosterone is still being studied, and your health-care provider will want to explore other possible reasons for this decrease in desire before prescribing testosterone.

Men produce less testosterone beginning in their 40s. But unlike women, whose hormone production falls off quickly with menopause, men have a much more gradual decline. The circulating testosterone levels of men tend to stay within a normal range even as men age. But if levels fall off to below the normal range, a testosterone supplement can restore libido along with a feeling of well-being. It can also boost cognitive function and energy levels.

Proceed with Caution

Taking testosterone supplements does have some serious risks, including an increased risk of depression and some cancers, so it is not a simple cure-all for low libido.

When women go through menopause, they often experience a lower libido. For some women, this is acceptable and not a problem. For others, it affects their quality of life and sexual health tremendously. If you find your sexual desire becoming less and this is an issue for you, check it out with your doctor and explore whether a testosterone prescription would be worth a try.

Estrogen, Progesterone, and the Female Cycle

Ask any woman in her fertile years and she will tell you that the state of her sexual health depends on what day of the month it is. As estrogen and progesterone cycle through their monthly ups and downs, a woman's attitude toward sex and her enjoyment of it can fluctuate a great deal.

Estrogen drops just before your menstrual period, as does progesterone, which causes premenstrual symptoms in some women. This can affect your interest in sex since it is sometimes a period of irritability and moodiness. On the other hand, some women report a surge in libido immediately prior to starting their period, when they feel an urgency about sex.

Estrogen peaks during the first half of the menstrual cycle and then falls off abruptly just before ovulation, when the egg is released. Progesterone begins to climb at ovulation and peaks in the second half of the cycle. It is common for women to feel more sexual desire at ovulation, followed by a general feeling of well-being for a week to ten days. Biologically, this makes sense because this is the most fertile time of the month. A woman's production of testosterone corresponds to that mid-cycle boost in libido, too, so it is often a time of both heightened enjoyment of and desire for sex.

The trick to maximizing your sexual health over the course of your cycle is to know your own patterns and "ride the wave." If you know there are times of the cycle when you don't enjoy being touched (or talked to!), discuss it with your partner and decide ahead of time how to handle it. And if you can predict your times of high desire when you find sex particularly satisfying, make a plan for that, too, since great sex is bonding and exciting for both you and your partner when it's that much fun.

Understanding your body and how to treat it can maximize your general health as well as your sexual health. You have a lot to say about the sort of body you walk around in, and you can contribute to your own sexual fitness by tending to your body's needs.

The Least You Need to Know

- Muscle strength is critical to sexual fitness.
- Becoming more flexible will increase your sexual choices.
- You can improve your sexual energy level with some simple lifestyle changes.
- Sexual fitness starts in your cells.
- Women need testosterone and men need estrogen to stay sexually healthy.
- Women can enjoy sex more if they understand their cycle.

Chapter 5

Your Five Best Bets for Improving Sexual Health

In This Chapter

- ◆ Diet hints for great sexual health
- ◆ Why exercise is critical for sexual function
- ◆ What maintaining a healthy weight can do to boost your sexual health
- ◆ How getting enough sleep gives you a real advantage in bed
- ◆ Which habits are killing your sex life

None of the suggestions in this chapter will come as much of a surprise. But usually when you make choices about what to eat, or whether exercise is worth it, or how much sleep to get, you don't really think about the effect it is having on your sexual health and fitness. It's the little choices you make every day that will keep you in the sexual running for years—or not.

Diet—Sexy from the Inside Out

We have a cultural obsession with food and diet—what we should eat, what we shouldn't eat, what movie stars eat, what athletes eat, which diets work, which foods will kill us, what tastes good, what doesn't. Yet for all our obsession with food, we still don't seem to have our act together. We are, as a nation, more overweight than ever.

We have a similar obsession with sex. Almost every magazine at the checkout counter has some version of both food and sex in the stories listed on the cover. And, as with food, we are all over the board about sex. We should. We shouldn't. We must. We can't.

So when you start talking about food and sex in the same paragraph, it opens a door that everyone wants to peek around but not so many want to walk through. But there is no getting around the simple truth: What you eat is the foundation of your body, your health, and your ability to stay sexually fit. Simple.

Simple, yes, but not so easy. Eating to get and maintain your sexual fitness needs to start as soon as you are aware of the connection between diet and sexual health, and it has to permeate your awareness with every vegetable on your plate and every doughnut you turn down. Staying healthy, and sexually healthy, is an accumulation of a hundred decisions a day that slowly change and improve the way you eat. This is not "a diet" that you go on and off. It is a decision to eat for a better life, not for the moment's taste.

Essential Nutrients

The term "essential nutrient" is used two ways. Sometimes it refers to nutrients that are required for metabolism but that your body is unable to make by itself. Most vitamins, minerals, and some of the amino acids (protein building blocks) and fatty acids fall into this category.

But in a more general way, there are "essential" components of any good diet. Your body needs protein, carbohydrates, and fat in order to work properly. It is the way you combine and proportion those elements that will make or break your efforts to be healthy. Add to the mix that you need water and fiber, and you can see that there are a million ways to do this food thing.

Try This! _____

> When you are dishing up your lunch or dinner, use a 10-inch plate rather than the largest dinner plate in the cupboard. Then divide the plate into quarters, with one quarter for protein, one quarter for starch/carbohydrate, and two quarters for vegetables and fruits. This is approximately the percentage of those food groups that you want to have in a day, and this is a visual way to remind yourself to eat a healthy, vegetable-packed diet.

For a diet to be sexually healthy, it has to minimize your chance of heart disease, support your needs for energy, and supply the micronutrients that keep all your cells in working order. As you make dietary changes, you need to stop thinking of it as "a diet for now" that you will abandon as soon as you have lost weight, attended your class reunion, or gotten into your wedding dress. You will have the best success if you see your food changes as "a diet forever" that will support your health and well-being for the rest of your life.

Good Fats and Bad Cholesterol

Your body needs a certain amount of fat to operate smoothly. But fats should make up only about a third of your daily calorie intake, and of that third almost none of it should be from trans fats or saturated fats. Unsaturated fats, such as those found in fish, nuts, seeds, and plant oils, can actually help lower your blood cholesterol levels, which helps protect your blood vessels from accumulating plaque.

Start reading food labels. If you see "hydrogenated" or "partially hydrogenated" on the label or if the foods contain lard or trans fat, put them back on the shelf. It's easy to get into food habits, but you can retrain yourself to choose the ones that will do your body the most good. Here are some suggestions for limiting the damaging fats and boosting the helpful ones:

- Replace one meal a week and then two meals a week with a fish or vegetable dish instead of meat.

- Limit your indulgence of trans fat treats like fast food or doughnuts to once a month.

- Switch to unhydrogenated vegetable oils such as canola, safflower, sunflower, or olive oil in your cooking.

- Substitute low- or nonfat dairy for whole dairy products.

- Monitor your calorie intake for a week and note how much of it comes from fat. Aim for 25 to 35 percent of your calories coming from fat.

- When eating out, choose "grilled" over "fried" for your entrée.

- Use soft margarine (tub or liquid) instead of butter.

- Get as close to "5 a day" servings of vegetables and/or fruits as you can. The many nutrients and micronutrients in vegetables and fruits will nourish you at every level.

Start making small changes in your food choices, and in a few short months you will be—literally—made of different stuff.

Hydration: Wet Is Good

Water is essential to keeping your entire system in running order. Sexual health depends not only on a well-running body, but also on lubrication and healthy mucous membranes, not to mention those sparkling eyes and moist lips. All these things require adequate water in your diet.

There are different opinions as to how much water is optimal, and it depends on how warm a climate you live in, how active you are, and what else you are eating and drinking. Most sources would set eight 8-ounce glasses a day of water—that's 2 quarts—as the minimum amount to drink every day. You actually put out more water than that in urine, breathing, and sweating, but there is water in the food you eat as well, so eight glasses is a good place to start.

Some situations will require more than eight glasses of water a day, including if you are …

- Extremely active and/or engaged in athletic activities.

- Living where the weather is extremely hot and you are outdoors.

- Exposed to high altitudes (over 8,000 feet).

◆ Breastfeeding.

◆ Ill with a fever, vomiting, or diarrhea.

Proceed with Caution _____

It is also possible, although rare, to drink too much water. If you drink large amounts of water, it is possible to dilute the amount of sodium in the bloodstream, which is a condition called hyponatremia or "water intoxication." This is a dangerous, sometimes fatal condition. If you are an athlete or drink large quantities of water in a short period of time for any reason, replace some of the water with a sports drink that restores sodium and other electrolytes.

The color of your urine is a good marker for whether you are getting enough fluids. Drink enough water to keep your urine very pale yellow or almost colorless.

Alcohol, caffeinated drinks, some medications, exercise, and illness can all make you dehydrated. As a rule of thumb:

◆ Drink a glass of water at each meal and one between each meal.

◆ Drink water or a sports electrolyte drink before, during, and after exercise.

◆ Substitute sparkling water for alcoholic drinks when you are socializing.

◆ If you do drink alcoholic beverages, drink a glass of water for each alcoholic drink you have.

Usually, it's a very natural thing to drink enough water. If you are rarely thirsty and if you produce 1 to 2 liters of very pale or colorless urine every day, you are probably drinking enough water.

Toxins

As important as it is to eat the right things, it is also important to not eat certain chemicals and toxins. Our environment, including the food we eat, is loaded with toxins (literally poisons) that can affect sexual health. Some of the more serious effects can be seen from *hormone disruptors*, which interfere with your natural hormone function, causing sexual side effects over time.

def•i•ni•tion————————————————

Hormone disruptors, also called endocrine disruptors, are chemicals that interfere with the normal function of your body's hormones. This disruption may be intentional, as with some hormonal drugs, or it may be unintentional, as with certain environmental toxins. Hormone disruptors can block the action of hormones, raise the levels of hormones, increase or decrease the production of hormones, or alter the transport of hormones. These chemicals are currently being studied to determine their impact on reproductive cancers, birth defects, sperm formation, human egg formation, obesity, and other hormone effects.

Hormone disruptors are one type of toxin found in your diet and in the environment, but there are others as well. Here is a chart of common environmental toxins and their possible effects on sexual and general health:

Environmental Toxin	Where Found	Possible Effects
Polychlorinated biphenyls (PCBs)	Banned in the United States, but still found in farm-raised salmon	Cancer, brain, and nervous system effects, endocrine system damage, reproductive and fertility problems, birth or developmental effects, immune system damage (including sensitization and allergies)
Pesticides	Most foods (including fruits, vegetables, commercially raised meats) and bug sprays	Cancer, Parkinson's disease, miscarriage, nerve damage, birth defects; blocks nutrient absorption from foods
Dioxins	Animal fats, farm-raised salmon	Cancer, reproductive and developmental disorders, skin rashes, skin discoloration mild liver damage, excess body hair

Phthalates	Plastic wrap, plastic bottles, plastic food storage containers, and fragrances (any of these sources can leach into food), cosmetics, soaps, PVC tubing	Reproductive system birth defects and hormonal alteration in baby boys; reproductive problems and hormonal changes in men
Mold and fungal toxins	Peanuts, wheat, corn, alcoholic beverages, contaminated buildings	Mild to severe allergic response
Volatile organic compounds (VOCs)	Drinking water, soft drinks, carpets, paints, deodorants, cleaning fluids, varnishes, cosmetics, moth repellants, air fresheners	Cancer, birth or developmental effects, brain and nervous system effects, reproductive and fertility damage, immune system damage (including sensitization and allergies)
Heavy metals (lead, mercury, arsenic, aluminum, cadmium)	Drinking water, fish, pesticides, preserved wood, antiperspirant, dental amalgams	Cancer, neurological disorders, fatigue, nausea and vomiting, decreased production of red and white blood cells, abnormal heart rhythm, damage to blood vessels
Chloroform	Air, drinking water, many foods	Cancer, reproductive damage, birth defects, dizziness fatigue, headache, liver and kidney damage

Adapted from: Environmental Working Group

If you want to minimize the impact of toxins on your sexual health, here are some tips:

- Try, as much as possible, to eat food products labeled "certified organic" and "organic free range."

- Avoid processed foods since many chemicals are used to process them.

- Avoid artificial sweeteners and food additives as much as possible.

- Boost your immune function by getting enough rest and by producing vitamin D through safe sunlight exposure.

- Use all-natural cleaning products and cosmetics.

- Avoid artificial fragrances in soaps, air fresheners, perfumes, cosmetics, fabric softener.

- Have your tap water tested for pollutants and impurities. If it fails the test, install a filtering system.

- Avoid medications whenever possible, including extended release versions with phthalates in the capsules.

The impact of toxins is one that accumulates over long periods of time. By the time we understand all the implications of these substances in our food and environment, the damage will be done. Your sexual health, and that of your children, depends on being as careful as possible now to minimize the impact of toxins on reproductive systems, hormones, and general health.

Sexy Foods

Food can be sexy in a couple of ways. It can give your body the necessary nutrients to keep functioning, and it can offer a sensual opportunity to suggest sexual activity for you and your partner. If you are curious about foods as aphrodisiacs, check out that section of Chapter 2.

Doses of these important nutrients, needed for good sexual function, can be found in common foods:

- Zinc in oysters, pine nuts, and pumpkin seeds.

- Vitamin C in tomatoes, chilies, and citrus fruits.

- Vitamin E in asparagus—lay it on the plate in cream sauce for a suggestive touch.

- B vitamins in whole grain breads and eggs.

- Folic acid in avocados, those "testicles of the gods."

- Allicin, an amino acid in chopped garlic, helps fight disease and has a reputation for improving blood flow and libido. Just be sure you *both* partake, or this little turn-on may drive your partner away.

- Phenylethylamine, the "love chemical" in dark chocolate—it's the perfect small dessert when you want to feel excitement like that tingle of a first crush.

Try This!

If you want to combine nutrient density with sensuality, go for fruit. Fruits contain many vitamins and micronutrients and can be prepared in many suggestive ways to tease and amuse. Try dipping fruits in sauces or yogurt; whipped cream on, well, anything is sexy; and blueberries are loaded with antioxidants. Is there anything sexier than fresh strawberries dipped in chocolate?

Supplements

Eating a healthy diet is the best way to assure good sexual health. But getting every last vitamin and mineral is hard to ensure without a nutrition text and a spreadsheet. So to make sure you are supplying your body with what you need, consider supplementing your regular diet with the following:

- A good multivitamin/mineral tablet taken every morning *or* a stress formula multivitamin if you have a particularly stressful job or are in a stressful phase. It will provide extra B vitamins that your body uses up more quickly when under stress.

- A calcium supplement to ensure that you are getting 1200 mg of calcium a day. The combination of dietary calcium plus supplements will keep your bones strong.

- Enough vitamin D to make the calcium absorb well. Either getting out in the sun or taking it as a supplement will help with calcium absorption.

In addition to vitamin supplementation, you may want to add herbal supplements to your campaign for sexual health. There are many supplements that have been recommended—some of them for centuries—by various types of health practitioners. But keep in mind that many of these compounds are strong medicine and can interact with other medications you are taking or can cause blood pressure changes or other physical symptoms.

Proceed with Caution

Supplements are not regulated by the FDA, so check with your medical provider before adding *any* supplement, no matter how innocent it may seem!

The following herbal supplements are most often recommended for a boost in sexual functioning:

◆ Ginseng has long been known for its restorative qualities and boost for nerve function, energy, and mood. It may improve blood flow to the genitals, helping with erectile and clitoral stimulation.

◆ Ginkgo biloba is an herb that reportedly improves circulation and desire.

◆ Cinnamon, in food or even the smell of it, may evoke an erection in some men.

◆ Yohimbe is an herb that has long been promoted for erectile dysfunction. The most active ingredient is Yohimbine, which is a prescription drug. Yohimbine is rarely used since the introduction of PDE-5 inhibitors, which are much more effective. It does seem to have some ability to increase blood flow. It may also step up your heart rate, though, so check with your medical provider before adding it to the mix.

Exercise

Exercise is a treatment for almost every body woe, and sexual performance is no exception. Your body works better when you use it regularly, and exercise sets in motion many physiological processes that make life—and sex—easier and more fun. Chapter 6 discusses in detail what it takes to maintain your sexual fitness, but let's take a look at the main reasons why exercise is one of your five best bets to keep your sexual health and fitness up to par.

Aerobic Exercise

Aerobic exercise, in which you improve the oxygen capacity of your heart and muscles, tones up and improves every cell in your body. The better the oxygen exchange, the more your cells can do their jobs, and the better your performance in everyday activities and in bed.

When you exercise regularly, you improve blood flow to your genitals, improve posture, ease joint pain, improve mood, maintain good balance, and decrease your risk for heart disease. All of these effects have sexual benefits, and if you can find a way to share aerobic activities with your partner, you have a ready-made opportunity to continue the aerobic activity under the covers.

Don't Resist Resistance

Like aerobic activity, resistance training (also called weight training or strength training) can make and keep you ready to enjoy sexual activities. Whether it is building arm strength so you can stay on top or doing lunges so you can enjoy standing sex, having strong muscles gives you sexual choices you never had before.

Add to the picture that building muscle increases testosterone levels and stabilizes your bones, and it's easy to see why everyone can profit from a weight-training program. Women in particular need to consider weight training as part of their regular routine.

Women do not have the natural muscle mass that men do, so in order to be comfortable with bedroom activities they gain more than men when they are strong. For women, strength training has the additional benefits of creating a faster metabolism to burn more calories in a day and providing an improved body image, which adds that sexy confidence that men find attractive. The goal is not to have a weight lifter's body but to have a body that has all the strength needed to participate in sex fully and in all the ways you desire.

Stretching and Flexibility

Just as women may need someone to point out the benefits of weight training, men will probably need someone to point them toward the yoga mat. Stretching and flexibility are key to minimizing injury, having stamina, and enjoying sexual positions. Ask any football coach about flexibility in his players—he will tell you that it makes a great performer even better.

Stretching exercises take the stress off joints, help muscles get rid of metabolites from other types of exercise, and improve your comfort level in and out of bed. Additionally, stretching is fun to do with a partner, and partner yoga or morning tai chi can open doors in your relationship by sharing the experience, especially when you tell each other explicitly that it's for sexual health.

Balance

Balance exercises are important at any age but become more important as you get older. Exercises that strengthen lower body muscles help with balance, as do those that require you to close your eyes or stand on one foot for periods of time. Being vigilant about your balance can reduce your chance of falling and can help combat the tendency to suffer from vertigo—dizziness—that sometimes happens as you age.

Like strength training, balance exercises prepare you for being flexible with your sexual activity. They improve posture and the way you carry yourself, and they help you present a younger, more vital version of yourself when you walk or dance. Balance is a subtle physical characteristic, and it gives a graceful quality to your movements that can be sexy at any age.

Maintaining Your Weight

As you move through your 30s and into your 40s, maintaining a healthy weight becomes more challenging and also more important. Many chronic diseases are associated with being obese, and maintaining a moderate and healthy body weight will postpone or prevent these diseases from ruining your health and your sex life. Contrary to what most people think, our partners are pretty forgiving about what our bodies should look like. Almost no one expects his or her partner to look like a model, but most people would like a partner to be within the normal range and healthy.

Waist Circumference: Measure Your Risk

Although maintaining a normal weight will help you stay sexually healthy, there are different risks associated with different kinds of weight gain. As most people know by now, when you gain abdominal weight it is more dangerous and can be a warning sign that you are at risk for heart disease.

Proceed with Caution

Women with a waist measurement of more than 35 inches or men with a waist measurement of more than 40 inches may have a higher disease risk than people with smaller waist measurements because of where their fat lies. The so-called "intra-abdominal" or "visceral" fat is associated with much higher rates of heart disease and diabetes.

As outlined in Chapter 15, many medical conditions can diminish your sexual function, and heart disease and diabetes are two of the main offenders. Having and maintaining a normal, healthy weight can help prevent and minimize the sexual problems that come with those diseases. While you don't have to be a fashion model to stay sexually healthy, it does help to keep your blood pressure down and your circulation at its best. Maintaining a moderate weight is a big step toward both.

Weight Loss Programs That Work

Next is the question of which eating program you should try in order to get, or keep, your weight at a healthy level. When retraining yourself to eat the right foods, you can start with a weight-loss program. But it is much better to think of it as a "long-life" program rather than a temporary fix.

There are many weight-loss and dieting programs available. It is big business in a land of big people, so how can you know which one might be right for you? The Federal Trade Commission has developed "Dietary Guidelines for Providers of Weight-Loss Products or Services." As you consider programs, look (or ask) to find out whether that program adheres to those guidelines. According to the commission, successful and reputable weight-loss programs will do the following:

- Not make miracle or exorbitant claims

- Encourage you to follow advice from the federal government's "Dietary Guidelines for Americans" (such as eating five servings of fruits and vegetables per day and choosing whole grains, low-fat dairy products, and lean meat)

- Suggest that your daily calorie intake be lowered by 500 to 1,000 calories but not more than that

- Encourage you to lose weight slowly, not more than one or two pounds a week

- Encourage you to check with your medical provider if you are going to have fewer than 1,500 calories per day

- Include a recommendation for daily exercise

- Design programs that can work in "real-world" eating situations

- Be open about the cost of the service or product

- Share the qualifications of their staff

- Include strategies for weight-loss barriers that you may encounter

- Offer studies and information about success rates and what follow-up services are available

- Be open and honest about the risks associated with the program

Keeping It Off

When you've lost some weight and are at a healthier body proportion, how do you keep the weight off? There is no simple answer to that question, or we would all be at a normal, healthy weight. Many diets and eating programs help people lose pounds, but staying at that healthier weight can be a monumental task.

Part of the answer, as noted earlier, is to see your eating plan as an "eating for the rest of my life" plan rather than a short-term attempt to lose weight. Making small changes slowly, and in ways that show modest, steady improvement in your body size, is the best way to go. With each little change, tell yourself that you are creating the healthy body you want to carry you through your long and happy life.

Beyond the Basics _____

Being aware of your hunger level is important if you are going to maintain a healthy weight. When your stomach is empty, it stimulates the release of ghrelin, a hormone that signals hunger. This in turn makes eating seem urgent and can lead to overeating. Eating foods high in fiber, like fruits and vegetables, with small amounts of protein will keep your stomach full longer and will trigger ghrelin release less often. Eating many small meals throughout the day helps prevent the release of it as well.

Sleep: The Other Reason to Be in Bed

Sleep is a component of good sexual health that is often minimized or overlooked. In our busy "do more with less" culture, sometimes people who do sleep enough are seen as slackers or underachievers. But actually the opposite is true. People who get the sleep they need are healthier in body and mind than their drowsy colleagues.

Sleep's Impact on Sexual Health

Sleep is essential for performance of all kinds, including sexual performance. Studies have shown that increasing sleep time improves the performance of athletes, and many Olympic athletes sleep in rooms controlled for temperature, light, and noise.

Being deprived of sleep affects mood, coordination, and mental acuity. In fact, sleep deprivation can impair motor coordination and judgment in much the same way as alcohol. Sleep deprivation also disturbs hormone function, which affects libido and sexual function in both men and women.

Lack of adequate sleep has been shown to increase the risk of many medical conditions and diseases. Poor or inadequate sleep has been associated with an increased risk of the following:

♦ Heart disease and stroke.

♦ Diabetes, probably due to changes in insulin regulation that occur with too little sleep.

♦ Breast and colon cancers, possibly because melatonin, a hormone that helps protect against these cancers, decreases when you are exposed to artificial light at night.

◆ Obesity. If you sleep only 5 hours a night, you are 73 percent more likely to be obese than your friends who get a full 8 hours.

◆ Depression, although depression can trigger insomnia, too, so it is hard to sort out whether too little sleep triggered the depression or vice versa. It is likely that insomnia and depression cycle, each making the other worse.

◆ Poor immune response. Without enough sleep, your body does not produce as many antibodies to fight disease.

◆ Motor vehicle accidents. It's estimated that as many as 20 percent of car accidents are caused by sleepy drivers.

Lack of sleep and fatigue are show stoppers in the bedroom, too, and during times of life when sleep is hard to come by—like when children are small and when women go through menopause—women especially are much more likely to suffer low libido.

What Is a Sleep Disorder?

A sleep disorder is any disturbance in sleep patterns, including difficulty falling and staying asleep, problems staying awake, trouble following a regular sleep schedule, and behaviors that disrupt or occur during sleep. Sleep disorders are common in both men and women and become even more common with age. About one in six people have a diagnosed sleep disorder, and estimates of undiagnosed disorders put them at about the same rate. That means there are 40 million people in the United States with a diagnosis and another 40 million who aren't getting good sleep and haven't yet sought care.

Beyond the Basics _____

Severe sleep apnea may reduce sexual desire, sensation, lubrication, and orgasm for women. This in turn can affect the quality of a couple's relationship. Although women do not have sleep apnea as often as men, researchers estimate that over 90 percent of women with the disorder don't even know they have it. So if there's a chance your sexual relationship is suffering from the poor quality of your sleep, talk to your medical provider about a referral to a sleep disorders clinic.

Sleep disorders leave you frustrated, tired, and not functioning at full capacity. Sex goes by the wayside as you toss and turn, relationships are strained, and your sexual health becomes the last thing on your mind as you cope with your exhaustion.

Lifestyle Changes That Can Put You to Sleep

If you think you have a sleep disorder (or if your partner thinks you do!), see a medical provider and get a referral to have it checked. If you have only occasional problems sleeping, here are some ideas that might help:

- Stop using caffeine after noon. Even if you think it does not affect you after that, it remains active and can keep you from falling or staying asleep much later that night.

- Don't use alcohol to fall asleep. Although it may make you drowsy at first, it will become an irritant later and will wake you before you can get enough sleep.

- Make your bedroom as dark as possible or use eye shades to block the light. Use room-darkening shades so that your body isn't cued by outside light to waken.

- Sleep without fluctuating noise like a television or stereo. The changes in tone can keep you from falling into the deep, restorative sleep you need.

- Whenever possible, exercise before dinner. Exercising later in the day can make it difficult to get to sleep. But *do* exercise since that will help your body feel tired enough to fall asleep.

- Learn relaxation or meditation techniques and use them in the last few minutes before sleep to ease your busy brain into restful sleep.

- If something wakes you up and you can't stop thinking about it, write it down quickly and then see if you can return to sleep. Sometimes capturing a thought will keep it from haunting you for hours.

- Manage stress. The more you learn to manage the stress in your life, the less it will interrupt you at odd hours. Cortisol, the hormone released with stress, disrupts other hormones, including the ones that regulate your sleep.

Medications That Can Help

There are many medications that are used to help with sleep disturbance. The over-the-counter medications are mostly mild antihistamines and can be helpful for falling asleep. Prescription medications
such as antidepressants, anti-anxiety agents, tranquilizers, hypnotic
sedatives, and other medications can also be prescribed to help with
sleep. Some medications are habit forming, and some can interact badly
with other medications that you are on, so talking openly with your
prescribing doctor is a must.

When sleep disturbance is caused by an underlying condition, treating the condition is usually the first choice. For example, insomnia is a
symptom of depression, and once the depression is treated the insomnia
may resolve on its own. Likewise, anxiety can cause sleeplessness, and
finding a way to deal with the anxiety will eliminate the need for sleep
medication. If you are regularly using over-the-counter sleep aids, talk
to a medical provider or counselor about your symptoms. The sleep
problems may be a sign that something else is going on.

Alternative Strategies for Getting Z's

Herbal sedatives are available over the counter as well, but they should
be used carefully and may interact with other medications. Some of the
common herbal solutions are valerian root, chamomile, catnip, ginseng,
hops, passion flower, kava, lemon balm, and skullcap. There are seda-
tive teas that combine different plants to help with sleep.

Getting exercise during the day can make sleep better, and learning
techniques such as meditation or progressive relaxation can help you let
go of the day and slide into a natural sleep. Acupuncture is also helpful
for balancing your system enough to sleep naturally.

Habits to Break

Even though you have heard these recommendations before, review
them in light of your sexual health. Some habits are truly the death
knell for your sex life, especially as you get past your 30s. The sooner
you consider their impact, the sooner you can do something about them
and prevent irreversible damage. If you are serious about improving
your sexual health, these have gotta go.

Smoking Strangles Your Sex Life

Smoking is a killer any way you look at it, and that goes for your sex life, too. Nicotine causes constriction of the small arteries that supply blood to the penis and clitoris, decreasing erection and sensation. It causes heart disease, which impairs sexual response. It also causes cancer and respiratory problems, which rob you of your vitality and sometimes your life.

That said, if quitting smoking were easy there would be millions of smoke-free people. Nicotine is highly addictive, and the longer you smoke, the more receptors your brain has created for the nicotine to bind to. That makes quitting tobacco one of the hardest habits to kick. Talk to your medical provider about using the patch, hypnosis, medications, and whatever it takes to break the hold tobacco has on your body. You (and your sexual partner) will never regret it.

Alcohol and Performance

Alcohol has an ironic connection with sexual performance. When you are under the influence, you will probably find that reducing your inhibitions raises your interest in sex. And the higher your interest, the higher your hopes. But alcohol impairs sexual function, and regular heavy drinking can impair it permanently.

Alcohol also impairs your judgment, prompting you to take sexual risks you would not take if you were completely sober. You could pay a lifetime with a viral sexually transmitted disease for one tipsy little lapse in judgment. It's a high price and can be devastating to your sexual choices. If you think you are hooked on alcohol, or if your partner and others have told you that you have a problem, talk to a counselor or medical professional about getting some help.

Other Lifestyle Adjustments Worth Making

Any lifestyle changes that walk you in the direction of good health are good for your sexual health. If you want to make a noticeable difference in the quality of your sexual performance and in the quality of your life and relationships, do the following:

◆ Get screened for chronic diseases like diabetes and high blood pressure so you can make changes early in the game.

- Take as few medications as needed to keep your body in running order. Don't go off medications without talking it over with your medical provider, but also don't take over-the-counter medications every day without realizing that they can take a toll on your body, too.

- Pay attention to what you eat. What you eat today becomes your body tomorrow, and you want your body to be a healthy, sexy version of your self.

- Move more. Introduce more moving and walking and stretching into your life. Do it in playful ways. Your body was designed to move, and moving it all day long will help you move it in bed.

- Don't use illegal drugs. They are tempting and seem to be a quick, fun high. But if you go for the hit, you will lose out in the long run. They misuse the body that you want to serve you well, and over time you will find that they—or the lifestyle you adopt to keep getting them—own you.

Remember that you are the one who decides which sexual life you want to lead. If you allow yourself quick jolts of instant pleasure with food and drugs, or if you insist on a couch potato lifestyle, you will rob yourself of a long run of sexual health and pleasure. Taking care of your body early in the game is your best bet for being able to enjoy it through the summer of your life and into the autumn years.

The Least You Need to Know

- Less animal fat and more vegetables in your diet will help prevent conditions that dampen sexual performance.

- Getting plenty of water and fewer toxins protects your reproductive health.

- Include aerobic exercise, weight training, stretching, and balance exercises if you want to be in top sexual shape.

- Don't diminish the importance of getting enough sleep. There are medications and strategies to help you get back to a healthy sleeping pattern.

- Cutting out tobacco, excessive alcohol, and other drugs will add years to your sex life and quality to your sex.

Chapter 6

Maintaining Top Sexual Health and Fitness

In This Chapter

- Three types of exercise for sexual fitness
- Different exercise needs for men and women
- Specific exercises for different sexual activities
- Physical exams and tests to help you stay on top

Whatever sort of shape you are in—totally buff, middle of the road, or on the pudgy end of the spectrum—you can improve and/or maintain your health and sexual fitness. It's not a matter of dramatic, life-changing diets or rigorous training routines as much as it is a conscious, persistent effort to work good habits into your days.

Research is finding ways to keep individual cells alive for extended life spans by preserving their energy-generating mito-chondria. But until researchers can offer this same technology to humans, we are each on our own to preserve our sexual capaci-ties and good health. Men and women usually have different goals and approaches but, acknowledging these differences, we also have a lot to learn from one another.

Maintaining the maximum sexual fitness for *you* is a combination of deciding what fitness level is reasonable and possible and then incorporating lifestyle elements that achieve it. Simple? Yes. Easy? Not so much.

Staying in Shape

"Staying in shape" implies that you are already in shape to start with. This may or may not be true, but this chapter is really about encouraging you to, first, not lose any ground, and second, improve your sexual fitness.

Staying in shape for sexual activity requires that you determine what that means in your unique life. What level of fitness does sexual activity require for you? Are you there and just want to maintain? Or do you want to be ready for increased or different sexual pursuits? Whatever your sexual fitness goals, there are ways to achieve them without turning your life upside down.

Daily Exercise

Your sexual fitness depends on your body's ability to respond to sexual cues and create opportunities for sexual expression. If you are too much out of shape or too tired, you will not welcome sexual adventures with the same enthusiasm as you could with a little preparation.

Exercise is heaven for some people but purgatory for others. You may be somewhere in the middle, willing to do the work but not eager to make it your life's mission. That's good enough for becoming more sexually fit.

It's important to know that, for getting ready for better or more frequent sexual activity, daily exercise is much more effective than the weekend warrior approach. Your body responds to the regularity of moving and working muscles, and after awhile it "asks" you to exercise.

Aerobic Exercise

A well-rounded exercise plan includes aerobic activities like walking, running, rowing, swimming, or biking (spinning, if it's indoors on a trainer). Choosing one of these that you enjoy, and doing it every other day for about a half hour, will bring some welcome changes to your sex life.

Research shows that both men and women who get regular aerobic exercise …

- Produce more testosterone, which boosts sex drive.

- Notice improvement in their mood.

- Sleep better—and a rested person is more ready for sex!

- Have more blood flow to the genital area, making them more responsive and sensitive to stimulation.

- Have better all-around stamina, including during sex.

- Have better lung function and therefore more oxygen during stressful or exciting activities.

In addition, men who exercise are about 30 percent less likely to have erectile dysfunction, and women who exercise have significantly fewer hot flashes during and after menopause. You now have plenty of reasons to add aerobic exercise to your days!

Anaerobic Exercise

Getting enough aerobic exercise will improve your endurance and your heart, but it's not enough to prepare you to fully enjoy your sex life. You also need *anaerobic exercise* to round out your sexual fitness program.

def•i•ni•tion

> **Anaerobic exercise** is exercise done intensely for short periods of time, and it uses a different process for making energy than aerobic exercise. It is primarily for building muscle strength. You may have heard anaerobic exercise called strength training, weight training, or resistance training. Whatever you call it, it can offer a big boost to your sexual performance.

Men and women who do two to three sessions of resistance training a week will notice results in the first month. The sexual benefits are obvious when you can hold positions longer and more comfortably, but there are other reasons to start with some sort of weight or resistance exercises:

◆ An increased feeling of well-being

◆ Improved balance

◆ Less joint pain, which makes sexual activity easier for longer periods of time

◆ Better bone density, making fractures less likely (for those more adventurous types!)

◆ Greater body confidence (reported by both men and women), a characteristic that's attractive to both men and women

Although it's women who are encouraged to do more weight training as they get older to maintain their bone mass, both men and women enjoy their (and each other's!) bodies more when they are stronger and toned.

Beyond the Basics _____

Don't get a "muffin top" abdomen that pooches out over your waistband. Strength training for women who have not yet gone through menopause can help reduce abdominal fat. Researchers found that when women added strength training to recommended physical activity, they gained less abdominal fat than another group that did the physical activity alone. In addition, the strength-training women lost an average of 4 percent of their body weight overall, compared to no weight loss in the "activity-only" group. Strength training is another weapon against the "muffin top" weight gain effect, which is so common in women as they age.

Stretching

Stretching or flexibility exercises are an absolute must if you are trying to improve your sexual fitness. Women tend to be naturally more flexible than men, but both men and women become stiffer and less agile over time, sometimes beginning as early as your 20s! If you want to avoid cramps during a romantic moment or pulling a muscle attempting a new position, now is the time to add stretching to your daily practice.

Stretching is easy to begin. It requires no equipment, no gym, no partner (although it can be fun with a partner), and not much time. You can start by stretching before you get out of bed in the morning by lying on your back and bringing your knees up to your chest—try doing it one knee at a time, and then both knees. You can cross one bent leg over the other and pull it up toward your opposite shoulder, then repeat that on the other side. Even this small amount of stretching reminds your body how to move.

Continue this stretching after you get out of bed, and warm up first by walking around, or doing arm circles and neck circles, or by stretching just out of the shower. Get a good book on stretches, choose just one or two for starters, and do them every morning. You will notice that you move more sensually, gracefully, and more comfortably after even a few days of stretching.

Extending the parts of your body to their full range of motion—arms, legs, torso, neck—takes only minutes in the morning, and you will feel the results all day long. Stretching can actually help your muscles recover from workouts or from sex that leaves you a bit achy.

If you have a partner who is willing to stretch with you, make it a sensuous shared activity. Play like a couple of cats in bed, reaching and extending arms and legs around and over each other. Take a yoga class together and practice at home naked or in silk underwear. Not only will it keep your muscles pliable and ready for fun, it might lead somewhere delightful whenever you practice. What a great way to start your day!

Regular stretching gives your body extra range for being creative in bed, but it's a multitasking activity because people who stretch regularly ...

◆ Cope better with stress, which is a major factor in sexual dysfunction.

◆ Have better circulation to *all* areas of their body.

◆ Move more lithely, which implies body confidence.

- Have more energy since muscles are more efficient.

- Are more aware of their bodies, which makes them more present to body sensations and pleasure.

- Have less joint and muscle pain, which can be a major distraction during sex.

When you decide to start a stretching program, take it easy. Never bounce to try to force your muscles, tendons, and ligaments to extend too quickly. This can cause tiny tears in the muscles and ligaments, or if you do it too quickly or dramatically, it can actually pull and injure the tissues. The last thing you want is to be able to move *less* in bed when you were hoping to move *more*.

Building Exercise into Your Life

When you first try to include exercise in your daily routine, you might be overwhelmed and feel stressed by the prospect. Or you might be gung ho and try to include so much that you can't possibly keep it up. The most successful exercise practices are the ones you like and the ones that you gradually increase over time until they just become a natural part of your day.

Choose activities that you enjoy doing. If you find running torturous, you are not going to keep at it. But if you like swimming or walking, start there. Whatever you do, don't train for a triathlon if you haven't been off the couch in months.

Sometimes setting a distant goal helps motivate you. If you want to run marathons, start with a 10K walk and train for that. Set yourself up for success. Once your body moves more, you will notice that you feel more confident about sharing it. Use activity dates to meet people or enjoy time with your partner. A walk in the woods could lead to more than grandma's house.

> **Try This!** _____
>
> Once you have decided on an activity that you will enjoy, start writing on a calendar or in a journal what you do each day. Here are some other ideas for easing exercise into your life:
>
> ◆ Design a simple goal sheet with dates for reaching some very reasonable goals (walk 8,000 steps a day, stretch for 10 minutes first thing in the morning, and so on) and keep track.
>
> ◆ Ask your partner what exercise he or she would like to do with you. Do that.
>
> ◆ Find a buddy who likes to do the same exercise and make weekly exercise dates.
>
> ◆ Add one tiny additional movement activity a week and try to do it daily (climb a set of stairs, walk an extra block from the bus stop, stand up from your desk once an hour and walk down the hall and back, stretch at your desk). Keep track.
>
> ◆ Find an event at least three months in the future. Set a simple goal to achieve by that event (walking a mile a day by the time your college roommate comes to visit, stretching every morning by your sister's wedding day, doing 10 pushups each day by the first day of summer). Keep track.

How Much Exercise Do You Need?

If you want to feel better, look better, and be ready for a little playful romance at the end of the day, how much exercise does it really take? Researchers agree that exercise is best if it is daily or as many days of the week as you can manage. At least a half hour each day will keep you aerobically fit and reduce your risk of heart disease. If you want to lose weight in addition to getting fit, then closer to an hour is probably what you will need and at least six days a week.

A great way to move slowly toward better tone and energy is to walk or do aerobic activities every day for about a half hour. Then three days a week, do some weight training for tone and muscle strength. If you add stretching on days when you don't weight train, you have a complete package of sexual preparation. And you don't have to do all your exercising at the same time—you can try smaller "exercise spurts" as long as they add up to at least half an hour a day, and you will notice your fitness level rising.

> **Beyond the Basics** _____
> Men who exercise regularly have better erections. Probably due to the combination of better circulation and more testosterone production, men over age 50 who are active are about one third less likely to be impotent. And it gets better: One study surveying men between 50 and 90 years old found that the more fit the man was, the better able he was to get and maintain an erection.
>
> Put down the remote control, men, and put on your running shoes—get that blood moving and those muscles working if you want to improve the quality of your sex life!

Men and Women: Different Strategies

Due to size, body composition, and hormone activity, men and women tend to have different challenges to becoming fit. Men have more muscle mass compared to women of similar height, and women are usually more flexible than their male counterparts. So getting men to try flexibility exercises can be almost as difficult as getting women to try weight training. But both need both, so a well-rounded exercise plan will not always come naturally.

Muscles Matter

Good muscle strength helps both men and women enjoy and sustain sexual activity until both are satisfied. Whether you want to be able to sit facing each other in a tantric position or you want to be able to lift your pelvis to meet your partner and maximize penetration, you need muscle tone to do it. If you have noticed that your muscles are sore the day after making love or that you don't seem to be able to hold sexual positions as long as you'd like, then you can use some improved muscle tone.

Besides making sex possible for longer, muscles step up your metabolism and burn calories even at rest. Building muscles protects your bones by helping maintain the calcium levels in bone tissue, and they hold your body in a youthful posture. Got it? Muscles matter.

Stretching: Why Limber Is Sexy

Ever think about why cats are seen as sensuous, sexy animals? It's not a mistake that we use the terms "sex kitten" or "tiger" when talking about sexually attractive people. Cats move in a way that is both athletic and sensual, and it's partly because they are such good stretchers. Being flexible as a feline is not just elegant, it enables you to climb around in bed in all the ways you want to.

A flexible body also has less pain, more range of motion, and fewer injuries. It's a characteristic that wears well over time, so pull out that yoga mat and reach out.

Energy and Stamina—Not Just for Guys

Both strength training and stretching result in better energy and stamina. Add aerobic exercise to the mix, and you will notice a marked improvement in your tolerance of taxing activities, including sex. And although stamina is often mentioned in the same breath as "male performance," women want to last in bed, too. The longer you can sustain sexual activity, the more time you have to do the following:

◆ Enjoy touch and foreplay

◆ Lubricate and anticipate orgasm

◆ Please your partner

So stamina is not just code for postponing ejaculation, it's a quality you want to cultivate to enjoy each other longer and to extend the pleasure of a sexual interlude.

Targeted Exercises

It's great to have a program of regular aerobic exercise and weight training, but sometimes it helps to work on specific areas to reach particular sexual goals.

Kegels: His and Hers

Probably the most well-known sexual exercise is the Kegel exercise. Developed by Dr. Arnold Kegel in the 1940s, it was originally intended to help women deal with incontinence after childbirth. But it has been used for years to tone up the pelvic floor muscles for other reasons, too—like sexual pleasure! Recent research with men using the Kegel exercise has shown that it is equally valuable to both genders.

Try This! _____

How to do a Kegel:

First, figure out which muscles are the pubococcygeal muscles by urinating and trying to stop the flow of urine. If you can stop your urine flow, then you have found the right muscles. Close your eyes and notice which muscles you are squeezing. Once you've discovered the right muscles, don't repeatedly stop your urine flow since this can confuse your bladder muscle about whether to relax or contract to release urine.

While you are sitting or standing, tighten the "Kegel muscles" as strongly as you can. Hold them tensed for a slow count to 10 and then slowly release them. Repeat this about 10 times. If you do this twice a day, you will probably notice a difference in two to three weeks. It's an "invisible workout" that really pays off!

The Kegel, or pelvic floor muscle training (PFMT), can help many conditions—in both men and women—that happen with normal aging or childbirth.

In women, PFMT may be used to treat or improve the following:

♦ Ability to achieve orgasm

♦ Urinary incontinence—a serious mood killer!

♦ Pelvic prolapse—a "sagging" or "dropping" of the uterus or bladder that can interfere with sex or with a woman's feeling that she is desirable

♦ Healing after childbirth

In men, this exercise proves just as important. With regular use, it may help or improve the following:

- Premature ejaculation

- The ability to have orgasm without ejaculating, helping men become multi-orgasmic

- Erectile dysfunction, both because it improves circulation and because it tightens muscle support

- Urinary incontinence, including after prostate surgery

- Prostate pain and swelling

PFMT is a great first step in dealing with any of these problems, and it is as low tech as it gets. You can do it anywhere (almost) and any time of day. You don't need any equipment, although for women there are assistive weights such as vaginal cones or Ben Wa balls that can be helpful. It's an equal opportunity boost to your and your partner's sexual fitness.

Upper Body: In Each Other's Arms

A strong upper body—shoulders, arms, and neck—will pay dividends in the bedroom. The stereotypical "man making a muscle" pose to impress the girls is not entirely without a basis. Not only do you want to be able to hold each other tightly to convey desire, but you need a certain amount of arm, shoulder, and neck strength to be the partner on top.

Even young men report being tired or sore after having sex for a longer period than they are used to. In the man-on-top position especially, you want to be able to keep yourself from crushing your partner and in a position to be able to move and thrust. This requires good arm strength, sturdy shoulders, and a strong neck. Your partner may be holding you, creating even more resistance, and you don't want to col-lapse in a heap halfway through.

Women, too, get tired when in the "on top" position. Although it is a fun position for both partners and gives her more control over the pen-etration, women are notoriously weaker in the upper body and can find it disappointing not to be able to hold themselves up as long as they want to enjoy the ride.

To avoid that "shaky biceps" moment, include lots of upper-body exercises in your workout. Two or three times a week is enough to keep you in shape for all but the most gymnastic versions of sex play. The classic pushup is excellent for upper-body strength, as is its gentler cousin the kneeling version. Working out with dumbbells to build up your biceps and triceps muscles can be done at home. If you have a pull-up bar, you can work gradually up to excellent arm strength, and no gym membership is necessary.

Back and Lower Body

Your legs and lower back are essential for enjoying sexual pursuits. Your back and legs are the foundation for most sexual activities, so a little proactive building up of your lower torso and legs will literally carry you a long way.

Whether you want to be able to wrap your legs around your partner or be comfortable during standing intercourse, some attention to the condition of your legs is central. Strong and stretched hamstrings give you flexibility and strength for standing positions. Quadriceps and calf muscles give you balance and lap strength for sitting and kneeling positions. If any of those choices are in your fantasies, it's time for some lunges and leg curls.

And don't forget your lower back. Men and women both can have a sore lower back the day after an energetic roll in the sack. Ask any chiropractor or orthopedic doctor and he will tell you that he has treated patients who "threw their back out" having sex. And plenty of people injure their backs during sex who never see a doctor—or don't admit how they hurt themselves!

Your lower back comes into play with any pelvic thrusting you do, which includes most genital-to-genital sexual activities. And the more vigorous you are, the more chance there is for injury or soreness. When sex is really exciting, you want to be lost in the moment, not calling a timeout for back pain.

Try This! _____

To protect yourself from back troubles, start a simple series of back-stretching and toning exercises that can be done on your living room floor. You will want to include the following:

- Hamstring stretches
- Lower-back stretches—like knees-to-chest positions
- Leg lifts and raises
- Abdominal strengtheners—like modified sit-ups—to balance and support your back

Add walking or other weight-bearing aerobic activities to support good posture and circulation, and you have a recipe to keep you at your sexual best.

A lower-back injury can take you out of the game for weeks. Back injuries tend to heal slowly and may keep your back unstable for long periods of time—even years. When you are not in pain is the best time to shore up your back to prevent injury, and simple exercises can create a great foundation for fun.

Abs: For Control and Leverage

Your abdominal muscles literally "girdle" your torso, combined with your lower-back muscles. They support your back and give you an attractive upright posture. You need good abdominal muscle tone for comfortable sitting and walking. If you aspire to any sexual positions that require sitting without support, such as sitting facing each other or woman on top, your abs are major players. Any tantric positions that include extended periods of sitting require good abdominal support. Thrusting (whether you are on top or bottom) and pulling your partner toward you both require abdominal strength.

Childbearing, weight gain, and just general sitting around can take a big toll on your abdominal fitness. Once you decide to regain some tone, take it slowly. If you start too aggressively, you'll be sore and that will discourage you from continuing. A little soreness is okay and even a sign of progress. But don't start out gangbusters because your body will object if it hurts to keep at it. Begin with a few crunches in the morning, maybe even in bed.

Abdominal muscles respond quickly to a program of sit-ups or crunches. Varying the crunches with twisting crunches (touching your elbow to the opposite knee) will add a stretch that increases flexibility along with your abdominal strength. Do your abdominal exercises at least twice a week, with a day in between for muscles to rebuild and recover.

It's impossible to "train" for a date this weekend when you haven't done anything active in months. A stretching and strength-building work-out two to three times a week keeps your body supple and will prepare you for the sexual activities you want to engage in. Even if you don't have a partner right now, it's a great time to ready yourself for a future relationship. If you *are* in a relationship now, talk to your partner about wanting to be toned again and engage him or her in the process. Maybe even share some exercise time together with the goal of having more fun in bed.

Your Annual Physical

Maintaining your sexual health is an ongoing process. Part of that process is keeping a watchful eye by having some regular exams and tests. Problems are easier to correct if you find them early, and a yearly physical is the reality check you need to know how you're doing. Staying ahead of physical problems assures you a good shot at an active, healthy life and an active, healthy sex life as a result.

Essential Physical Exams

Nothing replaces a yearly physical exam as a safety net for guarding your health. Having your doctor's or health professional's experienced eyes and hands checking for problems is a head start on finding any problems early enough to be able to do something about them. Your continued sexual health depends on a healthy body that you can count on.

Women are more often encouraged to see a doctor once a year, usually to monitor birth control methods and general gynecological health. But beginning around age 30 both men and women need to take an active—proactive—role in guarding their general and sexual health. To stay ahead of sexual problems, consider the following yearly exams by a health professional:

◆ A breast exam for women and for men who find a lump in their breast. (Men normally have small amounts of breast tissue and can develop breast cancer.)

◆ A pelvic exam for women to assure that your uterus and ovaries are normal and without any lumps or growths.

◆ A testicular exam for men. Unlike many cancers, this one tends to strike men at an early age, most commonly between the ages of 15 and 34. All men should feel their testicles carefully once a month. The shower is the best place to do this.

> **Beyond the Basics** _____
> After age 40, there's more reason to start keeping track of how often you visit your doctor or health professional. For the National Institutes of Health recommendations for how often to get physical exams at your age, visit this website:
> www.nlm.nih.gov/ medlineplus/ency/ article/002125.htm

◆ A prostate exam for men every year after the age of 40. If you are having problems with getting an erection, those problems may be related to an enlarged prostate and this is the time to check.

◆ A skin exam every year after you are 50. Your skin is a major sense organ through which you experience so much of your sexual pleasure. Be sure there are no cancerous areas to worry about.

Screening Tests

In addition to a hands-on (or "eyes-on") exam by your medical provider, there are also routine screening tests that can protect your sexual well-being. Check at your yearly physical about whether you need any of the following:

◆ **A pap smear and human papilloma virus (HPV) screen for women over 30.** If the pap and HPV are normal/negative, then this test can be done every three years. (Every three years is probably often enough for women who are in monogamous relationships, do not have HIV, and are not exposed to new HPV. But if you have *any* doubts about whether you've been exposed, ask for it annually!)

◆ **An STD check.** If you have had a new partner in the past year or if you are in a nonmonogamous relationship, these tests are essential. Be sure that your screening for sexually transmitted diseases includes HPV since that virus can cause several types of cancer.

◆ **Women should have a mammogram every year after the age of 40.** If you have any risk factors for breast cancer or find a lump, you may need mammograms or other tests even more frequently.

◆ **Everyone should get a baseline colonoscopy or sigmoidoscopy at the age of 50.** Colon cancer and other bowel diseases disrupt not only your sex life but every other aspect of life as well. If you have symptoms or a strong family history of colon cancer, you may need to be screened earlier than that, and if you have diabetes or are African American, get that colonoscopy at 45!

Your medical provider may suggest that you get other screening tests as well, but protecting your sexual health and well-being is a great excuse to get in for your annual physical.

Labs That Tell the Story

In addition to screening tests and an exam, there are probably lab tests that your health-care provider will want to see. If you are worried about any of these conditions, you can ask for the lab tests yourself:

◆ **Blood glucose check.** If you have any symptoms of diabetes or if it runs in your family, ask for this. Diabetes can cause sexual dysfunction in both men and women.

◆ **Hemoglobin.** If your energy is down or if you are a woman who has very heavy menstrual periods, your iron stores may be low. A blood test to check the iron level may be a good first step.

◆ **Cholesterol levels.** Heart disease has many implications for your sexual function. Keeping tabs on your cholesterol level can provide the first hint that you may be developing cardiovascular problems.

◆ **Pulmonary function tests.** If you have noticed that you are short of breath during sex or other strenuous activities, these tests can help determine if you need some sort of respiratory support such as inhaled medication.

- ◆ **At age 40, a baseline prostate specific antigen (PSA) test should be done.** This test can help detect prostate cancer in early stages when the physical exam is still normal. At age 50, this will probably be part of your annual checkup.

Any of these lab tests may be ordered as a routine part of your annual health exam. But if you have specific areas or conditions that you are particularly worried about, ask your provider whether the test is warranted. It's your body, and you have a right to the information that will help you make good decisions about it.

Check the Scale

People tend to gain weight as they get older. Your metabolism slows, and your activity is usually less than when you were younger. The best way to fight obesity is not to let it sneak up on you. If you are not someone who weighs him- or herself at home, be sure to get your weight at your yearly physical. It is much better, though, to invest in a good bathroom scale and "weigh in" several times a week.

Staying within normal limits on weight helps you keep your energy, flexibility, and youthful body. If you notice that your weight is beginning to climb, drop those pounds early rather than letting them raise your risk factors. It might help to know that many diet experts feel that "new" fat is easier to shed than older, established fat, so paying attention can make your job easier.

When you're done stepping on the scale, check yourself in the mirror. Are you developing a big tummy? Belly fat is not an innocent marker—not only does it give you an unattractive body shape (which can be murder on your dating self-confidence), it is actually dangerous. A yearly waist measurement will help you know if you are at risk for diabetes or heart disease.

Proceed with Caution

As an added incentive for guys, men who gain belly weight usually also add fat down in front of the pubic bone, which reduces the amount of visible (and available) penis. We all claim size doesn't matter, but it's a rare man who wants to see his penis shrink!

If you are a man with a waist measurement over 40 inches or a woman with a waist measurement over 35 inches, it is time to get into a serious weight loss program before you develop problems that can't be reversed. It may help you to keep an old belt to compare your waist measurement now to what it has been in the past.

Weight is a problem endemic to our high-fat, low-activity culture. Your sexual health will fare much better if you can manage to stay within a normal weight range. Your body looks better, moves better, and is more attractive to you and your partner if you work at keeping a healthy weight year after year.

Repairing the Damage: Sooner Is Better

We can't keep our bodies from aging. In fact, if we are lucky we get to age! But you can minimize the wear and tear of the years if you attend to problems early. Some potentially dangerous or debilitating conditions can be headed off at the pass if you catch them soon enough. Your sex life will be the last thing on your mind if you are faced with a life-threatening or handicapping condition. Here are some common early signs of trouble:

◆ New or more-severe-than-usual headaches

◆ Shortness of breath when you exert yourself

◆ Pain anywhere that is not explained by recent activity or injury

◆ Sudden or worsening low energy levels or extreme fatigue

◆ Any new or abnormal finding on one of your self exams, such as a breast or testicular exam

◆ Unexplained gain or loss of appetite or weight

◆ Unexplained sadness or emotional distress

Listen to your body, and if anything seems amiss, check it out with your health care provider. Even life-threatening conditions can often be treated or controlled with early care, diet, and appropriate exercise. Your love life follows your body, so pay attention and stay ahead of the game.

The Least You Need to Know

◆ A combination of aerobic exercise, stretching, and weight training will prepare you for most sexual activities.

◆ Starting with small exercise goals will help you succeed.

◆ Women tend to be more limber but need to work on muscle strength.

◆ Men tend to be muscular but need to stretch.

◆ You can prepare for specific sexual positions with specific exercises.

◆ Your yearly physical is a maintenance must.

Chapter 7

Cleanliness Is Next to Sexiness

In This Chapter

- Which types of body hygiene are good for your sexual health
- Why smelling "good" may not be so great
- Why it's a smart idea to keep from washing *too* much
- What you can do to help your body stay balanced and "self-cleaning"
- Differences in male and female hygiene

Clean is good, right? We live in a culture that encourages us to stay ultra clean and smelling "good." Sometimes it's easy to forget that your body was designed to stay healthy without constant scrubbing. But how do you know where to draw the line on germs?

No one wants to offend others with their bodily odors—least of all your partner or date—and *some* washing is necessary for sexual health. On the other hand, washing too much can break down your skin, which is a natural barrier and provides protection against infections and the microorganisms that cause disease. This chapter takes a look at what kind of clean is sexually healthy and what might be too much of a good thing.

Body Hygiene

Staying clean is good for your social life—you probably learned that part of the lesson in junior high school. Check out the personal ads sometime, and you'll see how often someone mentions "poor hygiene" as one of their personal turn-offs.

But there is more to hygiene than remembering to shower every day. There are good reasons to keep some things clean and good reasons to leave others well enough alone.

It's "Natural," But Is It Healthy?

Some people subscribe to the school of thought that declares, "My body smell is natural, so I don't need to wash it off." And to some extent, that may be true. But if you want to attract a sexual partner, it serves you well to pay attention to your "natural" odor.

Body odor is a tricky topic. If you have bad breath or smelly feet or a sweaty aroma, most people won't tell you. If you work outside or in an environment where no one gets close enough to take a whiff, how you smell is pretty much moot. But when it comes to being in close quarters—and definitely when it comes to being in intimate quarters—the last thing you want to do is offend someone with your odors.

Most unpleasant body odors are caused by bacteria. Bacteria grow best in dark, moist areas, which explains why certain parts of your body smell stronger than others—namely, your underarms, feet, and groin area. These areas are usually in the dark, and generous sweat glands see to it that they are usually wet or moist. This is a perfect recipe for bacteria and the odors they cause.

Beyond the Basics

Some people avoid dating or sexual intimacy altogether because they have been told they have a strong "fishy" or "garbage" odor. If you, or someone you know, have always had such an odor, it could be a disease called "trimethylaminuria," also called "fish malodor syndrome." People with this condition lack an enzyme that breaks down bacteria byproducts in the intestine.

Although there is not a cure for this inherited disease, it can be treated by avoiding certain foods such as fish, eggs, beans, and organ meats. Sometimes antibiotics can help for short periods of time. Researchers also found that increasing the daily intake of charcoal and chlorophyllin could also help reduce the odor. See a doctor (or have your partner see a doctor) if you think this might be affecting your ability to get close to others. You might have this treatable condition.

For normal amounts of bacteria, showering or bathing daily with mild soap will keep you smelling and feeling fresh enough. Antibacterial soaps are not necessary, and even deodorant soap should be saved for those with particularly strong underarm odor. Your genital area does not usually need any special attention unless you are dealing with an infection or overgrowth of bacteria, in which case you will want to check with your health-care provider to determine whether you have a treatable condition. If any of the following happen, check in with your doctor or clinic:

◆ You have a sudden increase in the discharge from your penis or vagina, whether it is clear, cloudy, or white.

◆ You or your partner notice a strong odor coming from your genitals.

◆ You see any unusual sores or redness on or near your genital area.

◆ You notice pain, itchiness, or burning that does not go away after a day.

◆ You or your partner notice a persistent sweet, sour, or "bad" odor in your sweat or urine.

When your natural body odor is kept in check by daily washing, it may be perfectly acceptable to dispense with antiperspirants. But listen to your partner or friends who tell you that you have a problem with odor. For every one who dares to mention it, there are many who will stay quiet or, worse yet, just avoid you. Nothing will turn a first date into a last date faster than an unpleasant smell that *you* might not even register. For those who have a steady partner, take the plunge and ask if you have any odor or hygiene issues. This kind of honesty is a part of intimacy building and can lead to many other interesting topics.

Odors, Scents, and Pheromones

Your sense of smell is primary—even "primal"—when it comes to your sex life. It cuts through all first impressions and overrides any logical conclusions you might have about a potential partner. Because smells and odors register in your hypothalamus, which is a very primitive part of the brain, smells sidestep any sort of "rational" approach you might have to deciding whether someone is appealing. If they don't smell good to you, you will have a hard time talking yourself into being happy with them.

Sex *pheromones* seem to clue in a potential partner to your mating availability. In the animal world, pheromones signal when a female is "in heat" or is ready to mate or when a male is searching for a mate. In the human world, they seem to have some of the same effects.

def•i•ni•tion

Pheromones are chemical messengers that send signals to another member of the species. In plants, insects, and animals they have many purposes, including marking food trails, sending an alarm, or initiating mating. Sex pheromones can signal attraction, interest, or mating readiness in some species.

Although there is controversy about whether humans have pheromones, there is some intriguing research about how we respond to the chemical messages from others. Some of the more interesting results are as follows:

♦ A male chemical called androstadienone boosted activity in the hypothalamus of heterosexual females and homosexual men but not in heterosexual males.

- A female chemical called estratetraenol triggered activity in the hypothalamus of heterosexual males and in some lesbian women, but not in heterosexual females.

- The smell of androstadienone boosted the level of cortisol in female test subjects. Cortisol is a hormone that causes alertness and is released during stressful or exciting events.

These results seem to indicate that we secrete chemicals that "wake up" the primitive centers of the brain that regulate hormone and sexual activity in the opposite sex. There will be plenty more research on pheromones to figure out the details of how they act on our brains and sexual behavior.

Another interesting note about smells is that women seem to be attracted to men who smell "different" from the woman's family members. Perspiration carries odors that show a person's "genotype," or genetic makeup. Research shows that when a woman smells the sweaty t-shirts of several men, she usually prefers the shirts of the men whose genetic makeup is *least* like her own. Presumably, this is a natural preference for people *least* likely to be genetically related to her and is therefore a protection against inbreeding. Since the women in the studies did not actually see the men whose t-shirts they were sniffing, it has nothing to do with a man's appearance and works at the much more subtle level of smell.

So since you send all sorts of chemical signals to your potential partners, you may want to forego some of the heavier perfumes and deodorant soaps. They might cover up your natural mating signals, and you don't want to do that!

Can You Wash Too Much?

The short answer is "yes," but how do you know how much is too much? Remember that skin is the first barrier to any germs or infection that might be harmful to you. You count on your skin, whether you are aware of it or not, to ward off attackers before you even know they are there.

When it comes to your genitals, anything that breaks down the integrity of your skin is an invitation to germs and infections, so you want every millimeter of skin to be as intact as possible.

Proceed with Caution _____

Washing with harsh soaps or too rigorously can weaken the skin, causing irritation, dryness, and tiny openings. These openings can allow infections to get a foothold where they might not have had an opportunity if your skin was in better condition. To avoid damaging your skin's protective qualities, be sure to ...

◆ Use mild soap without fragrances or deodorants.

◆ Wash gently with a soft cloth.

◆ Don't "scrub" delicate areas.

◆ If you have to bathe more than once in a day, go easy on your genital area.

◆ If you notice a sore or open area when washing, get it checked by a health-care provider before having sex.

Being too rigorous when you wash your genital area can irritate the follicles of pubic hair. This can break the hair, which may cause painful or inflamed ingrown hairs as it grows back. If the follicle remains irritated it can become folliculitis, which is an inflammation or infection of the hair follicle. Usually folliculitis goes away on its own, but an infection may need to be treated with antibiotics. See your doctor right away if the area is warm to the touch, stays red for more than a day or two, or if you notice pus.

When you shower, consider the type of soap or shampoo you are using. Soap has a combination of oils and alkali, and soaps with too much free alkali are very drying. You want a soap that is effective at taking off the dirt without taking all your natural oil with it. It's a delicate pH balance between acid and alkaline, or what is known as the *pH value*. When washing delicate areas like your face or your genital area, you may find that soap with a lower (more acid) pH is easier on your skin, but it also needs to be alkaline enough to clean well. Experiment with various types of cleansing agents, and pay attention to how your skin looks a few hours later.

"Natural" Hygiene

Your body is a magnificent organism that is designed to keep itself in running order. When all is operating smoothly, it is largely self-cleaning. You are most familiar with cleaning the outside of your body—skin, hair, nails. But there are a lot of cleaning and purifying activities going on beneath the surface all the time.

The areas of your body concerned with your sexual function do a great job of keeping themselves clean and working. There are different processes for men and women, but there is definitely a lot going on to keep your sexual equilibrium up and going.

Keeping the Body in Balance

Since your body has so much capacity for "self-righting," your main job is to give it what it needs to keep that process happening. There are many ways to do this through your daily habits and lifestyle. A little attention to some basic things will support your body and have long-lasting sexual benefits.

Eating the right foods can help your body keep itself rolling. (For more about a sex-healthy diet, see Chapter 5.) Choosing foods that have a low glycemic index—that is, that don't set your insulin into overdrive, causing highs and lows in energy and mood—is one of the big favors you can do for yourself. Having good sexual energy requires a steady supply of efficient fuel, so stay away from simple carbohydrates that make you unpredictable. And eating enough vegetables and fruits gives your body what it needs for repair work and fighting infection.

You also need to give your body time to recover from stress, and it's not only about getting enough sleep. A habit of having some quiet time in each day will help you recharge and make it possible for you to respond to social and sexual situations with ease and playfulness. Whatever it takes for you to return to a balanced perspective after a difficult day or a momentous event will put you in a good position to take advantage of romantic opportunities. Maybe it is a glass of wine with your feet up or some yoga breathing exercises before dinner. Anything you can do to let go of the day's stressors will pay off big time in your body's ability to maintain and restore itself.

All of your body's "cleaning" activities require lots of water. If your body fluids are busy carrying byproducts and toxins out of your system, they need enough water to keep replenishing themselves. Water is the magic ingredient that moistens your lips and softens your skin. No one wants a dry mouth when you are in the mood for a kiss, and both men and women need to drink enough water for their bodies to be able to lubricate during sex!

Your Body's Natural Cleaning Cycle

When your body is in balance, it can carry out its natural cleaning cycles. Most of your body fluids are in the business of cleaning up your system. Perspiration carries away waste products from the bloodstream to the surface of your skin, saliva in the mouth helps keep teeth and gums clean, and urine is the vehicle for many waste products to leave your body. Your body has a number of slow-moving "rivers" that transport waste products out.

Sexually this is true as well. Your reproductive organs are cleaned and maintained as part of your body's natural process. For men, this means that every time you urinate, you are not only eliminating all the unnecessary or harmful waste products that are in your urine, you are also flushing out your urethra and moistening the mucous membrane that lines it. This keeps that membrane in good health and working hard to protect you from invading bacteria or other microorganisms that might cause infection.

For women, it is often said that the vagina is self-cleaning. It is normal to have some regular vaginal discharge that carries out skin cells, impurities, and natural cellular secretions from the vagina. You are the expert on what is "normal" for you, and some women can have quite a lot of discharge that is still considered normal for them. It is when that discharge changes in some way—more than usual or with a different odor or accompanied with burning or itching—that it might be a sign of something going wrong.

> **Beyond the Basics** _____
> Normal vaginal discharge varies from woman to woman. Your discharge can be clear, white, or yellowish and still be normal. And it may vary in amount during different parts of the menstrual cycle. You may notice that it is clear and very "stringy" mid-cycle when you are fertile and rather thick and yellowish later in your cycle. You will probably notice more discharge after sexual activity when you have lubricated. Learn what is normal for you.

Good Germs/Bad Germs

Your body has many thousands of resident bacteria and other microorganisms that assist in biological processes. Most of these are normal, helpful organisms, and without them you would be less able to digest food or fight infection. When things get out of balance, your healthcare practitioner might recommend that you take "probiotics," or helpful organisms in the form of powders, pills, or foods to re-establish your normal healthy level of these beneficial organisms in your system.

For women, there are many helpful bacteria present in your vagina to keep the tissues healthy and ward off infections. If something happens to disrupt or destroy these bacteria, you can suffer some troublesome side effects.

For example, if you are on an antibiotic for a sinus infection, it will kill the bacteria in your sinuses but also in your vagina. These vaginal bacteria normally keep the yeast count in your vagina low, but when they are wiped out by the antibiotic, the yeast will have a chance to overgrow and take over. Then you have a yeast infection, which will cause itching and inflammation and might make you vulnerable to other infections.

In addition, if you have sex without a condom and your partner's semen has an alkaline pH, it may create a perfect vaginal environment for bacteria to grow well beyond the normal levels. Then you might develop an overgrowth of bacteria called "bacterial vaginosis," which, while not transmitted from your partner, may be caused by contact with his semen.

When your immune system is suppressed by chemotherapy, HIV infection, or some other reason, you are particularly vulnerable to infection. It is even more important for you to keep enough probiotic organisms in your system to help you fight unwanted infections. Here are some handy rules for keeping your good germs in the right numbers:

◆ Don't use antibiotics except when you really need them. Unnecessary antibiotics can wipe out the infection-fighting bacteria in your body and leave you vulnerable.

◆ Eat a healthy diet, including kefir, yogurt, or other cultured milk products.

◆ Limit the amount of simple sugar you eat since too much glucose in blood and body fluids can encourage the overgrowth of bacterial and fungal infections.

Personal Sexual Hygiene

The term "sexual hygiene" typically is used to mean either birth control or sexual abstinence. In this book, however, personal sexual hygiene refers to taking care of yourself in ways that enhance, protect, and maintain your sexual function. Everything from brushing your teeth to washing your genitals can contribute to your sexual health.

Maintaining sexual fitness requires you to do some simple maintenance in order to avoid certain conditions that can put a major crimp in your sexual activity.

Oral Hygiene

Whether it is a first date or a sexual encounter, your mouth is a major player in your sexual health and fitness. From the most fundamental aspect—your breath—to more delicate sexual encounters like oral sex, oral hygiene is essential.

Having breath that is appealing is obviously a first step toward physical intimacy. Research has shown that couples make decisions about whether to pursue a sexual relationship after the very first kiss. Women use that kiss to assess the intentions and commitment of their partner, and men use it to determine whether the woman is interested in a sexual response. You probably want to maximize your chances for a happy ending to that first kiss, and oral hygiene is a good place to start.

There are a number of medical conditions that can give your breath an unpleasant odor. Sinus infections, acid reflux, tooth decay, and gum disease are some of the common culprits. You may not even be aware of your breath odor since you quickly become accustomed to the taste and odor as your smell receptors fatigue.

Good oral hygiene is exactly as your dentist has described: thorough teeth brushing at least twice a day and flossing at least once a day. If you are a smoker or tend to get a coating on your tongue, scraping or brushing the tongue can help eliminate odors as well. Listen to your friends, and if one of them tells you that you have an odor to your breath, do some detective work to figure out the cause.

 **Proceed with Caution**

If you have a sweet or "fruity" odor to your breath, it's possible that it might be diabetes or another metabolic condition causing the odor. If someone tells you your breath smells fruity, check with your doctor since it could signal a serious condition.

If you are in a sexual relationship that includes oral sex, be aware of the membranes inside your mouth. If you notice any sores, white spots on your tongue or gums, or sores in the back of your throat, get them checked by a doctor or your dentist. You can get yeast infections and herpes in your mouth from sexual contact. You can also get other sexually transmitted diseases in your mouth, just as you can on your genitals. Use a good light and a dental mirror after you brush your teeth to check for any of these problems. If you notice any sores inside your mouth or cold sores around your mouth or lips, refrain from oral sex until you get it diagnosed or it is completely healed.

Finally, nothing puts the light out on your sex life like a heart attack. New scientific research shows that poor oral hygiene can lead to heart disease by causing chronic inflammation. Bacteria can also get into the bloodstream from your unhealthy gums. The last thing you want is a "broken heart" from poor brushing and gum care. Get your dental checkups, brush with good technique, and safeguard your heart, your health, *and* your fresh breath.

"Feminine Hygiene"

Girls learn at an early age that it isn't "feminine" to smell like a woman. There are many commercial products specifically designed to cover or eliminate odors associated with menstruation or normal vaginal discharge. Many women associate vaginal odor with being unclean and spend time and money to eradicate any sign of smells from the vagina and vulva.

As you learned earlier in the section on smells and pheromones, some natural odors are appealing to sex partners. Before you launch a major campaign to eliminate all your female smells, check with your partner about what he or she finds (or doesn't find) offensive. Many of the products used to cover odors can cause an allergic response or irritation, thereby opening your skin up to infections.

Simple daily washing of your vulvar area with warm water and a soft cloth is all you need to eliminate the buildup of oils and skin cells called smegma. When this sticky paste is allowed to collect, it can grow bacteria between the folds of your labia or under the hood around your clitoris. But it is an easy matter to wipe the area clean each day. No further deodorizing or treatment is necessary for healthy genital skin.

There are a couple of conditions that women should be aware of that can be worsened by either harsh washing or failure to wash your genital area.

The first is vulvovaginitis, which is an inflammation or infection in the vulva or vagina. Sometimes this is caused by a sexually transmitted disease, and those infections are discussed in Part 4. But infection and inflammation can also be caused by irritating or harsh chemicals that come in contact with genital skin. Products such as bubble bath, perfumes, feminine hygiene sprays, and shaving cream can irritate this sensitive tissue. Once irritated, it may become infected with viruses or bacteria.

Not washing can also cause irritation to the skin. Wearing tight clothing or underwear of nonbreathable fabric can create a moist environment where bacteria can take over and cause either external irritation or vaginal infections such as yeast or bacterial vaginosis.

Vulvodynia is a chronic pain in the external genitals that gets worse if you wash too often or too harshly. The cause of vulvodynia is not clear. It may be related to irritation of nerve endings from constant inflammation of the area, but it makes sexual activity at least uncomfortable if not out of the question.

In order to avoid or minimize the chance of developing these conditions, women should do the following:

◆ Gently wash the genital area daily with warm water only

◆ Avoid strong chemical cleansers and perfumes

◆ Wipe from front to back after using the toilet to keep fecal bacteria out of the vagina as much as possible

◆ Apply cool compresses to the area if it becomes painful or irritated

◆ Wear cotton underwear or panties made of wicking fabric to keep the area dry

◆ Use tampons and pads of 100 percent cotton

◆ Avoid hot tubs

◆ Use lots of water-based lubricant if you need it during sex to avoid friction to the area

Douching—Good or Bad?

The word "douche" comes from the French word for wash. Many women are taught that in order to be "fresh and clean" they need to wash out the vagina periodically. There are many commercial douching solutions on the market that appeal to women who believe this.

Your vagina does not need to be washed with a perfumed douche or any other product in order to be clean. In fact, these products can disturb the acid pH inside the vagina that helps keep bacteria in check.

Douching can also increase your chances of pelvic inflammatory disease (PID), which is a serious infection in your fallopian tubes or uterus.

Proceed with Caution _____

Here are six good reasons *not* to douche:

- Douching does not eliminate vaginal odor and will probably make it worse by disturbing your good bacteria.
- It doesn't prevent sexually transmitted diseases.
- It can push germs up into your fallopian tubes and uterus and cause a serious infection.
- It strips away the natural flora that keeps your vagina in balance.
- It does not prevent pregnancy.
- In pregnant women, douching is associated with delivering your baby too early and should be strictly avoided.

Sometimes women use a vinegar douche to fight yeast infections or bacterial vaginosis. While it does give the vagina a more acid pH, which helps fight these infections, even vinegar douching is not usually recommended. Research on whether vinegar douching is helpful has shown mixed results.

If you are tempted to douche because you notice an unusual vaginal odor, see your health-care provider to be sure you don't have an infection that needs to be treated. Douching can disguise symptoms and let an infection get out of control.

Male Hygiene

Good sexual hygiene practices for men are simple and pretty straightforward. You need to keep your penis and scrotum as free of bacteria as possible, and it's easy to accomplish with a daily bath or shower and a small amount of attention.

If you are uncircumcised, you need to wash the head of your penis every day with warm (not hot) water. No soap or other washing agents are necessary, but you do need to do it at least once a day. Pull the foreskin back behind the head of the penis and wash well with water. Use your thumb and forefinger or a cotton swab to get the area right where the foreskin joins the head, or glans. This is where skin cells and natural oils collect to form smegma, and it is a magnet for bacteria and debris. After you have washed the glans and the inside of the foreskin, gently replace the foreskin over the head of your penis.

The scrotum and shaft of the penis can be gently washed with a mild soap and water. Go easy on this sensitive area and dry it thoroughly when you are done. This simple daily routine will prevent an over-growth of bacteria and fungal infections that can cause unpleasant odors and skin inflammation. Scrubbing it too vigorously or with harsh soaps can also cause skin irritation and may cause ingrown hairs that can become infected.

There are some uncomfortable consequences for not washing daily, especially in uncircumcised men. For example, the head and foreskin of the penis can become reddened and sore in a condition called balani-tis. The space under the foreskin can harbor bacteria, yeast fungus, or other microorganisms, and the result is an infection. Balanitis can also be caused by a response to a harsh chemical or by an allergic reaction to soap, lubricants, fragrances, lubricated condoms, spermicidals, or other agents. The treatment for balanitis depends on what is causing it. Antibiotic ointments, antifungal medications, or antihistamines may be used depending on the cause. In any case, daily washing and drying of the area is important to prevent any infection from coming back.

Another possible result of ongoing poor hygiene can be phimosis, or the inability to pull the foreskin all the way back from the head of the penis. Usually this happens after an infection or other irritation causes the skin at the tip of the foreskin to develop scar tissue. This scar tissue will contract into a tight ring that will not go over the glans. Sometimes the inside of the foreskin can also stick to the head of the penis, making it painful and sometimes impossible to pull the foreskin back. In extreme cases you may not be able to urinate and might need surgery to correct the problem. The vast majority of uncircumcised men never have any problem with their foreskin, but a little preventa-tive care is very helpful.

Cleaning Up: Before and After

There is a "continuum of cleanliness" when it comes to sex. At one end are those people who are fastidious about having not a single germ on their bodies or genitals and who would be repulsed at the thought of being less than squeaky clean—and they may hold their partner to this standard as well. At the other end of the continuum are those who pay no attention to whether they have washed recently and may be unknowingly offending sex partners (or potential sex partners) with their indifference to personal hygiene. Most of us fall somewhere in between.

In general, you want to be clean enough that you are not forcing bacteria from your body into your partner's. A quick clean up before sexual activity can be a confidence builder for you and can help you feel freer and less anxious about what your partner is thinking.

On the other hand, it is also worth a conversation with your partner to see whether some odors are arousing or appealing to him or her. You don't want to wash so rigorously that you totally rule out that "animal attraction" that your partner feels for you.

After sex, don't scrub your skin too hard since this could actually open up tiny places where infection can get in. Uncircumcised men show a lower rate of sexually transmitted diseases if they clean under the foreskin every day, thus giving bacteria and viruses less opportunity to grow and multiply.

One study raised questions about how soon to wash after sex when it showed that uncircumcised men who washed immediately after sex (within three minutes) had a greater chance of getting HIV from their partners than those men who waited at least ten minutes to wash. Researchers aren't exactly sure why this would be true, although one theory is that contact with the acid vaginal fluids makes it harder for the virus to survive. The bottom line for uncircumcised men is to clean your penis thoroughly every day but not immediately after having sex.

You've probably heard that urinating after sex is a good idea, and that is true especially for women. Vaginal sex introduces bacteria up through the urethra and into the bladder. If you have the presence of mind to drink two to three glasses of water in the hour before you have sex, it will guarantee that you have enough urine in your bladder to be able to urinate after sex. Flushing out your urethra—the tube leading from your bladder to the outside of your body—can lower your chances of getting a bladder infection. Urine will also reestablish the normal pH in your urethra and make it harder for germs to set up camp.

It's also important to remember, however, that urinating does not prevent you from getting a sexually transmitted disease. It does not prevent pregnancy, and it does not guarantee that you won't get a bladder infection either. So while a post-sex pee is a great idea, don't expect it to protect you from infections or pregnancy, and don't believe anyone who tells you it will.

Shaving and Waxing—for *Both* of You

There was a time when the rules were pretty clear: Men shaved their faces, and women shaved whatever hair was considered "unseemly." Well, the rules have changed. Or maybe more accurately, there are no rules about who should shave what. Getting a bikini wax used to be just for women, but now men are waxing and shaving the genital area, too. As standards of beauty change and evolve, your ideas about what hair you want to keep—and what hair you want *not* to keep—may change as well.

Once again, a check-in with your partner might be in order. If your partner finds it a turn-on to see your _____ (you fill in the blank) bare and smooth, you might be willing to give it a go. Whether it is waxing and/or shaving your back, face, genitals, legs, armpits, or head, you will want to remove the hair in a way that does not cause any harm. Here are a few guidelines for removing hair safely:

♦ Take your time. Whether waxing or shaving, being careful pays off.

♦ Use a warm, wet towel to soften the skin around the area you want to shave or wax.

♦ For shaving, lubricate with shaving gel, gentle soap, or petroleum jelly. Leave the lubricant on for a few minutes before you shave.

♦ Shave in the direction of hair growth and not against the grain. Shaving directly opposed to the hair growth can cause ingrown hairs, which may become infected or inflamed.

- Waxing is okay for some areas, but it can be quite painful if the hair is long or the first time it is done. Waxing is *not* for the scrotum!

- Depilatories are not recommended for tender areas, and do not use them at all on the scrotum because they can cause a chemical burn to sensitive tissue.

- After shaving, use aloe gel or lotion, preferably one without fragrance. This keeps the skin in good condition and helps prevent ingrown hairs and itching.

- Pay attention to the shaved area and keep it clean and moisturized for several days to avoid infection.

- If you want to keep the area free of hair, consider laser hair removal or electrolysis. These methods are more permanent; however, they can be expensive.

The first time you shave or wax an area, you will probably get considerable itching and maybe redness. This tends to lessen if you keep the area regularly shaved or waxed, as your skin toughens to the process.

Shaving and waxing will often result in ingrown hair, and the closer the shave, the more likely that you will have ingrown hairs. Since an ingrown hair is an opening in the skin with an irritant under it, there is a fair chance of a skin infection as a result. Watch for signs of redness, warmth, or yellowish drainage. See a doctor or health-care professional if you notice any of these symptoms around an ingrown hair. Sometimes treating with a topical antibiotic ointment will heal the infection, but if it doesn't go away within a couple of days, see a doctor. You may need oral antibiotics.

The Least You Need to Know

- Keep your body clean enough to be safe but not so clean that you damage your skin or turn off your partner.

- Smells—good and bad—play an important role in sexual health.

- Your body does a lot of cleaning on its own, and you can help it by eating, resting, and giving it enough water.

◆ Men need to keep their penises clean, especially when uncircumcised, in order to prevent infections in themselves and their partners. But they should wait at least ten minutes after sexual activity before cleaning up.

◆ Women need to gently clean their external genitals, but douching is *almost never* recommended and can even be dangerous.

◆ Shaving can be very sexy, but easy does it!

Part 3

It's All in Your Mind

We've all heard that "the most important sexual organ is the brain." But how does that connection play out in real life? Your body and mind are not separate entities; they play off each other and affect how you perceive the world around you—and how you perceive that world affects your body and your health.

Your mind is also the source of your attractions. Understanding why certain people spark your sexual interest and how that affects your love life is not entirely a mysterious process. Much of it is biological, and some of that "magic" is also psychological. Attraction and love are critical players in your sexual health. The more you know about your own love tendencies and habits, the more you can attract healthy, loving sexual connections.

Chapter 8

Sexual Health and Fitness—The Mind/ Body Connection

In This Chapter

- ◆ How your mind affects your physiology
- ◆ Why stress derails sexual response
- ◆ Training your mind improves your sexual experience
- ◆ The role of optimism in sexual health
- ◆ How attitude contributes to sexual health

We've all heard the saying, "The brain is the most important sex organ." You won't get much argument that your state of mind has a tremendous impact on your sexual response. But what is that response really made of, and how can you work the mind/ body connection to your advantage when it comes to sexual fitness?

Your Body Listens to Your Thoughts

First, let's differentiate between *mind* and *brain*. While the mind and the brain are related, they are not the same.

def•i•ni•tion

The **brain** is the part of your central nervous system located in your cranium, or skull. It serves as the main receiver, organizer, and distributor of information for the body. The **mind** is your conscious awareness as it is demonstrated in thought, perception, will, memory, and imagination.

You need the physical cells in your brain functioning so that you can exercise your mind, and your mind can, in turn, cause changes to the chemicals of the brain.

Since sexual fitness requires a mixture of physical fitness and an awareness of how your mind affects your body, fitness improves if you understand what you can do to get your mind and body on the same wavelength, with the same goals.

When you are in any situation—work or play (sexual or nonsexual)—you respond to that situation based on what you *think* is happening, not necessarily what is actually happening.

For example, if you are with someone who keeps checking her watch and you think this means she is bored, you respond to that. You might be hurt, or angry, or relieved, but you are responding based on your perception—what you *think* is happening.

But what if that person is looking at her watch because she is parked at a meter and is worried that she is going to get a ticket? And what if she is really attracted to you, wants to continue the conversation, but doesn't want to get a ticket? You might end the date, or feel hurt, or get angry for nothing.

There are plenty of opportunities like this to misinterpret situations every day. We are stuck in "thought habits," and we don't even know it. We make automatic assumptions, behave as if they are true, and never know whether they are or not. Therefore, we have lots of chances to make mistakes—and lots of chances *not* to make mistakes.

Usually this goes on unconsciously, and most of the time we make good decisions about how to act. If you see a car coming toward you and you jump out of the way, you made the right decision. The problem is that because we are correct *most* of the time, we think we are correct *all* of the time. Your perception *is* your reality, and your perception may or may not be right.

So if we behave due to what we think is going on, how do we decide when to believe ourselves and when to check our assumptions? That takes some paying attention to thought habits. Your thought habits can be taking you for a spin, and you may not even know it.

Physiology and Thought

There are many things that affect the chemical environment inside your body—your genetic makeup, illness and disease, what you eat, what drugs you take, your thoughts. You don't have control over the genetic cards you were dealt, and you may have an illness or disease that is out of your control. But the other factors are ones you have choice about, and your thoughts are directing the show.

This is not a new notion, that you control your thoughts and your thoughts control your actions. Ancient wisdom such as yoga, Buddhism, Taoism, and others emphasized the mind as the way to change behavior. Yogis who can lower their blood pressure or slow their heartbeat were forerunners to people who learn biofeedback to lessen pain or calm anxiety. Thought leads to state of mind, which leads to state of body.

To be sexually fit, you need to understand the role you play in determining your body's well-being. Having the ability to calm your mind and think chosen thoughts will clear the way for you to build a history of positive sexual experience. You can make it possible for the release of endorphins and serotonin (chemicals that create a state of calm pleasure) to replace adrenaline and cortisol (chemicals that create a state of fear and/or stress). It could mean the difference between pleasant, relaxed sex and tense, anxious (or no!) sex.

Beyond the Basics _____

One dramatic example of how thoughts and your response can create a physical condition is something called "broken heart syndrome."
The clinical name is "stress-induced cardiomyopathy," and it occurs when
a person has an intense emotional response to an event, such as the
death of a loved one. The sudden release of stress hormones, like adrenaline, seems to temporarily damage the heart, causing heart attack symptoms. It usually resolves on its own, but it is painful and serious. Literally, a
broken heart.

Your body's response, including its sexual response, depends on your
ability to distinguish a true emergency from a perceived emergency and
act accordingly.

Stress Response

You've probably heard of the stress response. It is often referred to as
the "fight or flight" response. Research has refined our understanding
of the stress response and has found some gender differences as well.
Let's look at the stress response in stages and see how it affects your
sexual health.

Phase 1 of the stress response is the triggering event. The triggering
event is any event that threatens you in any way, whether it is an emotional threat or a physical threat. So let's say that the triggering event
is your spouse coming home and announcing, "I'm leaving you for
someone else." This would obviously be stressful for most people. But
any unexpected event or major change can be a triggering event for the
stress response.

Phase 2 of the stress response is your interpretation of that statement.
Chances are, you will perceive that statement as an emotional threat.
(Unless you were _hoping_ your spouse would leave you, which would
make it something altogether different.) So your thought is something
like, "Oh, no. I'm losing the most important person in my life. I won't
be able to survive! I can't do this!" Your mind is telling your body that
a life-threatening event is taking place.

Phase 3 of the stress response is where your physiology helps you out. Your body "understands" that you suddenly need to respond to a threat, and it kicks out stress hormones and shuts down all nonessential systems, putting the focus on your heart (which starts beating madly), your brain (which starts thinking a million thoughts a minute), and your muscles (which tense up ready for whatever action you decide to take.) For men, who have testosterone mediating their behavior, they are ready to fight or flee.

Women have a bit of a different response to this threat. They are apt to go into a "tend and befriend" stage that focuses on protecting the children and calling in their social supports. This makes biological sense because, if women had always had a "flight" response, they would have left the offspring behind. So women tend to think of how to protect the children and instinctively bond with other females about what to do. They have the same rapid heartbeat and stomach-in-a-knot response, but in the absence of all that testosterone, it seems to trigger the additional release of the hormone oxytocin, which creates the bonding and protective instincts.

Okay, so you are in a full-blown stress response. If the triggering event is something that is immediate and short lived, everything plays out well. You have an argument that resolves the issue, and your body recovers, returning to normal.

But if it turns into a long-term, chronic stressor—your spouse packs a bag and leaves, and you are faced with a long, drawn-out divorce—your body stays in this state of phase 3 stress response. Your blood pressure stays high, your digestive system is shut down, and your muscles stay tensed. You don't sleep, you get headaches, and your short-term memory is shot. When you are in this stage for a long period of time, you are prone to the following:

- Eating badly—probably sugary or high-calorie foods to give you energy

- Being emotionally labile, up one minute and down the next as you struggle to respond to each new situation

- Being forgetful since you are preoccupied with surviving this event

- Having high blood pressure, which can cause a stroke or heart attack

- Getting an ulcer because your stomach is not emptying properly and you are producing more stomach acid

- Using chemical "coping supports" such as nicotine, alcohol, caffeine, or other drugs to help you cope, sleep, wake up, etc.

It's not hard to see that a stress response shuts down your ability to respond sexually. Even if it's not an issue in your relationship that is the triggering event (it could be, say, losing your job or having a seriously ill child), the body's response to chronic stress is not conducive to closeness, playfulness, or positive communication, all of which are important in a sexual connection. You are busy saving your life—at least that's how your body sees it—and you have more important things to do than have sex.

Training the Mind to Calm the Body

So how do you short circuit the stress response so that you can cope and function? There are several places where you can break the cycle, but it takes some training. Everyone has strong, learned stress responses, and it takes energy, awareness, and effort to intervene.

The first thing you can do is avoid triggering events. If you know certain circumstances are stressful for you and they are avoidable, you can stop the stress up front. Say "no" to that speaking engagement; don't meet with your ex-girlfriend to divide up the CD collection; don't volunteer to coordinate the fun run at your child's school.

Even if you reduce the triggering events in your life, which is a very good idea, there will still be situations and events that provoke a stress response. So what then?

Well, next you can take a deep breath and decide whether this really *is* a threat. That sounds simple, but we are usually on autopilot about triggering events, and when you hear your ex-husband's voice on the phone asking when you can get together to go over that last credit card bill, you are conditioned to feel stressed. Give yourself some time to think about it. Tell him you will call him back. Take a deep breath and ask yourself, "Am I in danger here?" If the answer is "yes," then make a plan to protect yourself. Take a buddy with you to the meeting, or have him fax you the bill and tell him you will call him after you've had a chance to look it over. Whatever you can do to put some space between you and the "threat" keeps you from kicking into a full-blown stress response.

Find ways to reinterpret a stressful situation in ways that put a positive spin on it. Is there a way to find this just "interesting" or "informational" instead of threatening? Can you make a game of it or make a bet with yourself about how you will behave? Try to find a way to see it as difficult but not scary. In other words, if you tell yourself another story about the stressor, and it will become less of one.

Try This!

The next time you recognize yourself having a stress response to something minor but unexpected, do a progressive muscle relaxation. Sit or lie in a quiet room. Starting at your feet, practice tensing and then relaxing each group of muscles—feet, calves, thighs, buttocks, abdomen, chest, upper arms, forearms, hands, neck, face. Contract each set of muscles tightly, making it small and firm, and then relax it completely. Pay attention to what it feels like to be tense; notice what it feels like to relax. If you practice this enough, you will be able to consciously choose relaxation when you feel your muscles tighten up.

If there are elements in your sex life that make you anxious, practicing stress-reduction techniques ahead of time can minimize your stress. Whether it's a new date or an argument that comes up when you and your partner are together, being calmer will make it possible to be truly present in that moment and deal with the stressor in a productive or positive way. You can enjoy the date. You can resolve the argument.

Whether your stressors are sexual or otherwise, there are several things you can do to lower your response to stress:

- Eat properly so that your body has what it needs to respond to stressful situations.

- Exercise for 20 minutes a day, either aerobic or strength exercise.

- Learn stress-reduction exercises like progressive relaxation, visualization, or breathing techniques.

◆ Take a meditation class and practice for 15 minutes a day.

◆ If you feel stressed or anxious most of the time despite trying some of these things, check with your medical provider to see if anti-anxiety medications are worth a try.

Becoming familiar with the stress response is the first step toward not letting stress rule your life or your sex life. Once you understand what it means, it's time to put energy into de-stressing your life so that your mind is available for the sexual activities that you want to pursue.

Want Better Sex? Relax!

Now that you've had an introduction to the stress response cycle, we can take a look at what it means to your everyday sex life. There's plenty of room for you to take the pressure off and improve things in the bedroom.

Stress Can Kill Desire

How exactly does stress sidetrack your sexual response? There are several ways it can take a toll and several ways you can consciously minimize the damage.

Learning to deal productively with stress is important because your body needs to recover from stressors in order to have a healthy sexual response. It is an interesting dance between excitement and relaxation.

Your *autonomic nervous system (ANS)* is the conductor of the sexual symphony, bringing in first the *parasympathetic nervous system (PNS)* to get things started. This lets you relax and lets the spongy tissue around the penis or clitoris fill with blood—an erection.

Next, the *sympathetic nervous system (SNS)* revs up your system. Your heartbeat gets faster, you breathe heavier, your pupils widen, and your muscles tense. This is what most people recognize as sexual arousal. It's the I-want-sex-right-now feeling that you have when you are eager for sex.

def•i•ni•tion

> Your **autonomic nervous system (ANS)** is the part of your nervous system that regulates involuntary functions like heartbeat, breathing, digestion, gland activity, and sexual arousal. It has two "divisions" with separate responsibilities— the **parasympathetic nervous system (PNS)**, which is responsible for calming your body down when the immediate stress is over and the **sympathetic nervous system (SNS)**, which is responsible for initial stress response.

Sound familiar? Then it is a careful balance of PNS relaxation to keep the erectile sensitivity going but SNS excitation to bring you to orgasm. If everything works, then voilà—orgasm a la autonomic! If the parasympathetic system takes over after your orgasm and relaxes you dramatically, falling asleep is likely. (Guys, if your partner complains that you fall asleep too fast after sex, blame it on the parasympathetic nervous system!)

Understanding this process gives you a clue about the effect that anxiety can have on a sexual encounter. If he can't relax in the first place, a man may have trouble with an erection because his stress response is keeping the smooth muscle in his penis from relaxing to fill with blood. No fill, no erection. But being able to reverse his anxiety will let his body respond to his arousal, first with an erection and then with increasing excitement. It works similarly for women but more invisibly.

It's clear that staying on the good side of stress is a boon to your sexual response. The trick is to recognize the signs of your own stress response and then counter its effect with the strategies you've learned for calming the waters.

How to Let Go

If you find yourself in a situation where stress is messing up the moment (and if you are astute enough to realize that it's happening), you have choices. Learning how to make good choices can be the difference between a temporary blip on your sexual radar screen and a stress habit that digs you into a hole.

Probably the most important action is to call a "time out" for yourself and get a moment to decide how to react instead of reacting out of instinct. Let your body work *with* you, and use your mind to give your body some direction. Here are some things to consider:

- **Timing is everything.** If there is a time when you notice that you are more stressed than others or when you tend to be irritable, be aware of it. And definitely avoid it as the time for amorous advances.

- **Ignore the small things.** When there are small things that irk you, decide which ones you can just ignore. Picking your battles instead of letting them all trigger stress is one way to train yourself out of over-responding.

- **List your alternatives ahead of time.** Go over in your mind the other ways to deal with repeating problems or stress triggers; that way, you can make a better choice in the moment.

- **Try massage.** Having a skilled massage therapist work with your body and muscles can educate you about where and how you hold your stress and how to do it differently.

Beyond the Basics

You know that stress can short circuit your sexual response, but it can work the other way, too—sex can counteract stress. A British study asked men and women to keep a two-week journal of their sexual activities. They then underwent a stress test of public speaking and an oral math test, and their blood pressure was measured. Those who had engaged in penetrative sex—penis in vagina—showed the least stress, and their blood pressure returned to normal faster. This effect lasted for over a week, and the stress reduction was not seen in those who had other kinds of sex, like masturbation. Researchers theorized that the release of the hormone oxytocin with penetrative sex is protective for future acute stress.

Besides the strategies mentioned earlier in this chapter, try taking slow, deep breaths when you want to turn that stress train around. Stretching your chest muscles in a slow, rhythmic fashion will kick in your parasympathetic nervous system and give you the calm moment you need

to reconsider. This is also a good move if you are having trouble getting an erection since it might give you just enough relaxation response
to let that spongy erectile tissue fill up. You've got nothing to lose by
learning how to give yourself the space to make something positive
happen.

Reading Your Body

Assumed in all this "making choices" talk is that you can tell when you
are starting to get stressed. That can be a big assumption, especially for
people who are used to minimizing body sensations or pain. Both men
and women are guilty of this, and it is common for people to tune out
stress until some damage is done. It's often seen as a plus if you can just
"suck it up" and continue past your edge of tolerance. Too much of that
and you will have learned to ignore your body's danger signals.

Becoming aware of your body's response is a step-by-step process.
Practices such as meditation and relaxation exercises are a great place to
start because they require you to tune in to your body. Once tuning in
becomes a habit, you can use that information to actively choose how to
feel and behave.

Tuning in to your own body not only makes your sexual experience
more positive, but it can be extended to your partner. Being familiar
with your own stress and mood responses can key you into those of
others, including your partner. Nothing is sexier than someone who
knows when to give you a neck massage because they noticed that "you
look a little tense."

Exercise and Mood

Research shows that exercise improves your mood and your coping
ability. What the studies usually show is that regular exercise, both
aerobic and anaerobic, improves your mood, outlook, and general feeling of well-being. Exercise works best for temporary or situation-based
anxiety and stress and does not have as much impact on a negative
mood when it is your constant state.

Depression and Exercise

Exercising several times a week generally helps to lift depression. It's not clear whether it's the improved circulation, better nutrient flow to the brain cells, or more release of neurotransmitters like serotonin and endorphins that does the trick. But the effect shows up consistently in the research.

And it doesn't have to be a rigorous workout. Small and moderate amounts of exercise help lift mood as well as heavy workouts. Some research even shows that smaller, more moderate amounts of exercise work *better* because people are more likely to continue them over time if they are easier to work into their lives.

> **Proceed with Caution** _____
>
> Some antidepressants like selective serotonin reuptake inhibitors (SSRI) can affect your sexual response. If you are on such medications, you have to weigh the cost of being depressed with being slower—or unable—to reach orgasm. Sexual health for you may mean finding ways to enjoy sex in spite of the side effects, or it may mean finding other medications that will work as well for your depression.

Another benefit of exercise is the increase in testosterone. This enhances your sexual well-being by raising libido. That, along with improved mood and energy levels, can boost your sexual fitness score all around. If depression or mood problems are an issue for you, regular exercise is a perfect complement to medication and/or therapy, and it may make enough difference all by itself to lift your mood.

Walk in the Sunshine—Depression Buster

If you want to maximize the impact of exercise on mood, try walking outside every day. Receiving light through your eyes helps your body convert tryptophan to serotonin, which is a mood-elevating hormone. This is particularly helpful if you suffer from seasonal affective disorder (SAD), a depressed mood during the months of the year when sunshine is less available.

In one study, women who walked 20 minutes a day outside and took a vitamin supplement reported not only an improved mood but also decreased tension and anger. Exercising in the sunlight also increased self-control, energy level, and a sense of well-being. Because it was an easy regimen to follow (a vitamin pill and a 20-minute walk once a day), the women tended to continue the practice well beyond the study period. If you want to maximize your exercise benefit, exercise outside.

The Role of Optimism

When considering the way your mind can improve your performance—in sex and in life—don't overlook the impact and importance of optimism. By studying people who seem to persist despite problems and challenges, the benefits and attributes of optimism seem almost magical.

Studies show that optimistic people get sick less, live longer, and are more successful in work. A positive outlook and cheerful persistence seem to trump other characteristics like intellect and opportunity when it comes to succeeding in the long run.

Put On a Happy Face—Choosing Joy

The interesting thing about optimism is that, while some people are naturally inclined to be more optimistic, even pessimistic people can learn to be more positive. If you are not a "Pollyanna" sort of person, that's okay. You can still learn ways of thinking and interpreting life that will make you more successful and satisfied.

Optimism is a cognitive habit. Some people are consistently more positive in their outlook. They tend to be probability thinkers and adapt easily to change. Pessimists tend to see things as unchangeable and pervasive. In other words, no matter what you do, things won't get better—the Eeyores of the world.

Try This!

When you find yourself seeing things in a negative light, ask yourself whether the problem is ...

- ◆ Personal—Is this really about you?
- ◆ Permanent—Does it always happen this way?
- ◆ Pervasive—Is it this way in all situations?

Then decide whether there are ways to make it *not* about you, *not* permanent, and *not* pervasive. The more you do that and the more often you do that, the more you will benefit from optimistic thought.

If you can learn to interpret a situation differently, you can begin to behave like an optimist. In one study that followed men aged 65 to 85 for a decade, the most optimistic of the men were 45 percent less likely to die of any cause than the most pessimistic men. Particularly for cardiac disease, optimism seems to be protective. It seems that looking on the bright side can keep you around for many more years to do so.

How Optimism Improves Sexual Health

Your sexual health and fitness can benefit tremendously from learning a more optimistic approach to life. Couples who have a positive explanatory style—that is, who explain things as hopeful and globally positive—show greater satisfaction in their relationships. This, in turn, opens the door for trust and more closeness.

If you explain things to yourself in a way that gives you an "out," you are more likely to keep trying and eventually succeed. This is true sexually as well as in other spheres. If you tell yourself that you can figure this out—whether it is how to ask someone out a date or how to find your partner's clitoris—you will be more likely to persist until you *do* get the date or find that clitoris. And that, of course, gives you confidence that you will continue to succeed. Optimism breeds success, in and out of the bedroom.

Attitude Matters

Your attitude is what and how you think about a matter. Since it is pure thought and completely voluntary, attitude is something you have control over. Your attitude is a filter through which you see your world, and this filter affects your perception.

Your attitude about sex has a lot of influence on your sexual health. What you learned as a child, how you explored sexuality as an adolescent, and your experiences as an adult have all helped you form your attitude toward sex and toward your partner(s). If you are noticing patterns in your sex life that you are uncomfortable with, check your attitude for clues. How do you feel about women in general? Men? Is sex a positive aspect of your life or a chore? Do you think it is healthy to want sex? Is it okay for your partner to want more or less sex than you do? And if that's the case, what does it say about them? About you?

Exploring questions that reveal your attitude will give you clues about where to start. People usually get what they believe in, not what they ask for. If you are not getting what you want, take a close look at your attitude and what you believe about those things you want—or *think* you want. You may discover that your attitude about women is affecting how you treat your lover. You may realize that your attitude about living with your partner before marrying is making you feel bad about yourself and, therefore, about having sex with that partner. Talk about your attitudes with others and see how they see the same situations. Be prepared to learn things you may not expect.

Appreciation Is Sexy

One attitude that is never out of style is appreciation. Appreciation of your partner is something you can always afford. Whether it is his or her body, smile, supportive behavior, cooking, willingness to pick up his or her socks—there is always something you can appreciate. If there isn't, or if you can't find something, your attitude will reflect that, too.

Having a general attitude of appreciation takes two things: noticing what you appreciate and communicating that to your partner. Appreciation is something that grows as you share it, and sharing it opens doors to understanding what you value in each other. It builds your emotional bank account for those times when you make a "withdrawal" by arguing or failing to appreciate. Building this bank account makes you both feel rich.

What About Your Partner's Attitude?

What if you think it's your partner's attitude that needs adjustment? When your partner has a negative attitude, it can wear away at the relationship and at your enjoyment of each other. You can't change your partner's attitude, but you can decide how you will respond to it.

First, check your own attitude. What would your partner say is the problem? Is any part of it something you can change or adjust? Do you resist making that change? Why?

If your attitude is positive, hopeful, and appreciative, then what? Communication is the order of the day when two people have vastly different attitudes toward a relationship. Can you talk to your partner about his or her attitude? If not, it may be time to let a professional help you get your attitudes on the same page. Don't put it off. It's not unusual for couples to fade into a sexless marriage or relationship because one or the other didn't know how to adjust his or her attitude to keep the spark alive. Don't be afraid to get help—this is not a simple conversation.

It is also not a matter of blaming one another. Couples often find that there are differences in hopes, desires, and goals in a relationship. You may have different libidos, different priorities, or different levels of fatigue. There are many reasons why you get out of sync, and attitude is a symptom that you could use the trained ear of a skilled professional to get you back on track.

Making Positive Choices

Making positive choices is up to you. Your mind can have a profound impact on your sexual health, and it takes one good decision after another to lead you to a satisfying sex life. Once you begin to use your mind to create your reality, your goals will become clear, and you will discover there are many right ways to get where you want to go. Learning how to interrupt the automatic choice maker inside you will be the beginning of creating the sex life you've always wanted.

The Least You Need to Know

♦ Your behavior depends on your assumptions, and some of your assumptions may be wrong.

♦ Your autonomic nervous system takes your sex life for a ride, and it might be a good ride or a bad ride.

♦ When stress takes a bite out of your sexual response, you can intervene early in the process by using relaxation and breathing techniques.

♦ Exercise improves mood and is even more effective when it's done in the sunlight.

♦ Optimism is good for your sexual health, and you can learn how to think like an optimist.

♦ Your attitude toward your partner is a conscious choice, and you can improve your connection by working with your attitude.

Fateful Attraction: Can Love Make You Fit for Sex?

In This Chapter

- Two ways to understand "having chemistry"
- How love changes our physiology for the better *and* the worse.
- Why oxytocin is called "the trust chemical"
- How the health of your marriage and the health of your body are linked
- How love and sex enhance each other to the benefit of your sexual health

Can falling in love be good for you? Bad for you? Love and sex seem inextricably connected, but are they always so? And how will your sexual health or fitness benefit from love? There may be more questions than answers about love, but there is no question that it has an effect on your body's health.

One of the questions is whether "falling in love" and "being in love" are made of the same stuff and whether they have a similar impact on your health and your sexual health in particular.

That heady, freefall experience of head-over-heels falling in love is responsible for one set of chemicals released into your body. Coined by Dorothy Tennov as "limerence," this experience is what all the songs are written about. It is the high and the low, the Romeo and Juliet, the "can't get her out of my mind" experience that some people are prone to and others aren't. If you are the sort of person who experiences love in that Shakespearian way, you understand well what limerence is.

Lust is something different. The urgent, "gotta have it" sort of desire for sexual union can be very strong. Like limerence, people have it to varying degrees, and also like limerence, it can override your sense of reason, cloud your judgment, and rule your life.

The pair-bonding, forever after, till-death-do-us-part kind of love is yet another version, and it gives rise to its own set of chemicals in the body. What are the differences between these experiences of love, and what price does your body pay for them? Knowing the answers to these questions may not change your experience of love, but it can help you understand what is happening to you.

What is sexual attraction made of? Will understanding it change the nature of it? Can it be healthy? Is it love? These are the topics of this chapter.

What Is "Chemistry" Anyway?

Using the term "chemistry" when discussing love and sex can be taken two ways. When you say "we have chemistry," usually you mean that you feel a draw to each other. Something inside "clicks," and you both feel a rightness about the connection. If you can't always articulate what makes for sexual chemistry, you usually know it when you feel it.

But there is another meaning for chemistry in sex and love, and that involves the chemical responses of your body. In recent years, science has begun to examine the neurophysiology of "love" and "attraction" so that we can better understand the experience and its implications in our lives. The study of this area is as much art as science since it is necessarily based partly in measurable results and partly in subjective experience and ancient bodily responses.

I've Never Felt Better: That Lover's High

Being in love feels good. No, being in love feels great! Particularly for those who are limerent—capable of limerence—being in love is the experience they seek and, in some cases, seek often to maintain the high.

Scientists are just beginning to analyze the reasons for this experience. Some of the love light, it seems, is chemical. People in the initial phase of romantic love have elevated levels of dopamine in their system. Dopamine is a neurotransmitter that is involved in the reward system of the brain. Research is trying to sift through its role in behaviors like sex, eating, and attraction. There is some evidence that it seems to increase "wanting" rather than "pleasure of having." This would explain the experience that so many people have of urgent longing when they are in love.

The initial phase of love also raises levels of phenylethylamine (PEA). This acts much like amphetamine and raises heart rate and blood pressure and decreases appetite. The "high" associated with early love is a bit like a hit of cocaine. No wonder you want to feel it again and again.

Proceed with Caution

On the other side of that high, when it wears off or when your affection is not returned, is the low side of being in love. Just as withdrawal from cocaine leaves you strung out and depressed, withdrawing from limerent love is a feeling of terrible sadness and desperate longing. All your recently stimulated receptors are asking for more chemical reward. People deal with this sudden drop in many ways, including eating, drinking alcohol, and using illegal drugs. It is common to feel sad or even depressed, and grieving lovers are famous for their suicidal tendencies.

Clearly, as good as it feels to be in love, it may not be worth the low of being "out of" love. When Dorothy Tennov described limerence in her research, she was not making the point that it is a preferred state. She was making the point that it is a common experience, generalizable to many people, and that it is tumultuous and draining when it isn't euphoric and sublime. Like any mountaintop experience, there's always that trip back down the mountain. The limerent moment is memorable but not necessarily enviable. Overeating, alcohol and drug use, and suicide are not on the list of sexually healthy habits.

The Rules of Attraction

There are many rules of attraction. There are biological tendencies, personal idiosyncrasies, and cultural standards. There are many ways to determine whom we should be attracted to, but there are also all the inexplicable subtleties of whom we are attracted to. This chapter can't sort out all the variables, but it can introduce a few.

First, there are the biological odds. When studies are done on people's tendencies toward attraction to sexual partners, we seem to be unconscious "choosers," preferring some candidates over others. What connection do these choices have to our sexual health, and how can we incorporate this knowledge into our plan to be sexually healthy?

One of the clear preferences that studies have revealed is the preferences for body proportion. As cited in Chapter 2, men in general prefer a woman with a smaller waist and larger hips. Women prefer men to have small hips and waist, with more chest. Biological underpinnings of these choices are easy to deduce. Men want a woman who can safely bear children; women want a strong man who can protect and provide for the family. These preferences operate on a subconscious level. We prefer people who are healthy and who appear to have the capacity to carry on the species. Even when we have found a partner, we will be drawn to those who are biologically attractive.

In the larger scheme, though, what do these preferences mean? They tell us that health is the marker of attractiveness. All the things that we gravitate toward sexually—waist/hip ratio, clear skin, symmetrical features—are markers for health. They are subliminal cues that "this person is healthy and going to be around for a while." For sexual health, you want to send the message that you are strong and healthy and that your body can sustain the wear and tear of life. This means that exercising is more important than expensive jeans and that proper diet is sexier than short skirts.

Beyond the Basics _____

We are drawn to people who "feel" familiar. Sometimes that is healthy and sometimes not. In order to change the sense of "rightness" about someone who is damaging to us, we require changes to the limbic portion of the brain, where emotions are interpreted and regulated. This is a complex and daunting process, and this "limbic revision" requires healthy relationships with people who are emotionally stable and available to us. These could be close friends, a new partner, or a therapist. Changing your ability to manage attraction takes energy and time, but if it results in a satisfying, happy pairing with an equal, it could be the best decision you've ever made.

Beyond our biological leanings, where does attraction come from? One theory that has gained support is from medical psychologist John Money, who proposed that as small children we form "love maps" that are the template from which we choose our sexual and life partners. These preferences are a subconscious "check list" that we measure people against, and when you are attracted to someone but can't say exactly why, it is probably because the person meets the criteria on your love map list. The closer the match, the stronger the pull.

These love maps can interfere with your sexual health if you are persistently drawn to people who are destructive to your psyche, who tend toward violence, or who do not reciprocate your affection. Making these templates conscious can at least make you aware of your automatic choices. If you see a pattern of making destructive, unhealthy choices, the difficult work of changing (or ignoring) your love map can become part of your quest for sexual health.

Attraction is an alchemy of biology, upbringing, culture, and self. Why we love the people we love will always be something of a mystery, but the more conscious you can be about it, the more likely you are to find someone who supports your sexual health, your emotional well-being, and your satisfaction with life.

Loving Is Good for You

The highs and lows of limerent love are arguably worth it or not, depending on the person who is experiencing it. But the positive health effects of longer term loving and of caring for another person are well documented in the research. Whether it is recovering from an illness or keeping your blood pressure lower, people in relationships have an advantage over those on their own.

Loving someone else boosts your immune function and teaches you empathy. Once the initial excitement of infatuation wears off, you have the chance to create a sexually healthy life with someone else who can meet your needs for intimacy and companionship well beyond the honeymoon period. In surveys to measure the level of sexual satisfaction, all ages show higher scores when they have a regular, familiar partner with whom to share sexual experience.

The Cuddle Principal

Part of the reason that a regular partner improves your life and health is the impact it has on your physiology. Living in close proximity to someone you love has a soothing, regulating effect on your life and on your body. Unless the relationship is marked by frequent conflict, it does a body good to reach out and touch someone.

Trust Opens Sexual Doors: The Oxytocin Effect

Benefiting from the full range of physiologic effects of sex includes experiencing the trust-building release of *oxytocin* that accompanies sexual expression.

def•i•ni•tion

Oxytocin is a hormone that is released during childbirth and labor, breastfeeding, and following orgasm. To a lesser extent it is released with touch, massage, and during loving verbal exchanges. It has the effect of bonding mother to baby and lover to partner. It is probably biologically significant in that it ensures that mothers will strive ferociously for a child's survival and that pair bonding will continue long enough to raise a child. It initiates the release of endorphins, rewarding these activities with a feeling of calm well-being.

Experiments have demonstrated that not only does a person trust others more when oxytocin is released, but they also become more trustworthy in an effort to win social acceptance. As men get older, they begin to experience the expansive quality that oxytocin is famous for. When testosterone drops a little, men begin to appreciate that the afterglow is a considerable part of sexual pleasure.

When trust is established in a couple, there is more room for sexual play and satisfying sexual experience. Intimacy is more than sexual contact, and emotional intimacy leads to physical openness with one another. Rather than seeing comfort as "taking each other for granted," you can also see it as the relief of not having to be anxious about the relationship. Pair bonds, with the ongoing help of oxytocin, can open the door for deeply gratifying sexual and emotional connection.

Beyond the Basics

One slight deviation from the oxytocin effect is in ovulating women who are not as trusting as others when given oxytocin. It is theorized that this is because fertile women need to be more discriminating about sexual partners and therefore can't afford to trust everyone. During the mid-cycle period of high desire, it may ensure that a woman will choose her regular partner and not the first appealing stranger she meets on the bus—something we can all be grateful for. (Except maybe that appealing stranger.)

Touch and Bonding

Emotional stability and bonding are the hallmarks of a secure relationship. Touch is one way to maximize these qualities in your sexual and emotional life. The limbic part of your brain, mentioned earlier in this chapter, is responsible for your experience of emotion. Touch, and even just being in each other's company, can begin to regulate and stabilize that part of the brain for both of you. In that way, relationship becomes physiology. The interaction of two people creates a constant feedback loop that calms and changes the limbic brain. You begin to count on each other for this regulating quality, and it in turn brings you closer.

When you add calm, persistent touch to the equation, you have the makings of a deeply bonded couple. There is tremendous comfort and pleasure in the familiar closeness that evolves over months and years of contact. Your brain literally changes as you accommodate each other, and your body relaxes into the cushion that is your union.

The down side of this, if there is one, is that once you are so accustomed to another person's presence and touch, it is a difficult transition if you lose him or her. Because limbic regulation is so intrinsic, losing a person with whom you have bonded in this way is like losing a piece of yourself. If you feel more whole because the relationship is satisfying, you will feel "dismembered" if it ends. Letting go of a partner to whom you are bonded, whether because of death, divorce, or long separation, can be like losing a limb. Your body and your rhythm of life are altered, and you become vulnerable to illness and grief. You have a partner-shaped place in your heart, and there is no substitute.

Taking the Spotlight Off Your Genitals

If you want to spice up your sex life and enhance the sexual health of your relationship, try not having sex for a while. Many sex therapies start with an initial period of refocusing your attention to your body but not your genitals. Holding hands, kissing, cuddling, romantic dinners—these are the things of sexual health. Forget about erections, orgasms, and penetrative sex. At least for now, remember each other's bodies as responsive and playful but don't take it all the way to the bank.

It is easy to slip into the idea that sex represents acceptance, attraction, and reward. You can find yourself making assumptions that aren't true and that hurt your relationship if you equate intercourse with your self-worth. If your partner is too tired or seems disinterested, it is natural to feel hurt or insulted, but it may not be about you or your attractiveness at all. It is much more likely to be about his or her capacity or energy level. Turning it into either a popularity contest or an expected behavior can take the fun out of sex and make it the focus of conflict.

Instead, back off entirely. Talk about "taking a sabbatical" from sex and be teenagers for a while. Remember when you weren't supposed to have sex? Try that on again and remember the pleasure of heavy petting. (A great little oxytocin producer!) Touch each other for the sake of saying, "I like that you are here with me" instead of "How about it, baby?" Settle for "outercourse" on the couch instead of intercourse in the bed. Even if it leaves one or both of you a little frustrated, be playful about it and trust that you are finding your way back to each other.

This sort of unconditional touching sends a powerful emotional message. It creates a shared history of positive physical experience. That can be important if one of you is not feeling sexually available for a while or if you have drifted apart sexually. Touch without focusing on the "payoff" builds trust. It makes some major deposits in your emotional bank account and gives you an emotional nest egg for those times when you have less flexibility and might make a withdrawal from that account. It's easier to cut each other slack if you have a recent experience of caring physical contact.

Try This!

If one or the other of you has trouble becoming aroused, try agreeing to a "no sex" month but with permission for loving touch during that time. With the pressure off, you can remember the pleasure of cuddling, sample the joy of old-fashioned necking, and remind each other in nonverbal ways that you desire and enjoy each other's company. It's like starting from the beginning and can refresh your memory about how sweet your partner can be. A little chocolate with that neck massage isn't such a bad idea either.

Why Married People Are Healthier

Many studies have shown that married people live longer and are generally healthier. This seems to hold true in all age groups and for most health indicators. Married couples report more satisfaction with their sex lives, especially in older groups, and in general a higher satisfaction with life.

It's hard to know exactly why married people are healthier, but there are several factors that may be in play. First is the tendency for marriage to change health behaviors for the better. Marriage reduces alcohol use and increases physical exercise. Married people tend to have more balanced diets and usually are more inclined to attend medical appointments and be screened for physical problems.

Marriage seems to have a consistently positive effect on mental health measures, too. Getting married reduces the symptoms of depression, and getting divorced increases those symptoms—sometimes for years.

Survival rates from heart attacks and cancer are higher in married people than in their single counterparts. Whether it is the support of a caregiver or the physiologic stability that caring provides, having a loving partner makes recovery from life-threatening events more successful.

The one health indicator that is less healthy in married people is body size. Married men and women are more likely to be obese than their single colleagues. Regular access to good cooking is something of a liability, so if you and your spouse are part of that obesity statistic, consider some married exercise to buck the trend.

New Horizons

If love is marked with comfortable, companionable caring, it can also be the victim of boredom. Although the health benefits of caring are many, familiarity also takes away some of the novelty that relationships need. To combat those doldrums, couples have to make a conscious effort to introduce new elements that surprise and delight each other.

Imagination and Fantasy

Imagination is another sort of sexual lubricant. It can counteract the routine of being together in ways that make the partnership new and exciting. If you are in a couple, one of you may be more naturally imaginative than the other. Give each other permission to play with fantasy and novelty in ways that you can both enjoy. Just as children can play the same game every day with infinite small variations, adults can take advantage of their own playful nature to invent variations on a sexual theme that both will welcome.

Erotica vs. Pornography

It's been said that if something depicts sex with ostrich feathers, it's erotica, but if it depicts sex with the ostrich, it's porn. The line between erotica and pornography is sometimes very blurry, and one person's erotica is another person's porn.

> ### ☼ Try This!
> Have a fantasy discovery dinner with your partner. Over a dinner
> at home or in a quiet restaurant, make an evening of revealing your
> fantasies to each other. Abide by the rule that you won't judge or laugh
> at any ideas, and bring to the table at least three fantasies that you've
> thought of but never tried. They can be simple things like wanting to take
> a bubble bath together, or they could be elaborate role plays where you
> will pretend to be strangers and pick each other up in a bar. Whatever
> your partner's fantasy, listen for the parts that you would feel comfortable
> offering. You may learn some fun ways to surprise each other that would
> never have occurred to you. You may even want to skip dessert and get
> straight home to try one out.

In general, erotica is defined as images or writing that is intended
to be suggestive or symbolic of sexual desire or pleasure. It usually
involves emotions, passion, love, and tender expressions and allows
the participants to be represented as equals. Pornography is usually
seen as a coarser sort of art or writing, depicting sex graphically and
intended to arouse lust and sexual desire and to elicit overt excitement.
Pornography may depict men or women in humiliating or demeaning
roles, in which one or the other seems to be exploited and objectified.

While there is overlap between erotica and pornography, either one
can be a useful tool for exciting you as a couple and prompting exploration of new sexual ground. Talk to your partner about whether there
are writings or images that you find arousing or exciting. Don't rule it
out without some discussion of what would and would not be okay with
you.

If you are comfortable doing so, go on an "erotoshop" and check out
a local adult store. There are mainstream places in or near shop-
ping malls that have toys, videos, lingerie, and other sexual items. Go
together and look at the various movies. Talk about the themes of the
movies—they can be hilarious as well as arousing. Look at the toys.
Marvel at the ingenuity of some of the "sexual aids" in the store. Even
if you don't buy a thing, it opens up the chance to talk about ideas that
you would never have had opportunity to discuss. If going to a store is
too exposed for you, look at a catalog together of erotic materials. Even
the act of talking about these things can break up a sexual rut.

Talk to Each Other—Building the Excitement

Nothing says loving like a great conversation. If you have fallen into the silence habit with your partner, talk about talking. One thing that new lovers do is talk, talk, talk. They can't get enough of each other's thoughts and ideas.

Communication is the life force of a loving relationship. You can't be known unless you are heard, and you can't be heard unless you say something. Having a regular time when you can discuss things that matter to you is a way to keep your relationship relevant. It can be first thing in the morning or last thing at night. It can be on the phone or back and forth in a notebook. But it has to be respectful and safe. If you have trouble communicating in a respectful way and you want to be closer, find a counselor who can teach you the rules of intimate communication.

Don't underestimate talking as an aphrodisiac. Whether it is revealing a fantasy or telling your partner what part of his or her anatomy drives you crazy, words are potent love medicine. If you are comfortable with your communication style, try a little phone sex to get the engines revving. Just before it's time for your partner to call it a day, phone him and tell him that you've been thinking about his _____ (fill in the blank with your favorite body part) all day. Tell him that you are hoping to get a glimpse of that lovely _____ before you go to sleep tonight. Chances are that he will meet you at home eagerly and with some ideas of his own.

Or as you are drifting off to sleep, mute the television and tell your partner what you most appreciate about him or her. Be specific and positive, no buts about it. Then hand the remote control back over and cuddle up close. The more sensory cues you give, the more he or she will feel connected to you with that little bit of loving information.

Fantasy and sexual exploration are a way to say, "I trust you, and I want to be excited with you." Words that strengthen your connection are a sort of "oral sex" that you can almost always perform. Every word is a step toward a closer bond that enhances your sexual health and enriches your life together.

The bottom line on sex and love is that love makes you stronger. Your body and mind were designed for closeness and intimacy and are rewarded by both. If you experience love, you play more and you live longer. Bathed in the chemicals of caring and harmony, the tissues of your body are better able to withstand the rigors of life and sex.

The Least You Need to Know

♦ Chemistry is more than the "click" when you meet someone new. It's also the body's response to relationship.

♦ Limerence—the freefall feeling of being in love—is a double-edged sword and a chemical bombshell.

♦ The oxytocin and endorphins released during cuddling will reinforce your closeness and raise trust.

♦ Marriage and health are linked, and married people enjoy many health benefits of their long-term connection.

♦ Fantasy and imagination can keep your relationship new and exciting, reviving the spark and improving the bond.

♦ Relationship *is* physiology, and physiology determines your sexual health.

Part 4

Protecting Yourself

As much fun as sex is, it also carries some responsibility and risk. Some sexually transmitted diseases are forever, whereas others are easily treated. Some sexual practices are more dangerous than others, and preventing pregnancy can spare you a whole world of trouble if you are not ready for that step.

Engaging in sex in a way that lowers risk is one way to preserve your sexual health and fitness. Having the facts about sexually transmitted disease, contraception, and risky sex will help you safeguard your sexual health so that you can be well, play fair, and stay in the game for a long, long time.

Chapter 10

Viral Villains

In This Chapter

- ◆ What makes viral STDs so dangerous?
- ◆ The symptoms and treatments for common viral STIs
- ◆ Which viral STIs are most easily spread through sexual contact?
- ◆ How to minimize the way viral STIs affect your sexual health

Everyone wants to avoid getting a viral sexually transmitted infection or disease, but how much harm can they really do to your sexual health? Is it possible to be sexually healthy and have an incurable sexually transmitted infection? What should you do if you have symptoms, and are there ways to prevent STIs and still enjoy your sex life?

This chapter covers sexually transmitted diseases and infections caused by viruses. Viral STDs are often treatable, but not curable. Bacterial STDs, which are usually curable with antibiotics, are covered in Chapter 11.

This chapter explores these questions and describes the common viral sexually transmitted infections, as well as their diagnosis and treatment. Any sexually transmitted infection or disease affects your sexual health. Some only briefly—until you are treated. Some have lifelong consequences. Forewarned is forearmed, and a little knowledge can save you a lot of trouble.

STDs and STIs

A *sexually transmitted infection (STI)* is an invasion of the body by a microorganism that was transmitted through sexual contact. An STI may or may not have symptoms. A *sexually transmitted disease (STD)* is a sexually transmitted infection that has progressed to the point where there are symptoms or tissue damage from the infectious process of the organism. Not all STIs go on to be STDs, but you can transmit an STI that becomes an STD in your partner.

def•i•ni•tion

Although many clinicians use STD and STI interchangeably, for the purposes of this book, a **sexually transmitted infection (STI)** means any invasion of your body by a sexually transmitted organism, and a **sexually transmitted disease (STD)** refers to an infection that has reached the symptomatic or tissue-damage stage.

Protecting you and your partner from STIs and STDs is critical for preserving your sexual health. Remember that you can have an STI and be unaware of it if you have no symptoms.

Condoms are the first line of defense against STIs and should be used every time you have sex unless you are in a monogamous relationship in which *you and your partner have been tested for STIs.* If you and your partner have had any sexual relationships with other people prior to each other, either or both of you could have an STI and not know it.

Some STDs are more difficult to treat than others. The viral infections are the ones that, while usually treatable, are not really curable. Viral STDs are a great reason to carry condoms with you *and use them.*

If you have, or have had, a viral STI, there are precautions that can prevent you from passing it along to your partner. There are also symptoms and conditions that you will want to be on the lookout for since these infections can continue to damage your sexual health in the aftermath of the original infection. Viral STIs may be short lived and mostly a nuisance, or they may change the way you live your life.

Human Papilloma Virus: HPV

The human papilloma virus (HPV) causes warts of all kinds. At least 30 strains of this virus are genital infections, and the genital strains can be either high risk or low risk. HPV is extremely common, and some estimates are that as many as 80 percent of sexually active people will have this virus at some time in their lives.

HPV is spread by close genital skin-to-skin contact. You don't need to have a visible wart to have the virus in your skin, and therefore you can pass the virus to your partner when you don't even know you have it.

The symptoms of this virus are extremely variable. If you have one of the external wart strains, you will see fleshy or grayish warts on or around your genitals, your anus, or your urethra. If you got it from having oral sex, you can find the warts in your mouth and throat.

Beyond the Basics

Two of the high-risk strains of HPV cause *almost all* cervical cancer in women. Two of the low-risk strains cause *almost all* of the visible genital warts in both men and women. Ironically, genital warts are not a sign of the highest-risk HPV. But they are a sign that you have been exposed to HPV, so screening for the more dangerous types is in order.

You may have HPV and have no symptoms. Sometimes women have a clear discharge or vaginal pain, but that is rare. There may be some itching. For men, the only obvious symptoms are the visible genital warts on the penis or in the genital area.

The diagnosis of HPV is usually made either by pap smear in women or by noticing external warts in men and women. Sometimes a vinegar solution is "painted" on the area to make the warts show up better. There is no test to confirm that someone does *not* have the virus.

Treating HPV depends on what type you have. If there are external warts, they can be treated by freezing them or by putting chemicals on them. Warts usually need to be treated in some way, and if they are extensive you may need to be treated with a laser or surgery. Many HPV infections without visible symptoms go away on their own.

Since the high-risk strains can cause cancer of the cervix and anal cancer, HPV is an STD that you want to get screened for. If warts get large, they can block the urethra, interfering with urination.

If you are screened for HPV, you will not be treated unless there are external warts or precancerous changes of the cervix or vagina. There is no treatment for the presence of HPV without symptoms. Screening for it is done to find women at the highest risk for those problems. The recommendation is to continue annual pap smears in those women who test positive for HPV and for all women under 30.

> **Try This!**
>
> Get a pap smear and HPV screening test every year once you are sexually active. HPV screening is quickly becoming the best test to predict and prevent cervical cancer.
>
> Quitting smoking can also help minimize your cancer risk with HPV.

Prevention of HPV takes some planning. Condoms offer some—but not perfect—protection from HPV. There is now a vaccine that is recommended for women and girls from ages 9 to 26. Ideally, women would be vaccinated before their first sexual contact, but the vaccine does offer protection from the higher-risk strains even after you are sexually active. The current recommendation is only to age 26 and only for women, but this may change as research provides more information on the vaccine.

Molluscum Contagiosum

Molluscum contagiosum is a benign viral infection that is usually spread by skin-to-skin contact, but it can also be spread by using towels or sharing a bath with someone who is infected.

The symptoms are tiny, raised bumps that have an indentation in the middle. They are not usually itchy or painful and can be located anywhere in the groin area, buttocks, or lower abdomen. Usually the infection goes away on its own, but this may take up to a couple of years.

Once you have this infection, you can spread it by scratching one of the lesions (bumps) and spreading the virus. If you have a low immune system because of HIV, chemotherapy, or some other reason, you may have a major outbreak of this virus.

Diagnosis is usually made by a health professional by looking at the lesions. Sometimes they scrape a lesion onto a slide and look at it under the microscope to confirm the diagnosis.

Although it usually goes away on its own, removing the lesions will often end the outbreak. They can be removed with chemical agents or by freezing, and your health-care provider can help you decide what sort of treatment is best.

It's rare to have complications from molluscum contagiosum. Sometimes scratching at the bumps can leave you open to a bacterial skin infection. Preventing it may be difficult since it only requires skin-to-skin contact, and condoms don't protect all your skin in that area.

The main thing with this benign infection is to be sure the "bumps" you find are not something more serious. If you develop bumps in your genital or groin area and suspect that it is only molluscum contagiosum, get it checked to be *sure* that is what you are dealing with and not something that can do more damage.

Herpes: HSV

Herpes simplex virus (HSV) is also a very common STI. As many as one in five sexually active adults may have this infection, and many of them do not know it. This virus is not curable and lives in nerve fibers, often causing multiple subsequent outbreaks. Even though it is not curable, it is treatable and does not have to ruin your sexual health.

Proceed with Caution

One type of herpes simplex virus (HSV-1) is responsible for cold sores and fever blisters in the mouth and face. This strain is not the one that usually causes genital herpes, but it can. The other type of herpes simplex virus (HSV-2) is the one usually found in genital outbreaks. You can get or spread either type of herpes to the mouth or genitals by having oral sex with an infected partner.

The herpes virus is spread by skin-to-skin contact. It spreads best when there is a break in the skin or through mucous membranes (like in the mouth or genitals) because the skin is thinner and allows the virus to gain entry. It is actually a rather fragile virus and does not live for long on objects, so using towels or wearing clothing of someone with the virus does not spread it.

The symptoms of herpes, when there are symptoms, are tiny sores on or around your mouth or genitals. These sores start out as small, blister-like bumps, eventually becoming larger and breaking open. They may be completely painless or (especially with the first outbreak) extremely tender. As many as 60 percent of people with herpes simplex do not have any symptoms at all and are unaware that they carry the virus.

Diagnosis of HSV is usually done by a medical provider, who might either use a swab to take a bit of the fluid from one of the sores and send it in to a lab for testing, or send a blood sample to check for new antibodies to the virus. The blood sample is more accurate and gives fewer "false negative" results.

If there are no sores but you want to be tested to see if you have or have ever had the virus, blood tests can be done to check for the antibody, which tells you whether you have had the virus yet. Sometimes the diagnosis is done on the spot by examining you, and medications are prescribed to lessen and shorten the outbreak.

The treatment for HSV is antiviral medications, along with other measures to relieve symptoms. If the area is very painful, sometimes pain medication or creams to numb the area are used. For people who have severe or rapidly recurring outbreaks, antiviral medication may be prescribed on an ongoing basis to prevent skin eruptions and/or decrease viral shedding in the genital area.

HSV takes up residence in the nerve tissue near the spine, where it becomes inactive for periods of time. Outbreaks are unpredictable and depend on many factors, including how good your immune system is, how stressed your body is, whether you have some exposure to HSV from having cold sores or other previous infections, and whether the skin around your genitals is in good condition. Some people have one outbreak and never have another one. Some people have them every few weeks. If you have this virus, talk to your medical provider about what it takes in your particular case to keep the outbreaks to a minimum.

> **Beyond the Basics** _____
>
> The timing of HSV outbreaks is something of a mystery. Each person has to pay attention to his or her own set of triggers and then try to avoid the triggers or take antiviral medications when the outbreaks are most likely. Common triggers for HSV flare-ups include the following:
>
> ◆ Change in hormone levels, such as during pregnancy or menstrual periods
>
> ◆ Times of high stress
>
> ◆ High fever or illness
>
> ◆ Having surgery
>
> ◆ Relationship stress or change in sexual partners
>
> ◆ Trauma to the genital area, such as from another infection like yeast or another STI
>
> Learning to keep well within your body's stress limits can help prevent and minimize HSV outbreaks.

Herpes is an infection that can have a tremendous impact on your sexual health. Once you have it, you become aware of the need to disclose it to partners and to protect your partner from getting it. It can be an enormous relationship issue, and there are organizations and dating websites devoted to coping with this STI.

People with HSV often have a lot of shame or embarrassment about having the infection. They feel "untouchable" or "flawed" in some way and can suffer depression and great discouragement. Add to that the unpredictability of the infection and the fact that you can spread it even when you don't have symptoms, and it can feel pretty overwhelming.

If you have HSV or are in a relationship with someone who has it, there are ways to cope and continue to be close. Using antiviral medications and keeping yourself healthy so that your immune response is strong can make a big difference in the frequency of outbreaks. Condoms, although not foolproof, are very good at preventing spread of the virus to your partner.

If you don't have HSV, the best way to prevent it is to use condoms every time you have sex and to stay in a monogamous relationship. Every time you have unprotected sex with a new partner, you open yourself up to HSV and other infections. If you or your partner has cold sores (HSV-1), don't have oral sex when there is a sore since you can spread it to your partner's genitals. When the symptoms are gone, use a barrier (like a dental dam) to limit contact of the virus with vulnerable skin.

HIV: Think Twice

The human immunodeficiency virus (HIV) is a retrovirus that damages the immune system and can lead to acquired immunodeficiency syndrome (AIDS). It is pandemic and is responsible for about 15,000 deaths a year in the United States.

HIV is transmitted in semen, blood, pre-ejaculate, vaginal fluid, and breast milk. Sexual contact and sharing of needles in intravenous drug use are the main ways to get this infection. Mucous membranes, and the special skin cells of the mouth and vagina, are very vulnerable to the virus, making unprotected genital, anal, and oral sex very high-risk activities.

Symptoms of HIV are subtle, and about a quarter of the million or so people in the United States who have the virus don't even know they have it. The initial infection may have some flu-like symptoms, which eventually fade. After that, it is virtually impossible to tell that you have the infection.

The diagnosis of HIV is made with a blood test. There are quick tests that give results in about a half hour, and then the test is usually confirmed with another blood test. Some testing places send the blood away and results take about two weeks. There is also a home blood test that allows you to take the blood sample at home and send it to a lab for testing.

It takes anywhere from three to six months for the HIV antibody to be present in your blood, so testing for HIV immediately after having sex with someone will not tell you whether you got the infection from that person. It will tell you whether you have the virus now, though, and if you want to be tested immediately and again in several months, it would show whether you have the infection now and whether you became infected from that partner. If you are worried about whether you are infected, it's a good time to think about changing your sexual practices to avoid not only HIV but other STIs as well.

Beyond the Basics

Home testing for HIV may seem like a good way to get anonymous results, but beware of Internet or magazine advertising of test kits. People who are worried about their HIV status are prime targets for shady marketing of products that promise to diagnose, prevent, or cure HIV. There is currently only one HIV test kit approved by the FDA for home use. For a listing of approved test kits for HIV, check the FDA website: www.fda.gov/cber/products/testkits.htm

The great danger of HIV, of course, is that it will progress to AIDS. A person with AIDS has a compromised immune system and begins to experience opportunistic infections and diseases that his or her body cannot fight. Deaths from AIDS are due to one of these conditions.

Treatment of HIV has progressed tremendously, and people with this disease are living much longer lives than in the early days of the disease. Antiretroviral medications have helped people with HIV live relatively normal lives and for much longer periods of time. But treatment does not cure the disease, and these medications have some unpleasant side effects.

You should be tested for the HIV virus if you …

- Have unprotected sex with men who have sex with men (MSM).
- Are a male having sex with men.
- Use intravenous drugs.
- Have sex with an intravenous drug user.
- Have unprotected sex with a new partner.
- Have a history of any of the above and have not been tested.

If you want to know where you can get anonymous testing, call your local health department for a list of sites in your area.

Preventing HIV is critical to your sexual health—partly because HIV can go on to cause such serious disease but also because preventing one STI protects you from getting other STIs as well. The only sure way to prevent HIV or any other STI is to abstain from sexual activity. For some people, this is the preferred choice, and it can be a sexually healthy one if it is what they want. For some, the relief of not worrying about sex, STIs, or pregnancy is worth abstaining. Usually this is a temporary choice, but it can be a sexually healthy one if it increases the person's health and well-being.

For sexually active people, preventing HIV requires planning and maturity. The best prevention is to have sex with only one partner (who is also monogamous) *after* you have both been tested for STIs. Staying in a one-person relationship is the most reliable way to avoid all STIs. Other ways to prevent HIV infection include using latex condoms every time you have sex, insisting that your partner use condoms, avoiding sex with high-risk partners (MSM or IV drug users), and keeping your body healthy so that your immune response can fight off illness and disease.

Once you have HIV, the most important thing is to get appropriate care as soon as possible. Talk to your medical provider about your HIV status and get a referral to a center that specializes in HIV care. The sooner you can be started on appropriate therapy, the better your chances to live a long, normal life.

> ### Proceed with Caution
> Smoking and drinking can damage your immune system. If you have a diagnosis of HIV, stop both in order to maximize your body's response to treatment.
>
> If you do not have HIV, stop smoking and drink only moderately. Too much alcohol will affect your sexual decision-making and increase the likelihood that you will engage in high-risk sex. Smoking and excessive drinking are never sexually healthy.

Be sure that your partner or partners are tested for HIV once you have the diagnosis. If he or she is still negative for HIV, then you can take precautions to minimize the chance for transmission of the virus. Obviously, this would be a serious relationship issue, and you may want to talk with an HIV counselor about how to preserve your relationship after the diagnosis and even about how to tell your partner(s).

HIV is a serious, devastating diagnosis. Your sexual health will suffer, and eventually your physical health could also suffer. People who get this infection usually have relationship and psychological issues to deal with. Don't be afraid to get help. This is not a condition you can handle by yourself. If you can't talk to your partner about it initially, find some professional help to get you started. Get the medical care you need, and find counseling services to support you as you deal with the aftermath of your diagnosis. Isolating yourself will only make it more difficult to manage your life and health.

Hepatitis

Hepatitis is an inflammation of the liver. There are several varieties of viral hepatitis, but we will focus on the hepatitis B virus (HBV) and hepatitis C virus (HCV) because they have the most implication for your sexual health.

Hepatitis can cause liver damage, and hepatitis C is the most common reason for liver transplants in the United States. There are ways to prevent hepatitis, and there is some treatment for it, but it is not a curable STI. Many people have liver disease and don't know it. As with HIV, not knowing can let the disease get a foothold in your body, so paying attention, getting tested, and getting good care make all the difference in how much these infections damage your sexual health.

Beyond the Basics _____

When you are trying to differentiate between hepatitis B and hepatitis C, the main thing to remember is that hepatitis B is usually sexually transmitted but can be transmitted other ways as well. There is a vaccine for hepatitis B, and that's a great way to prevent it.

Hepatitis C is usually transmitted through blood, especially with IV drug users, but it can be transmitted in other ways as well, including sexually. There is no vaccine for hepatitis C.

Know your partner and get tested before you have sex for the first time with that partner. If you have any question about whether you have HBV or HBC, get tested!

Here is a chart comparing hepatitis B and hepatitis C.

Comparison Chart for HBV and HCV

Feature	Hepatitis B Virus (HBV)	Hepatitis C Virus (HCV)
Transmission	Unprotected vaginal, anal, or oral sex	Sharing needles with an infected person during intravenous drug use
	Sharing needles with an infected person during intravenous drug use	Needle stick injury (health-care workers)
	Needle stick injury (health-care workers)	Blood transfusions and organ transplants that occurred before 1992
	Sharing personal items like a razor, toothbrush, or nail clippers used by an infected person	Unprotected vaginal or anal sex (rare, usually with rough sex or when there are other STDs present)
	Bites from an infected person (rarely)	
	Tattoos, body piercings, acupuncture needles (rarely)	
	Blood transfusions that occurred before 1992	
Symptoms	Loss of appetite	In the acute phase, often no symptoms but may be jaundiced.

	Malaise (feeling of ill-health)	If HCV persists, the person may have:
	Fatigue (feeling tired all the time)	Loss of appetite
	Nausea and vomiting	Malaise (feeling of ill health)
	Abdominal pain	Fatigue (feeling tired all the time)
	Dark urine	Nausea and vomiting
	Jaundice (yellowing of the skin and eyes)	Jaundice (yellowing of the skin and eyes)
	Rash or arthritis may occur before other symptoms (during the "prodromal" or early acute stage)	
How it is *not* spread	Food, water, kissing, casual contact	Food, water, kissing, casual contact
Diagnosis	Blood tests	Blood tests
Treatment	There are no treatments specific to HBV, but if it persists, treatment may consist of antiviral and other medications to slow the growth of the virus.	Many HCV infections resolve on their own. When it becomes chronic, or if there is liver damage, Interferon may be prescribed.
Complications	Cirrhosis (scarring) of liver Cancer	Cirrhosis (scarring) of liver

continues

continued

Feature	Hepatitis B Virus (HBV)	Hepatitis C Virus (HCV)
Prevention	HBV vaccine: a series of 3 shots	There is no vaccine for HCV.
	Avoid sex with infected people and those at high risk of infection	Avoid sex with infected people and those at high risk of infection
	Use latex condoms or dental dams with all sexual activity	Use latex condoms or dental dams with all sexual activity
	Clean up any body fluids or blood spills with a solution of 1:10 bleach and water	Clean up any body fluids or blood spills with a solution of 1:10 bleach and water
	Avoid contact with infected blood or body fluids found on needles, razors, toothbrushes, and nail clippers	Avoid contact with infected blood or body fluids found on needles, razors, toothbrushes, and nail clippers
	Cover cuts, sores, and rashes with bandages	Cover cuts, sores, and rashes with bandages

People most at risk for getting HBV or HCV are …

- People who have unprotected sex with lots of partners.

- Men who have unprotected sex with men.

- People who use intravenous drugs, especially if they share needles and other drug equipment, or "works."

- Sex workers (prostitutes).

- Health-care workers if they used needles around high-risk people.

- Sex partners of infected people.

- People who got blood transfusions or organ transplants before 1992.

- Travelers to, and immigrants from, countries with a high incidence of hepatitis (HBV only).

Hepatitis is a serious disease. Like HIV, it continues to affect your sexual health well beyond the initial infection and often for the rest of your life. Because the symptoms in the early stages are difficult to notice, you may have hepatitis for a long time before you get care. And, as with HIV, you may not feel sick much at all, or you may be very ill from the disease. Prevention is best, but early diagnosis can also make a big difference in your long-term outlook.

Viral STIs and STDs cannot be cured, but with early care they can be treated, and their impact on your life can be minimized. The most important thing you can do to maintain your sexual health is to get tested at the first sign of an STI, and if you test positive, get treatment right away.

The Least You Need to Know

- Viral sexually transmitted infections are often treatable but not curable.

- Herpes, HIV, and hepatitis B are easily spread by sexual contact, whereas hepatitis C is not easily spread through sex.

- Sexual health depends on getting screened and treated promptly for both viral and bacterial STIs.

- Minimizing the damage of viral STIs depends on early treatment and on protecting your partner from becoming infected.

Chapter 11

Bacterial Bad Boys, Fungal Infections, and Critters

In This Chapter

- ◆ What makes bacterial STIs so dangerous?
- ◆ The symptoms and treatments for common bacterial STIs, insect infestations, and fungal infections
- ◆ How bacterial STIs affect your sexual health
- ◆ How to minimize the damage of bacterial STIs, fungal infections, and infestations

Bacterial STIs, for the most part, are easier to deal with than viral STIs. Although some are resistant to antibiotics, most are curable with medication. The implications for your sexual health are significant, however, even though they are mostly curable. If you have a bacterial STI, then you ...

♦ Are at risk for other STIs/STDs.

♦ May have scarring and damage to your internal reproductive system that will affect your fertility.

♦ May have sexual partners who are high risk.

♦ Need to pay attention to your sexual decision-making.

There are a few common bacterial infections that you will want to be aware of and avoid. All of them are treatable, but this doesn't mean that they are without risk or without consequences to your sexual health.

Gonorrhea

Gonorrhea, also known as "GC" or "the clap," is caused by bacteria called Neisseria gonorrheae. It attacks the mucous membranes found in your urethra, vagina, cervix, uterine lining, throat, anus, rectum, and even the lining of the eyelid if it is exposed.

You get gonorrhea when the secretions (fluids) from an infected mucous membrane touch the mucous membrane of an uninfected person. This means that you do not have to have penetrating sex to get the infection, and you can spread it from one mucous membrane to another by touching the infected skin and then touching uninfected skin—as with touching your eye after sex or wiping from vagina to anus.

Symptoms, when there are any, are usually obvious in men and occur two to five days after being infected. They include a yellowish discharge from the penis (sometimes called a "drip"), burning or pain when urinating, urinating more often than usual, and/or swollen testicles.

Women may not notice symptoms right away, but when they do occur it is usually about 10 days after being exposed to the infection. In women, the symptoms to look for are a yellowish or bloody vaginal discharge and burning or painful urination. If the infection gets as far as the fallopian tubes, the woman may experience lower-abdominal pain, lower-back pain, pain with intercourse, nausea, fever, and vaginal bleeding.

Proceed with Caution _____

When the infection has progressed up to the uterus and fallopian tubes, it is called pelvic inflammatory disease (PID). PID can be very damaging to a women's reproductive system and is caused by many types of STDs that are not treated early. PID may cause scarring that makes "tubal" pregnancies more likely or may close off fallopian tubes, making it difficult to get pregnant when you want to.

If you have symptoms such as abdominal pain, nausea, lower-back pain, fever, painful sex, and vaginal bleeding, see your medical provider. PID can endanger your fertility and, in some cases, your life.

Depending on where the GC infection is, there may also be redness or pain in the eyes, throat, or anus. But there may be no symptoms at all, so if you are being tested for gonorrhea and you have had anal or oral sex, ask for the swab test to be done from those areas as well.

The test for gonorrhea is usually a urine test. A urine sample is collected and tested for the bacteria. Sometimes a culture is required. For a culture, the medical provider will swab the infected area to get a sample of the fluid or discharge to send to the lab. If the test comes back positive, it is automatically sent to the local public health department, and sexual partners are contacted and treated.

Treatment for gonorrhea is antibiotic medication. If you have gonorrhea, your medical provider will probably treat you for chlamydia as well because they so commonly occur together. There are rare cases when gonorrhea is resistant to certain antibiotics, so if you continue to have symptoms after the treatment, return to the doctor so that a culture can be sent to determine whether you have a resistant strain of the bacteria. Once you are diagnosed with gonorrhea, your partner(s) must also be treated to prevent spreading it. Abstain from sex until the medication is gone and you have no more symptoms.

Preventing gonorrhea is a matter of protecting your mucous membranes from being exposed to the bacteria. The surest way to do this is to abstain from sexual activity. If you decide to have sex with a partner, both of you should get tested before you do so that you will know about any STIs, including gonorrhea, and treat them appropriately. Using condoms every time you have sex will help you to protect yourself from getting gonorrhea (but keep in mind that they are no guarantee of safety).

Although GC is relatively easy to treat, it can also pose a serious threat to your sexual health. Untreated, it can cause PID, which increases your chance for an ectopic (sometimes called "tubal") pregnancy in the future. In men, it can cause inflammation of the prostate gland or epididymitis (a painful inflammation in the testicles), which can also cause infertility if untreated.

Left untreated for a long time, GC can spread to the blood, spinal cord, and joints. This may be life threatening. Having a GC infection can also make you more vulnerable to other STIs like HIV. The inflamed membranes are easily infected with other organisms, including viruses.

If you have any suspicion that you may have GC, get tested. It is easy to treat in early stages, and your sexual health is definitely at risk if it goes untreated.

Chlamydia

Chlamydia is the most common bacterial STI in the United States, and it is caused by a bacteria called Chlamydia trachomatis. There are frequently no symptoms of chlamydia in either men or women, so it is often screened for at a women's annual exam. Women can easily be reinfected if their partners do not get treated when the woman is diagnosed with chlamydia.

Chlamydia is easy to get and easy to pass along to your partner because it so often has no noticeable symptoms. It is called the "silent STD" because the majority of people who have it are unaware that they are infected. The more sex partners you have had, the more likely it is that you have (or have had) chlamydia.

Symptoms, when they are present, are very similar to gonorrhea. Women may have a discharge or pain or burning with urination. They may also have the symptoms of PID such as lower-back pain, abdominal pain, vaginal bleeding, pain during sex, fever, or nausea.

Men sometimes have a discharge from the penis or pain and burning with urination. They may also have burning or itching at the opening of the urethra and/or swelling in the testicles.

As with gonorrhea, some cases may cause symptoms in the anus or eyelid if the bacteria infect those areas. Also similar to GC, rare cases may cause redness or pain in the throat.

Treatment is one dose of antibiotic or a week on an alternative antibiotic. If you have this STI, your partner(s) must also be treated, or you could get reinfected.

The best prevention of this STI, as with others, is to either avoid sexual activity or use latex condoms every time you have sex. Being in a monogamous relationship in which you have both been tested is also a way to avoid infection.

Chlamydia has many of the same long-term risks as gonorrhea. It is even more dangerous, though, because it goes undetected for longer periods of time and has more time to damage your reproductive system.

> **Beyond the Basics**
>
> Non-gonococcal urethritis (NGU) is an STI caused by many organisms but usually by chlamydia. It may be present in men and women and can go undetected. Symptoms are usually a discharge from the urethra and pain with urination. If you have a diagnosis of NGU, you and your partner must both be treated to keep from reinfecting each other.

Both women and men can have fertility problems after having this disease. Women may develop PID, and men can experience inflammation of the prostate and testicles and may have scarring of the urethra or other tissues. In women, this can cause ongoing pelvic pain and in men trouble urinating.

In rare cases, chlamydia can cause reactive arthritis or "Reiter's syndrome." This is a systemic rheumatic disease that is difficult to treat and can be debilitating. The symptoms of it include reddened eyes (conjunctivitis), joint pain, and inflammation of the genito-urinary system. Your sexual and general health could be compromised by untreated chlamydia, making early diagnosis and treatment (or, better yet, prevention!) critical for avoiding these serious conditions.

Trichomoniasis

Trichomoniasis is caused by a protozoa, which is an organism a bit different from bacteria. Like bacterial infections, trichomoniasis (also known as "trich") is curable with antibiotic medication.

The symptoms of this STI are almost always absent in men. In women there may also be no symptoms, but usually women have a frothy discharge, yellowish-green in color. There may be a strong odor with the discharge and pain with urination and intercourse.

Trichomoniasis is diagnosed by taking a small amount of the discharge and looking at it under a microscope, where the protozoa are visible. It is easily cured by taking an antibiotic called metronidozole.

The main threat to your sexual health is in letting the infection go untreated for long periods of time. It, like other bacterial STIs, makes it easier to get viral infections like HSV and HIV. Once you are diagnosed with trichomoniasis, your partner must be treated, too, since he or she almost certainly has it and will reinfect you with the next unprotected sex.

Syphilis

If "syphilis" sounds like an old fashioned STD, think again. An organism called a *spirochete* causes this infection, and there are about 32,000 cases a year in the United States. Left untreated, it can cause damage to many internal organs, including the brain.

def•i•ni•tion

A **spirochete** is a spiral-shaped bacterium whose structure makes it able to move about vigorously. Over time, spirochete bacteria can cause serious organ damage and are responsible for a number of different diseases, including syphilis, yaws, and Lyme disease.

The symptoms of syphilis can be similar to many diseases, and it is sometimes called "the great imitator" because it is so often mistaken for other conditions and diseases. The first symptom is a sore, called a chancre, which appears where the spirochete first makes contact with a mucous membrane. The next set of symptoms includes the following: a rash, seen on the soles of the feet and palms of the hand; raised white wart-like lesions on the genitals or groin; hair loss; and a feeling of generalized illness. All of these symptoms will go away without treatment, but the organism will not stop its infectious activity.

If left untreated, syphilis will become "latent" or seemingly inactive. But it can be silently damaging body organs. Later, when it is in its "tertiary" stage, symptoms may appear again in the form of tumors, heart damage, or neurological problems like blindness and mental illness.

Syphilis is diagnosed either by sampling the chancre and looking at the sample under a microscope or, more commonly, with a blood test. If your medical provider is quite sure that the history and symptoms make syphilis the likely diagnosis, he or she will probably treat it immediately while waiting for the lab results to confirm it.

Treatment is simple and very effective. It is an intramuscular shot of penicillin. The earlier you are treated for this disease, the less harm will be done to your body. While treatment helps at any stage, it cannot undo the damage already done.

> **Beyond the Basics** _____
> The incidence of syphilis has been extremely low since the availability of penicillin to treat it. In 2001, the number of cases began to climb again, especially among men who have sex with men and in African American people. It's hard to say exactly why these two groups are experiencing an increase, but if you are in one of these groups and are sexually active, be aware that you may be more likely to get syphilis and get tested as soon as you notice symptoms.

You can prevent syphilis by avoiding sexual contact or by limiting it to a monogamous relationship with someone who does not have the infection. Using latex condoms whenever you have sexual contact will diminish your chances of getting this STD.

The two really dangerous aspects of syphilis are that, left untreated, it can do so much organ damage and that, in early stages, it makes you more vulnerable to viral STDs like HIV and HSV. If you think you have been exposed to syphilis or if you have any of the symptoms of it, get to a clinic or medical provider right away.

Chancroid

Chancroid is a bacterial STD that causes painful sores on your mouth, throat, lips, and genital and/or groin areas. You can get this condition from skin-to-skin contact or from touching a mucous membrane to an object that has touched a sore. This STD is not common in Western countries, but it is seen in people who have traveled in or come from developing countries.

The symptoms of chancroid are painful sores anywhere that you have sexual contact. Women may notice no sores but may have painful urination or pain with a bowel movement, pain with intercourse, vaginal discharge, or rectal bleeding. Since these symptoms can be similar to syphilis, herpes simplex, or other STIs, it is important to get a diagnosis from a medical provider or clinic.

Testing is done by sampling one of the sores and examining the sample under a microscope. Sometimes the diagnosis is made based on symptoms alone.

Treatment is one of several courses of antibiotics. Preventing this STD can be done by using the safer-sex recommendations described in Chapter 10 for viral STIs.

Chancroid can be a marker that you have other STIs or STDs. Since it is rare, your medical provider may take an extremely thorough history to determine where and how you might have acquired the disease. He or she may also want to treat you for other sexually transmitted conditions at the same visit to assure that you are not infected.

Bacterial Vaginosis

Bacterial vaginosis (BV) is not technically a sexually transmitted infection because you can get it with or without sexual activity. But since BV is often associated with sexual activity or changing sexual partners, it is mentioned here.

Because BV is an overgrowth of bacteria already present in your vagina, you can get it when you take broad spectrum antibiotics because the antibiotic may disrupt the normal balance of bacteria. You can also get BV when you douche, for the same reason.

def•i•ni•tion

Bacterial vaginosis (BV) is an overgrowth of several bacteria in the vagina. It occurs when the normal bacterial flora are disturbed by antibiotics or with a change in the pH of the vaginal environment. It can mimic other sexually transmitted infections and, in some cases, progress to PID.

The symptoms of BV are an odorous vaginal discharge, pain in the vulva, itching or burning, and pain during urination. Untreated it can cause PID with the symptoms mentioned earlier in the section on gonorrhea. It has a characteristic "fishy" odor and may be mistaken for a yeast infection if the discharge causes intense itching.

Diagnosis is made by taking a sample of the discharge and examining it under the microscope. Usually your medical provider will screen you for other STIs when you have BV.

Treatment is a course of oral antibiotics. Sometimes intravaginal creams are prescribed to treat symptoms. You can usually prevent BV by using latex condoms when you have sex or by abstaining from sexual activity. Getting diagnosed early when you have infections that cause a vaginal discharge is important to prevent them from progressing to PID.

Any of the viral or bacterial STIs and STDs can permanently affect your sexual health and fitness. They can cause ongoing problems with your sexual comfort and can change the direction of your sexual life. The best way to approach a sexually transmitted infection is as follows:

♦ First, prevention. Avoid high-risk partners and use safer-sex practices such as latex condoms with every sexual encounter.

♦ If you *do* develop symptoms, get them checked immediately. Early treatment can make all the difference.

♦ Talk to your partner about getting tested, and if you or your partner is diagnosed with an STI, both of you should get treatment right away.

Critters

Some sexually transmitted conditions are actually infestations of tiny insects. These conditions not only can be very uncomfortable but can irritate your skin and make you more vulnerable to other STIs. By treating these infestations early, you can limit the damage.

Pubic Lice

Pubic lice, also known as "crab lice" or "crabs," are spread by close physical contact with someone who is infected. Clinically, they are known as pediculosis pubis. Sometimes these lice can be spread by wearing clothing or using towels after someone who is infected or by sleeping in bed sheets of an infected person, but this is rare.

The symptoms are usually intense itching in the genital area and the presence of "nits" or small lice eggs that cling to the pubic hair. Diagnosis is made by observing these or the adult lice in the pubic area.

Pubic lice are treated with a shampoo containing chemicals that kill the lice and their eggs. After washing with the shampoo, you need to comb out the nits and lice with a tiny comb. You and your partner must both be treated, and any clothing or sheets that you used while infected must be washed and dried in the dryer on the "high" setting.

Pubic lice, once treated, will probably not cause any permanent damage. While you are infected they may cause irritation to your skin, which is then vulnerable to other infections. Having an infestation of pubic lice is embarrassing, but if you get treated promptly, it should have no lasting effect on your sexual health or fitness.

Scabies

Scabies is an infestation under the skin by a tiny skin mite. It is spread by close physical contact and is spread easily during sexual encounters, especially if they are prolonged and involve long periods of closeness, as in spending the night together. The mites enter the skin and lay eggs, which hatch about 10 days later and begin to cause the symptoms.

The symptoms of scabies are intense itching, especially at night; streaks on the skin outlining the mite burrows, usually in an "S" or zigzag pattern; and small brown bumps, or pimples, or a rash in the itchy area. It is common to get these mites in areas that are warm and that fold, like the inside of knees or elbows, the groin area, buttocks, and under breasts. But they can be present anywhere and are found in many areas of the body, depending on where the mites first enter.

Diagnosis is made by history and symptoms, but sometimes a scraping is taken, and the mite can be observed directly under the microscope. Your medical provider may use chemicals on the skin in order to view the characteristic zigzag formation of the burrows.

Treatment is with a lotion that kills the mites and their eggs. Depending on which chemical is in the lotion, it must be left on for several hours and then washed off. All linens and clothing worn while the person was infested must be washed and, whenever possible, dried in a dryer. Items that cannot be laundered may be dry cleaned or placed in a sealed plastic bag for two weeks to decontaminate them. There is oral medication that is sometimes used to treat scabies, but it is not typically the first line of treatment.

Preventing scabies is a matter of not being exposed. If you know your partner has this mite, do not have close physical contact until he or she has been treated and all linens and clothing have been treated as well. Avoid exposure to towels, sheets, and clothing of the infected person. If you develop symptoms, get treated promptly so that you will not spread this to other close household contacts.

Try This!

Even if treatment for scabies is successful, the itching and rash may continue for another two to four weeks. Sometimes an over-the-counter oral anti-histamine (not an antihistamine lotion because the skin is sensitive) or special oatmeal bathing products will help ease the itch until the skin heals.

Fungal Infections

Fungal infections are inflammatory conditions in which several types of parasitic plants may invade body tissues and cause irritation and damage. The types of fungal infections that are sexually transmitted are skin infections, also known as "tinea," and yeast infections. Fungal infections are not always sexually transmitted, but they can be.

Yeast

Vaginal yeast infection, or yeast vaginitis, is an overgrowth of the fungus Candida albicans in the vagina. Many women have yeast as part of the normal vaginal flora, but when something happens to upset the vaginal environment, yeast can grow and cause problems.

Sometimes the semen of a new partner will change the pH of the vagina to support growth of yeast, or if a woman is on antibiotics for another infection, the bacteria that usually keep yeast in check may be destroyed, allowing yeast to grow unchecked. Both men and women with diabetes, or who have a low immune response due to HIV, chemotherapy, or some other reason, are more prone to yeast infections and may need to be treated more aggressively to keep the infection from intensifying.

The symptoms of a yeast infection are inflammation of the vagina, itching, and a white or "cottage cheese" discharge. The vaginal tissue is sometimes quite inflamed and vulnerable to other infections and organisms. There may be itching and inflammation of the labia and vulva and pain with intercourse or with urination.

Proceed with Caution

Although yeast is mostly a woman's infection, it can be spread to male partners. In men, a yeast infection can occur under the foreskin of the penis and may cause the same intense itching that women experience. Treatment for men is to wash the area with gentle soap and water and apply an antifungal medication such as one of the over-the-counter yeast treatments available in drug stores. Rarely does a man need to see a medical provider for a yeast infection.

The treatment for yeast infection is an antifungal medication. This may be in the form of a cream applied directly to the area of the infection, or it may be an oral medication given for a period of time. Since oral antifungals can have serious side effects, including damage to the liver, they are not usually used unless the infection doesn't respond to topical remedies.

Preventing yeast infections requires several things. First, staying in good general health helps your body keep yeast fungus under control. Women should wear cotton underwear so as not to create a moist, airless environment for yeast to grow. Avoid taking oral antibiotics unless they are truly indicated. If you are on prednisone, are diabetic, are immunocompromised, take antibiotics often, or douche frequently, you may be prone to yeast infections. Add yogurt to your diet to reestablish some of the bacteria to fight yeast, and use lots of lubricant during sex to minimize irritation to your vagina. Talk to your medical provider when you have symptoms and discuss how to keep yeast infections to a minimum.

Tinea

Tinea is the name for a type of fungal skin infection. When it is present in the groin area, it is called "tinea cruris" or "jock itch." Like yeast vaginitis, jock itch is not usually sexually transmitted. In some cases, though, it can be passed to a sex partner during vaginal or anal sex.

The symptoms of tinea are raised, itchy, scaly patches, with the edge of the rash a bit redder than the center. The groin area is ideal for this sort of infection because it is warm and moist and dark. The first symptom is often the itching caused by the fungus and is noticed after exercise or sweaty activity.

Diagnosis is sometimes done by examination alone, but it may also include scraping the scales and observing them under a microscope.

Treatment is almost always with an antifungal cream or powder. Tinea is present in the outermost layer of skin and usually responds well to topical treatment. If you are prone to this sort of skin infection, you may want to use small amounts of antifungal powder in the groin area after thoroughly drying from your bath.

Prevention requires avoiding contact with infected skin, wearing loose-fitting clothing, drying completely after bathing, and avoiding shared towels or washcloths.

Fungal infections do not usually have a permanent impact on your sexual health or fitness. Once successfully treated, they can often be prevented or promptly treated if they recur. While you are experiencing a fungal infection, however, either yeast or tinea, your skin is open to bacterial and viral infections, so getting treatment is important.

The Least You Need to Know

◆ Many bacterial infections are curable with antibiotics but are dangerous because they make you vulnerable to infection with viral STIs.

◆ Sexual health depends on getting screened and treated promptly for both viral and bacterial STIs.

◆ Pubic lice and scabies are infestations that are uncomfortable, but they can be successfully treated and prevented.

◆ Fungal infections are sometimes spread during sex, but if treated right away they do not permanently damage your sexual health or fitness.

Chapter 12

Contraception and Sexual Health

In This Chapter

- ♦ How hormonal birth control can affect your sexual health
- ♦ Which barrier methods are best at protecting your sexual health
- ♦ Permanent methods of contraception and when to use them
- ♦ Abstinence and fertility awareness as sexually healthy choices

When couples want the freedom to enjoy their sexual choices but don't want to deal with a pregnancy at this point in their lives, it's time for contraception. This chapter highlights the impact of various types of contraception on your sexual health and fitness. When you choose a way to prevent pregnancy, find one that keeps the love light on without dimming your health.

Hormonal Contraception

Hormonal contraception is a combination of estrogen and/or progesterone—two female hormones—that is available for women. There is no acceptable form of hormonal contraception for men. It comes in a variety of forms, and most women can find a hormonal method of birth control that works for them. This type of birth control works because the progestin inhibits ovulation, so there is no egg released each month. It also changes the cervical mucous to a thick, sticky type of mucous that reduces the ability of sperm to penetrate into the uterus.

Hormonal birth control offers excellent protection from pregnancy, but some of the side effects can be challenging to your sexual health and to your sex life in general.

Possible Benefits of Hormonal Contraception

Hormonal methods of birth control have many benefits. They are usually easy to use—whether by taking a pill, changing a patch, or getting a shot. They are extremely effective, working about 98 percent of the time if used correctly. There are many combinations of hormones and forms, so if one doesn't work for you, another one probably will.

Beyond the Basics _____

Hormonal contraceptives can be delivered in many ways. If you are a good candidate for this type of contraception, you can use pills, intravaginal rings, skin patches, a three-month shot, implants under the skin, an intrauterine device, or even emergency contraception (the "morning-after pill") as a method to prevent pregnancy. The main way to protect your sexual health while you use hormonal contraception is to talk over the choices with your medical provider and decide which has the lowest risk for damaging your health or your sexual relationship.

Some of the side effects of hormonal methods are welcome ones. These hormones often reduce menstrual cramps, acne, and premenstrual syndrome. If you are someone with heavy periods, they reduce the blood loss from menstrual periods, which can boost your hemoglobin, giving you more energy.

Hormonal methods give you the freedom to have sex without worrying about pregnancy. This can be very freeing for women and men alike. Because these methods are always working in your system, they don't interfere with a romantic moment. You can even use them continuously to control when you have your "period" (the withdrawal bleed between cycles) so that your menses don't ruin a vacation, romantic weekend, or honeymoon.

Another plus of using hormonal methods is that some women notice an increase in breast size, and if it's not associated with breast tenderness, they may like having a "new figure." Also, cervical mucous is thicker when you are on hormonal birth control, and this seems to be somewhat protective for pelvic inflammatory disease (PID). As discussed in Chapters 10 and 11, PID can be a major threat to your physical and sexual health.

Possible Risks of Hormonal Contraception

While some of the side effects of hormonal contraception can enhance your sexual health, some can put a dent in it.

Proceed with Caution

The most worrisome side effect of hormonal birth control is the chance of blood clots. The hormones in these methods can cause a clot to form in one of your blood vessels, which can move to the lungs—a life-threatening condition. Because of this clotting tendency, smoking while on the pill also makes the risk of heart attack higher in women over 35. Women who have a history of blood clots are not usually good candidates for these methods.

You may notice irritability or even depression when you are on hormonal contraception. Because of this mood shift, you and your partner may find that your sex life is at a standstill because you are sad or irritable, which interferes with closeness and sex.

Similarly, you may feel a decrease in your libido when taking hormonal birth control. This, of course, is an enormous issue in your sexual health. You probably won't enjoy sexual activity if you "just don't feel like it." It can be frustrating to be free of the fear of pregnancy, only to find that you are indifferent to—or rejecting of—your partner's advances.

Another side effect that affects your sexual health is weight gain. When you put on weight as a result of being on hormones, you may feel unattractive or less sexy, which makes you hesitant to initiate sex or respond to your partner's overtures. Sometimes the weight gain is due to an increased appetite, or a tendency to retain body fat. Women almost always experience this weight gain as a damper on their self-esteem and find it discouraging because the extra weight doesn't respond well to dieting.

> **Proceed with Caution**
> Another possible side effect of hormonal birth control is an increase in blood pressure. If you are on hormonal birth control and find yourself saying, "Not tonight, Hon, I have a headache," because you *do* have a headache, get your blood pressure checked.

Choosing a hormonal contraceptive can give you freedom and peace of mind. But pay attention to the way you feel and how responsive you are to your partner in case it has side effects that diminish your sexual well-being.

Barrier Contraception

Barrier contraception is an excellent way to protect your sexual health. Methods like condoms and female condoms give you good protection from pregnancy but also protect—at least in part—from STDs. Anyone can get these methods, and anyone can use them. There are plenty of barrier methods to choose from, which is always a plus.

Condoms: His and Hers

There are many reasons to incorporate barrier methods into your sex life, and condoms are a great start. They have lots of benefits to your sex life:

- They protect you and your partner from sharing germs.
- They are readily available—drug stores carry them.
- They can be used during sex as part of the pleasure—putting a condom on your partner can be very sexy.

♦ You can take turns being responsible for protection.

♦ Condoms come in flavors and colors and textures to add to your fun.

♦ They are very effective in protecting you from pregnancy and disease, *if you use them properly.*

The negatives of using barrier methods include the physical side effects and the "interruption factor" during sex. Some couples complain that they don't like interrupting the momentum of excitement to put on a condom. As noted earlier, this can be dealt with by seeing condoms as part of the foreplay.

Physical side effects might include an allergic response to the latex or the lubricant. If you or your partner has an allergic response, it can create itching or irritation and make the genital tissue vulnerable to other infections.

Another complaint from condom users is a decrease in sensation. For some men, this may lead to difficulty keeping an erection. For others, it may make it more difficult to reach orgasm. Using very thin, ultrasensitive condoms can minimize that side effect without eliminating the protection.

Try This!

Sometimes decreasing sensation can be a good thing. For men who have problems with premature ejaculation due to hypersensitivity, wearing a condom can keep them from ejaculating right away. (But don't use two condoms because the friction can make sex less fun and more irritating—literally.) The trick when you use a condom to decrease sensitivity is to tune in *more* to your sensations, not less. Paying close attention to the sensations in your penis, while reducing the stimuli, can help you learn to control your ejaculatory timing.

Diaphragms, Caps, and Sponges

There are several forms of barrier methods that are inserted into the vagina and cover the cervix. These methods can actually enhance your lovemaking because you can place them ahead of time, with no need to interrupt sex to have protection from pregnancy.

Diaphragms and cervical caps are fitted by a medical provider and are available with a prescription. Sponges are saturated with spermicide and are available over the counter. As with condoms, if you have an allergic response, stop using these methods since the irritation can open you up to other infections.

Proceed with Caution

The contraceptive sponge must be left in for six hours after sex to be effective and give the spermicide time to work. But it should *not* be left in more than 30 hours total, or you are risking toxic shock syndrome from the bacteria that grow after that period of time. If this is your method, plan accordingly!

Sponges, diaphragms, and cervical caps are best used by committed, monogamous couples who could cope with a pregnancy if one resulted. They are only about 85 to 90 percent effective, so they are not foolproof. And they do not protect from STDs, so if they are the only method you are using, you want to be sure that you are not taking the chance of getting an unwanted infection from your partner. If you have any doubt at all about whether your partner is a risk, use condoms, too.

Permanent Contraception: Freedom to Play

If you are in the stage of life where you have decided not to have more children, permanent contraception may be a perfect choice for you. If you are in a relationship, this is usually a two-person decision. The procedure for men is less expensive and has fewer risks. However, since it is the woman who bears the pregnancy, she may opt for her own permanent method for the peace of mind of not having to worry about that eventuality.

Tubal Ligation and Hysterectomy

A woman's sexual health is enormously impacted by pregnancy, so once you have decided not to have children, if you are convinced that you won't change your decision, you might want to consider a permanent method of birth control. But the procedure itself can also affect your sexual health, so it's not a light decision.

Tubal ligation is more than 99 percent effective for preventing pregnancy. If you are one of the very few who get pregnant after this procedure, there is a 50 percent chance of it being an ectopic pregnancy in the fallopian tube or outside the uterus, which is dangerous. Once you've had a tubal ligation, you must see a medical provider right away when you have symptoms of a pregnancy or if you develop abdominal pain.

Tubal ligation is, generally speaking, a very effective contraception method, and women tend to be quite satisfied with it. It does not typically change libido or sexual function, and therefore, tends to enhance rather than impair your sexual health.

Hysterectomy is the surgical removal of a woman's uterus. Often one or both ovaries and tubes are removed as well, resulting in infertility. Although hysterectomy is not a good choice all by itself to prevent pregnancy, it does result in the same freedom from pregnancy that tubal ligation does. Depending on whether the ovaries are removed and what the reasons were for removing the uterus, it may or may not affect sexual health. If the ovaries are removed, then estrogen levels drop, and there may be sudden, dramatic symptoms of menopause including hot flashes, mood changes, and sleeplessness. If you have had a hysterectomy, stay well connected to your medical provider until the hormone shifts have settled down.

def•i•ni•tion

Women can have a **tubal ligation,** which is a surgical procedure to permanently seal a woman's fallopian tubes—the tubes leading from the ovaries to the uterus. Also called "tying your tubes," it is an outpatient procedure that can be done in the hospital or a surgery center.

Women may welcome or grieve their newfound freedom from pregnancy, depending on how old they were at the time of hysterectomy and the reasons they needed it. Therefore, your sex life can be boosted or subdued as a result of this surgery. If you find your sexual health is declining after hysterectomy, talk it over with your medical provider.

Vasectomy

Men can have a vasectomy, which is a procedure to block the vas deferens—the tube through which sperm travel to join with the semen that comes out of the penis during ejaculation. Once the vas is cut and tied, there will no longer be sperm in the ejaculate, but there will still be fluid. A physician can make small incisions or punctures in the scrotum through which to cut the vas. This procedure is usually done in the doctor's office and takes less than half an hour. This method of permanent contraception has fewer complications than a woman's tubal ligation and is considerably less expensive. Once a man has decided not to father any more children, it affords him freedom from the fear of pregnancy.

> **Beyond the Basics**
>
> The only notable complication from vasectomy is epididymitis or orchitis—an inflammation of the epididymis or testis. This inflammation can cause tenderness and pain and may interfere with sexual activity for a while. It is usually easily treated with heat and goes away in about a week.

Men are not immediately free of sperm after a vasectomy. It usually takes 10 to 14 ejaculations and 1 to 2 months until there are no more sperm present in semen. Usually there is a checkup a month or two after the procedure to see whether there are sperm in the semen. Until you are sure that the "coast is clear," you should use another form of birth control after a vasectomy.

Some side effects of permanent contraception can damage your sexual health. In women, there may rarely be scarring or abdominal pain that results and makes sex uncomfortable or impossible. Men may have scarring as well but less often than women. For either gender, if reproduction was part of your sexual identity, you may experience a grief at the loss of your fertility, including sadness, lowered libido, or depression. If you experience emotional distress that lasts more than two or three months after such a procedure, seek some professional help to sort out what's going on.

Permanent contraception isn't for everyone, obviously. But for some people it offers great freedom and can make sex more playful and spontaneous because they are not worried about pregnancy for the first time in their adult lives.

Deciding to have a permanent procedure for contraception should be done only when you are certain you will not want more children. Reversing either a tubal ligation or a vasectomy is delicate surgery and is successful in restoring fertility only about half of the time.

Behavioral Methods

Behavioral methods of contraception are those that depend on making behavior choices to avoid pregnancy. They are usually used by people who are motivated and who have good control over their own behavior. They may choose these methods because other methods are contrary to their values or because they don't want the costs or risks of other methods.

Abstinence/Celibacy—Is It Sexually Healthy?

Abstinence or celibacy, which is choosing not to engage in sexual activity, can be a sexually healthy choice. Sometimes men and women find that they want to take a break from sexual activities. There are many reasons for this—religious, health, stress management, or psychological. Sometimes just refraining from an activity, whether it is sex, food, alcohol, or other appetites, helps you get some perspective.

Your friends (or the media or our culture in general) may make it seem as though everyone should want sex every day. But many people find that taking a break helps them decide what they really want and need from a sexual relationship. If you are sorting out how you feel about a particular partner and you want to think more clearly, or if you wonder how your life would be without sexual desires clouding your decisions, take a break. Give yourself a set period of time—two months, for example—and observe your emotions and sensations and longings. It may help you clarify your feelings and intentions about sex or about sex with a specific person. It's okay! And it's okay for as long as you want. You may even find you have more energy for other pursuits while you sort out your thoughts and feelings about sex.

Coitus Interruptus—Playing the Odds

Coitus interruptus—the voluntary withdrawal of the penis during intercourse before ejaculation—is not a preferred method of contraception if you are serious about not having a pregnancy. Also called "withdrawal" or "pulling out," it has a failure rate of between 4 and 30 percent, and the pre-ejaculate fluid can contain sperm and all the same microorganisms that semen contains.

Withdrawal is better than using no method, but it's not recommended as a primary form of contraception. This method can be good or bad for your sexual health, depending on how both partners feel about using it. If the chance of pregnancy makes either of you anxious, this can damage your sexual relationship and lower your enjoyment of sex. It can also be frustrating to one or both partners not to "finish" having sex with the penis still inside the vagina. On the other hand, it can offer some lowering of the odds of pregnancy for a couple who wants unprotected sex and who will be okay if a pregnancy results.

This method does not protect from any STDs. Because there is skin to skin contact and because the pre-ejaculate fluid contains many of the elements of ejaculate, you are only lowering the amount of body fluids exchanged, not eliminating the risk of spreading an STD.

Fertility Awareness: When Is It a Good Choice?

Fertility awareness can be a method of either planned conception or contraception. It is using one of several methods to determine when a woman is fertile and then either having sex (to get pregnant), avoiding it (to not get pregnant), or using a barrier method when she is fertile and otherwise no method. Determining fertile days can be done with a basal thermometer and/or by checking cervical mucous.

Fertility awareness can be good for your sexual health in several ways. If you are a committed couple, it can be a bonding "shared project." Because you both have to cooperate and be aware of the woman's fertile times, it creates a strong connection. If you are trying to get pregnant, it allows you to thoroughly enjoy the ovulatory time when a woman's libido is often higher. If you are trying to avoid pregnancy, it offers some control over your fertility by abstaining from sex during that time or by switching to a barrier method for those days of the cycle. It is low cost, has none of the risks of hormonal methods, and does not require a prescription.

The down side, as with withdrawal or abstinence, is that it can be frustrating for one or both partners, and this can cause problems in your relationship or tempt you to take chances that end in pregnancy. Also, fertility awareness does not protect you from STDs, so if one of you has an STD or STI, you have a good chance of passing it on.

Contraception is a broad topic, and this chapter is not intended to give you all the ins and outs of preventing pregnancy. But the method you choose does have implications for your sexual health. Choosing a method that suits your sexual goals and style is a good investment in ongoing sexual well-being for you and your partner.

The Least You Need to Know

- Hormonal birth control methods can offer you great freedom, but you need to know about side effects.

- Barrier methods can be good STD protection with minimal impact on your sexual health.

- Permanent methods of contraception may give you peace of mind, but you need to be sure that you no longer want to have children.

- Behavioral methods do not protect you from infections and may not be as effective for preventing pregnancy as some other methods.

Chapter 13

Risky Sex

In This Chapter

- ◆ How the excitement of risky sex can jeopardize your sexual health
- ◆ The signs that you might be having compulsive sex
- ◆ How using drugs and alcohol increases your risk
- ◆ Which sexual practices are riskiest?
- ◆ How to decrease risk and still have fun

When you push the edges of sex to increase the excitement, you can push yourself and your relationship over that edge and pay a price higher than you bargained for. Risky sex might offer you a momentary thrill, but you can spend the rest of your life regretting that moment.

Sexual health requires a certain amount of good judgment on your part to keep yourself and your body safe. This may seem like a simple matter, but in the case of sexual risk it is actually pretty complicated.

Safe Sex Is Sexier

Sex, as you have probably noticed, is a pretty reinforcing activity. No one has to tell you that it feels good, and for many people feeling good leads to a quest to feel even better. Part of this "feeling better" is finding sex that is not just satisfying but truly exciting as well. When you begin to risk your health in the search for excitement, you are in dangerous territory.

What's Really at Risk?

Lecturing people about the risks of sex doesn't usually change their behavior. If you are a person who likes the charge you get out of a risky encounter, you aren't likely to change easily or at least not unless you perceive yourself as vulnerable to getting a life-changing STD. And even then, you have to care enough about your health and/or that of your partner to take steps.

But the risks are real. Most new cases of HIV in women are from sex with men who engage in risky sex. Often the women are unaware—until they get their diagnosis—that their partners are having high-risk sex. Sometimes it's because the men don't want to be perceived as "gay" that they hide their sexual practices. They may even lie to themselves about it. But keeping this secret puts them at risk and eventually puts their partner at risk, too.

> **Beyond the Basics** _____
>
> Men who have sex with men (MSM) may or may not consider themselves gay. But if you are a man having sex with other men (or with strangers, multiple partners, or an IV drug user), you are having high-risk sex. Label it whatever you like, but protect yourself by using condoms with every encounter. Don't kid yourself—your health, and your sexual health, is in danger.

Compulsive Sex

Some people get hooked on sex the way others get hooked on alcohol or cigarettes or cocaine. Because of the dopamine "payoff" that sex offers, people who are vulnerable to becoming addicted to the dopamine release can get pulled into dangerous or risky sex for the excitement it offers. And just like alcohol or drugs, this dependence on sex can have disastrous consequences in their lives.

Your risk of getting HIV or other viral STIs is high if you are engaging in frequent high-risk sex. This "need" for sexual excitement is what drives the Internet pornography business and the adult entertainment industry. Like drug dealers and cigarette manufacturers, these industries prey on your continued desire for their product.

Compulsive sex not only threatens your health with the risk of STDs, it also threatens your ability to have a stable relationship and endangers your partner. For some people, it can affect their ability to function at work or can put them in danger of being arrested.

But, as with any compulsion or addiction, the more you indulge yourself, the more you *need* to indulge yourself. It can be overwhelming, and it can ruin not only your sexual health but your psychological health when you begin engaging in practices that you consider wrong or that you know hurt other people in your life.

If you are experiencing any of the following, you may be sexually compulsive or addicted:

- ◆ You engage in high-risk sex that is not fulfilling.
- ◆ You feel ashamed or embarrassed after sex.
- ◆ Your sexual activities create problems in your relationships or marriage.
- ◆ Your work performance is affected by your search for sexual experiences or by intrusive fantasy about them.
- ◆ You have a lot more sexual partners than most people you know.
- ◆ You can't seem to commit to a caring relationship because you don't want your sex life to be limited.
- ◆ You have been arrested for a sexual offense.
- ◆ You spend increasing amounts of time on the Internet or in adult stores looking for sexual material.
- ◆ You don't feel in control of your sexual attractions or activities.

♦ You often wish you "hadn't done that" after a sexual encounter.

♦ You spend a lot of time and effort arranging for sexual encounters, always thinking ahead to the next one.

♦ You sometimes feel as though you are living "two lives," one "normal" one and your sexual one.

♦ You have sex with someone even if you know it could give you an infection or ruin your relationship with someone else.

♦ You use sex to cope with difficult things in your life.

♦ You have trouble being "faithful."

These are signs that sex is ruling your life and therefore that it can lead you into risky situations. If you think that your eagerness for the next sexual experience is jeopardizing your relationship or your health, find a sex therapist who will listen. If you are unable to control sexual thoughts, are lying about sex to your partner, or are suffering consequences like STDs or being arrested, it's time to get some help. Chasing a sexual "hit" can be exciting, but it is never satisfying. You are missing out on deeper fulfillment, and you are courting poor sexual health.

Sex Under the Influence

Movies and novels often paint a romantic evening with a glass of wine in hand. Alcohol can reduce inhibitions and relax you enough to feel less anxious, a sort of "social lubricant." Like so many aspects of the sexual world, what is normal and fun in one context can be risky or dangerous when carried to an extreme.

Substance use is a major risk factor for ruining your sexual health. At the point where substances—legal or illegal—start to influence your judgment, you're in trouble. Some drugs like cocaine or methamphetamine have legendary impact on your sexual judgment and raise your risk of getting HIV and other STDs to dangerous levels.

Proceed with Caution

For both men and women, rates of STDs rise with increasing alcohol use, but women who use alcohol and illicit drugs have an STD rate of almost 8 percent. Men who use the same drugs have an STD rate of 1.5 percent. The difference may be that women get in for treatment more, or that women get STDs more easily because the vagina is so vulnerable, or that women are more affected by the drugs, and therefore, have even worse judgment. Whatever the underlying connection, ladies, all too often: DRUGS + SEX = STD.

The other effect of that glass of wine is that, while you may feel sexier after you drink it, you may actually be less able to perform sexually. It's a frustrating irony that when your desire rises after you've had a few, it's probably the only thing that will. Erectile dysfunction and arousal disorders increase with alcohol use.

Let's face it: sexual arousal alone is an altered state. All by itself it can impede your judgment and decision-making. Add substances to that, and you have a recipe for a very bad outcome and a serious decline in your sexual health.

Consider Your Partner—Taking Responsibility

If you are taking chances with your sexual health, you are taking chances with your partner's sexual health. It's one thing to take a risk and be the one who suffers, but if you are having multiple partners or engaging in risky sexual practices, you can be endangering your partner without even knowing it. You could have an STD or STI without symptoms, like HIV, HPV, or others, and pass it to your partner.

Talk to your partner about your sexual needs and behaviors. If you think he or she will be angry or terribly upset with what you have to say, do it with a counselor in the room so that you can work through the aftermath. If you are in a relationship that you care about, getting resolution about sex is a very big deal.

Beyond the Basics

Men who have more sexual partners also have an increased risk of prostate cancer. The research isn't clear about exactly why this connection exists. It could be that there is an infectious agent like HPV involved, and the more partners you have, the more likely you are to get it. Or it could be that prostate cancer occurs in men with more androgen hormones—the same hormones that increase libido. If you are a man who has had many sexual partners, be aware that you are more likely to be diagnosed with this disease.

Considering the health of your sexual partner or partners is a measure of your maturity and sexual judgment. At the very least, use condoms with every sexual encounter. If you are trying to change your sexual behaviors and you don't want to involve your spouse or committed partner right now, get some help. Sexual desires and behaviors are very strong, and they are hard to change. There are medications, therapies, and self-help groups that can support you to reduce your sexual risks. Explore the ways you can reduce your risk, and think about your partner when you are making those decisions.

Potentially Dangerous Sexual Practices

We've talked about compulsive sex, sex under the influence of chemical substances, and the importance of having good judgment when you are protecting your sexual health. But there are some types of sex that are just inherently more risky and that therefore have a greater chance of affecting your sexual health and fitness.

It's possible to have exciting, satisfying sex and still reduce your risk of STIs and other bad outcomes. If you are engaging in any of these high-risk behaviors, be smart about making rules for yourself that minimize your risk. No sexual encounter is worth losing your health or even your life. Know the risks. Plan ahead.

Unprotected Sex

Unprotected sex is sex without a condom or other barrier to bacteria and viruses. It's a relatively safe way to have sex if you are with only one partner, if you have both been tested, and if you are sure that neither of you has other partners. Even if all those criteria are met, though, there is a chance that one or both of you could have an STI without symptoms that you give to the other. But generally speaking, unprotected sex is a low-risk activity in a longstanding, monogamous relationship.

On the other hand, unprotected sex is a risky enterprise with almost anyone else. And the more "anyone elses" that you have sex with, the higher the risk. You only have to guess wrong once about the "safety" of a sexual partner to pay a high price.

Any sexual contact without a latex barrier between you and your partner has the potential to spread an STI. That goes for oral sex (either giving or receiving), genital sex, anal sex, and any combination of these. You don't have to have an orgasm or ejaculate to be at risk; any contact is an opportunity to share microorganisms.

Practicing *safe sex* means planning ahead to protect yourself. Carry condoms and/or dental dams if there is any chance that you will be having a sexual encounter. Tell yourself that unprotected sex is for later, if things work out between you. But for now, better safe than sorry.

def•i•ni•tion

> **Safe sex** is defined as the use of protective barriers and practices that reduce the risk of infection during sexual activity with the goal of preventing an STD. Safe sex is a misnomer since there are always unknown risks even for the most cautious partners, so "safer sex" or "harm-reduction sex" would be more accurate terms for practices that reduce risk.

Anal Sex

Anal sex is not usually considered a topic of polite conversation, but it is a sexual practice that is high risk, so we will talk about it here. And if not many people discuss anal sex, plenty of people are having it. Some studies estimate that as many as a fifth of all sexually active adults— men and women—have had anal sex.

The vagina is made for sexual activity. It is stretchy, and the walls are relatively thick. The anus and rectum, on the other hand, are not designed for sex and have a thinner wall, made of a fragile sort of tissue that tears more easily than vaginal tissue, making it easy for germs to penetrate and cause infection. It doesn't heal as quickly as the vagina

Proceed with Caution

Unfortunately, when people engage in anal sex they are *less* likely to use condoms than when they have penile/vaginal sex. This may be based on the incorrect assumption that anal sex is less risky than vaginal sex, but the opposite is true.

either, and because there are many sorts of bacteria in the area from fecal material, there is a good chance of a tear or cut becoming infected.

For those same reasons, it is also easier to get an STD through anal sex. Unprotected anal sex is one of the riskiest types of sexual encounter you can have, so it is more, not less, important to use condoms with every anal sexual encounter.

If you and your partner agree that anal sex is something you want to try, here are some things to remember to reduce the risk:

♦ Use a condom on your penis or anything else you use in your or your partner's rectum.

♦ Use plenty of lubricant—not petroleum based—to cut down on friction and the chance of making a cut or tear.

♦ Be very slow and patient, letting the person on the receiving end control how fast and how far. If the receiver says "stop," you stop.

♦ Don't have vaginal sex right after anal sex without removing the condom, washing both of you, and putting another one on.

People have very strong feelings about anal sex, and it's critical that you listen to your partner before trying it. If he or she doesn't like the idea or finds it disgusting, then find another way to enjoy each other. If you are both into it and are very, *very* careful, it can be an exciting addition to your sexual sharing. But you both have to want it, and you both have to play it safe.

Sex with Strangers

Sex with someone you don't know, or know only a little, is the riskiest sex there is. Dating scenes, including the Internet, make meeting people easy. But knowing someone takes time. Sex with a new partner, and especially an anonymous encounter, puts you in the path of every sexual hazard there is. If you are someone who is serious about your sexual health, this is not a road to go down.

Sometimes it is tempting to flirt with someone and tease the person along. Or it may be your fantasy to take up with a lovely stranger and get carried away on a sexual high. But unless you fancy having an STD, getting assaulted, being rejected, or all of the above, save your fantasies for role-playing with your regular partner.

When you are going out on the town or to a club or a big party where you don't know everyone, play it safe. Plan ahead of time what you will do with stranger temptation and stick to your plan. Here are some thoughts for keeping yourself safe to play another day:

- ◆ Go with a buddy. Don't leave without your buddy, and don't let your buddy leave without you. Use each other as an excuse not to take a stranger to bed.

- ◆ Remind yourself of your bottom lines—no sex on the first date; no secluded encounters unless you've known someone at least _____; no more than two drinks all evening if you aren't familiar with the surroundings.

- ◆ Meet for the first time in a public place if you are meeting an Internet friend.

- ◆ Have a "safety buddy" who you always tell where you are going, with whom, how you know the person, and how to find you (and that person) if anything happens.

- ◆ Best of all, don't put yourself in a situation where you will be tempted to connect too soon with someone you don't know.

Not only your sexual health but your safety and well-being can be sacrificed to a really bad decision. Even experienced people can underestimate the risk, and there's too much at stake to gamble with your health and future.

The dangers of risky sex are pretty high, and the consequences can be forever.

Try This!

If you are someone who loves the edge, think about ways you can spice up your sex life without ending it—role-playing with a trusted partner, phone sex with explicit language, or masturbating with erotic movies are daring, but safe. Taking pretend chances can be gratifying, but taking real ones can put you out of commission.

If you struggle with wanting to take risks, talk to a counselor who specializes in working with addiction or impulse-control disorders. Someone who understands the compelling nature of your desires can help you find a balance between exciting, satisfying sex and ongoing good health.

The Least You Need to Know

- Chasing sexual highs, intrusive sexual thoughts, lying to your partner, and living from one sexual encounter to the next are all red flags that you may be compulsive about sex.

- Alcohol and drugs can exponentially increase the risk that you will make a bad sexual decision.

- Putting your partner at risk of STDs is never okay.

- Unprotected anal sex is a very high-risk activity—it is especially easy to get and give STDs through this practice.

- Sex with strangers is courting trouble. There are safer ways to satisfy your desire for something edgy.

Part 5

Challenges and Solutions

The road to sexual health and fitness is not always smooth. There are plenty of challenges and barriers that can interfere with healthy sexuality. Some challenges are easily dealt with, but some require your full attention and professional help.

Whether it is a medical condition, a medication you take, or a full-blown sexual dysfunction, you need to know your options in order to make good decisions. Some sexual difficulties are common, while others are rare; some are easy to talk to your doctor about, and others embarrass you. Whatever the problems are, there are ways that you can tackle them that will improve your sexual health and upgrade your quality of life.

Chapter 14

Sexual Dysfunctions

In this Chapter

- ◆ Defining sexual dysfunction
- ◆ How to understand and treat low desire
- ◆ What to do when arousal is limited
- ◆ Dealing with the frustration of orgasm problems
- ◆ The reality of pain disorders

Everyone wants to be sexually healthy and fit, and this book has talked a lot about ways to get there. But what if you or your partner is sexually unhealthy, or sexually unfit to the point where things just aren't working? Sexual dysfunction is finally an acceptable topic to bring up with your medical provider, as well it should be. With drugs like Viagra to treat male sexual dysfunction, and with women stepping up to claim their own sexual fulfillment, it's time to take these conditions seriously.

These sexual dysfunctions used to be lumped into two categories. Male disorders were generally called "impotence," and female disorders were called "frigidity." Luckily, medical and psychological researchers are exploring the underlying causes of sexual dysfunctions, leading to more effective treatments.

Sexual dysfunction is a difficulty with any stage of your sexual response that interferes with your or your partner's satisfaction and enjoyment of sex. These conditions usually fit into one of four categories:

♦ Problems with desire

♦ Problems with arousal

♦ Problems with orgasm

♦ Pain when you have sex

Sexual dysfunctions can be devastating to your sense of self and to your relationship, and they can rob you of the pleasure and closeness that sex offers.

Desire Disorders

Sexual disorders of desire are those in which you feel like "I just don't want to." They are more common as people get older, but they can happen at any time of life. Sometimes it is just a temporary dip during a stressful time or a response to a difficult turn in a relationship. But if low desire lasts for weeks or months, it can threaten your relationship and your sexual health.

Low Libido in Men

Men are less likely than women to complain of low libido. When they do experience low desire, they tend to be more distressed than women who have the disorder. With so much circulating testosterone, men have usually taken sexual desire for granted, so it can be alarming when it drops.

Men can have a low libido for many reasons, including the following:

♦ Lower testosterone levels that come with age

♦ Depression

♦ Side effects from medication

♦ Dissatisfaction with a relationship

♦ Performance anxiety

◆ Byproduct of another sexual dysfunction

◆ Stress

Sorting out the cause(s) of low libido can be complex. It is often a combination of causes, and treatment may include more than one approach. If the cause is strictly a diminishment of testosterone, and if testosterone levels are below normal, they can be boosted with testosterone shots, creams, or patches. But desire can wane even if testosterone levels are normal, and that makes treatment something of an art.

It will probably help to discuss your low level of desire with a medical provider. It may take some combination of hormones, antidepressants, counseling or therapy, and/or the treatment of a co-occurring sexual disorder to get you feeling like your sexual self.

Low Libido in Women

Women are much more likely to report low libido than men are, and the tricky part with women is that they may or may not see this as a "problem." (Men almost always see low libido as a problem!) As many as half of all women report loss of sexual desire at some point in their lives, and it is more common as they age.

The causes in women are similar to the causes in men, including dropping testosterone levels, depression, relationship problems, and as a side effect of another sexual dysfunction. It makes sense that you won't "feel like it" when other things are going wrong or when your hormone levels are low.

Women also struggle with feelings of attractiveness as they age or with any weight gain. This, too, can lower libido if they think they are unappealing to their partner.

For women, it becomes a major problem when their level of desire is vastly different from their partner's. Either they grieve their former level of libido, or they worry that the relationship is

Beyond the Basics

There is some research suggesting that it is not the actual level of testosterone in your body that causes low desire, but the fact that it is dropping from the previous levels. You may have normal amounts of testosterone and still find that you are losing your sexual appetite.

suffering because they have such a low desire compared to their partner. Or both.

Stress and hormone levels are major players in female libido. The two groups of women most likely to say that they have lost their desire for sex are women with small children and women around and after menopause. For both of these groups, hormone levels and life stress can really impact the level of sexual desire.

Aversion Disorder

Sexual aversion disorder is one in which you become extremely anxious or frightened when faced with the possibility of a sexual encounter. This fear and/or anxiety has a detrimental impact on your relationships and prevents you from engaging in satisfying sexual activities. It can be mild or debilitating, and sometimes people use many "good" reasons for not having sexual encounters—not enough time, too tired, career focused, no suitable partners, etc.—without even realizing there is an underlying anxiety or fear of sexual contact.

Usually treatment for sexual aversion disorder requires counseling or therapy to understand why sexual contact provokes anxiety or fear. This aversion may have been present from childhood, or it may not occur until adulthood. The reason for sexual aversion may be rooted in sexual trauma or may result from being spurned in love or from a single disastrous sexual experience. If you notice that you consistently forego situations that might offer sexual opportunities, or if you are repulsed by the idea of genital contact, it's possible that you have developed an aversion to sex. Even if you are well aware of why this has happened to you, it's likely that you will need some professional help to overcome your feelings. There are therapies and medications that can help you discover the reasons behind your aversion. Reaching out to explore treatment is the first step to a more satisfying and healthy sex life.

Beyond Testosterone

Testosterone can be a very effective treatment for disorders of desire, but the reasons and causes for these disorders are sometimes complicated. A dose of testosterone is not going to solve the problem, for example, if you are angry with your partner and want a divorce.

Proceed with Caution _____

Testosterone can be a very effective treatment for low libido, but it also has some negative side effects. It can cause depression, mood disturbance, liver damage, and headache. In women it can result in acne, facial hair, deepening of the voice, and male pattern baldness; in men testosterone can cause changes in testicular size, acne, and trouble urinating. These and other side effects can be dangerous, so testosterone is *not* a simple cure-all for low sexual desire.

If your level of desire is wildly different from your partner's, and if it is affecting your relationship, it is probably time to get some help. Start by exploring treatment with a medical provider or counselor. In order to unravel the cause, they will want to know the following:

◆ Whether this is a new problem or has always been present

◆ What other sexual problems you may be having

◆ How you and your partner perceive your lack of desire

◆ What medical conditions you suffer from

◆ What medications you are taking

◆ What you consider a satisfactory level of desire

The treatment plan for low desire will probably involve physical as well as psychological elements. Finding the right combination will enhance your sexual health and restore a spark to your relationship.

Arousal Disorders—SAD Facts

Sometimes the problem is not that you don't want to have sex but that you can't seem to get and stay aroused long enough to enjoy sex. These problems of arousal—sexual arousal disorders (SADs)—happen to both men and women and can radically diminish sexual health.

Erectile Dysfunction

Erectile dysfunction (ED) is seen much more as a treatable medical problem than as a shameful condition since the development of medications such as sildenafil citrate (Viagra). Suddenly, talking to your doctor about problems with your erection has become not only more acceptable but more hopeful.

Erectile dysfunction is the inability—either totally or in part—to get and maintain an erection. Previously called "impotence," it is a source of enormous distress to men who suffer from it. The causes are varied, but you could suffer some degree of ED from any of the following:

♦ Poor circulation from diabetes, smoking, or heart disease

♦ Nerve or blood vessel damage from surgery on the bladder, prostate, or genitals

♦ Side effects from medications such as blood pressure medications, acid reflux medications, antidepressants, and others

♦ Psychological or mood disturbances such as depression or anxiety

♦ Fatigue

♦ Neurological conditions such as multiple sclerosis, Parkinson's disease, spinal cord injury, or diabetic neuropathy

♦ Stress

♦ Alcoholism

♦ Low testosterone levels

Proceed with Caution

Priapism is a condition wherein the penis stays erect for over four hours. It is often a side effect of injury or certain medications, including some used to treat erectile dysfunction. Priapism is a medical emergency because, as the penis stays erect, blood supply is cut off and permanent tissue damage can result. If you or your partner has an erection that won't go down, it's time for the emergency room.

Anything that damages your circulation or the tissues around the penis or that affects your attitude toward sex can contribute to erectile dysfunction.

Diagnosis of ED is made by taking a careful medical history to establish the timing and possible reasons for the dysfunction. In order to sort through the possible causes, your medical provider will probably want to do a thorough physical exam, some lab tests, and possibly a psychological exam.

Treatment for erectile dysfunction depends on the cause, as with any sexual dysfunction. Medications such as sildenafil citrate, or others in that category, have been quite successful in treating some men for ED. But if you are on nitrite-based medications for heart disease, these ED drugs are not an option. Hormones, antidepressants, and anti-anxiety medications are also sometimes prescribed.

Other treatments include injectable medications (injected directly into the penis) that improve blood flow, surgical implant devices that enable the man to create an erection with inflatable rods in the penis, surgery to repair blocked blood vessels damaged with injury, and vacuum devices that pull blood into the penis, where it is trapped using an elastic ring at the base. Any of these treatments can be effective, but all have risks and benefits that should be carefully explored with your medical provider.

Female Sexual Arousal Disorder (FSAD)

Arousal disorder in women is usually more complicated than in men and can have a number of sources. FSAD happens when a woman is unable to become physically aroused or stay aroused or lubricated during sexual activity. If you are a woman who finds that even when you *want* to have sex you don't feel physically aroused, despite sexual stimulation and foreplay, you may have FSAD.

Arousal is always more than just a physical response, and this is truer for women than men. Here are some of the causes to consider if you think you have an arousal disorder:

- Medical conditions and infections such as endometriosis, bladder infections, sexually transmitted diseases, thyroid problems, diabetes, and high blood pressure

- Hormone changes such as those that occur during and after pregnancy, during and after menopause, and with treatment for some cancers

- Medications such as contraceptives, antidepressants, tranquilizers, and blood pressure medications

- Surgery that alters your view of your feminine sexual self (such as mastectomy or hysterectomy)

◆ Use of alcohol, illegal drugs, pain medications, and nicotine

◆ Stress

◆ Injury to the genital area or traumatic sexual experience

◆ Depression

Women who have FSAD may or may not consider it a problem, depending on whether they desire more sexual activity in their lives. Diagnosis is a process similar to that used in male SAD, and your medical provider will use history, physical exam, lab tests, and psychological tests to determine what might be causing the disorder.

Female arousal disorders such as FSAD and *persistent sexual arousal syndrome (PSAS)* are very destructive to the sexual health of those who suffer from them. It's likely that any successful treatment will be a combination of therapies, including medications, behavioral therapies, and sometimes techniques such as relaxation exercises or biofeedback. Communication is essential between the woman and her medical provider and between the woman and her sexual partner. Arousal disorders are delicate ground, and a woman needs supportive, compassionate people around her in order to navigate that territory successfully and return to sexual health.

def•i•ni•tion

Persistent sexual arousal syndrome (PSAS) is an arousal disorder in women that is not well understood. Women who have it become physically and genitally aroused for long periods of time but are not desiring sex. The arousal is seemingly unprovoked and unwanted. Orgasm does not relieve the arousal and may even make it worse. This sensation can be very painful and may last hours or years. Physicians may not be familiar with the condition, and women often report being dismissed or embarrassed by medical providers who do not listen to their complaints. The causes are unclear, and PSAS may be due to hormone changes, medication reactions, neurological sensitivities, or other causes.

Orgasm Disorders

Orgasm disorders, which can affect both sexes, are a persistent delay or absence of orgasm following sexual excitement. A disorder of orgasm can mean no orgasm, or it can mean having one too soon, too late, or inconsistently.

Absent Orgasm

Not being able to achieve an orgasm is a condition called anorgasmia. Both men and women can suffer from this sexual dysfunction, and it is the inability to have an orgasm despite sufficient stimulation and sexual response. It can be terribly frustrating and can lead to depression, anxiety, or arousal problems.

There is a continuum of orgasmic disorders, and some people are unable to achieve orgasm under specific conditions or with a particular partner but are able to successfully orgasm when masturbating or with other partners. Sometimes ambivalence about a relationship will make it difficult or impossible to have an orgasm with a partner with whom there was previously not a problem.

There are several causes of anorgasmia, and sometimes a combination of elements leads to this disorder. Some medications like SSRI antidepressants are known for affecting the ability to have an orgasm. Other medications can cause this side effect as well. Also, psychological conditions such as anxiety, depression, guilt, shame, and other cognitive/emotional responses can interfere with orgasm.

Any of the other sexual disorders already described in this chapter can lead to an inability to have an orgasm, as can neurological disease and injury. Traumatic sexual experience such as abuse or rape can destroy the ability of either men or women to have an orgasm.

Treatment is aimed at the cause, so a careful diagnosis must be made by a medical or mental health professional. Once the cause is determined, treatment may consist of changing medication, behavioral or couple's therapy, treatment of an underlying medical condition, or some other appropriate reversal of physical symptoms.

Delayed Orgasm

For some people, orgasm is possible but only after prolonged stimulation, and it may be of low intensity when it finally happens. There are many reasons that orgasm could be delayed, including the following:

◆ Medications that decrease the ability to achieve orgasm (such as SSRI antidepressants)

◆ Hormone changes or imbalances, including sex hormones and thyroid hormones

◆ Inadequate sexual stimulation either physically, emotionally, or mentally

◆ Neurologic conditions such as spinal cord injury, multiple sclerosis, and epilepsy

◆ Unresolved relationship issues

◆ Stress, depression, and anxiety

◆ Diabetes

Try This!

If orgasm is delayed or diminished for you or your partner, try taking the spotlight off of it for a while. Sometimes the focus on orgasm as the gold standard has a dampening effect on the whole process. Try spending a few weeks with no expectation that either of you will be aroused or will have an orgasm, but spend time together regularly to do things that "feel good." Set aside safe, private times to cater to each other with foot rubs, back massages, shared baths, brushing each other's hair, or doing whatever the other person finds pleasurable. Growing close and just enjoying your bodies can open the door to a different sort of intimacy. Later you can think about orgasm again, but for now have a no-orgasm holiday.

Delayed and absent orgasm can be frustrating. If you or your partner notices a change in your ability to have an orgasm, discuss it with a professional. Talk about it so that you can get a diagnosis that will lead you back to a satisfying sexual connection with one another.

Once you have determined what the cause of the orgasm delay is, support each other in whatever appropriate treatment you and your medical provider or counselor agree on. If you are single, give yourself permission to get help so that you can enjoy your sexual encounters. As with other sexual disorders, treatment will probably be a combination of medical and behavioral approaches. Be patient—this is probably something that can be resolved over time.

Ejaculatory Disorders

There are a number of ejaculatory disorders that can put a crimp in your sexual health. You may find that you ejaculate too soon, too late, or only with certain activities. Any of these can cause personal, mental, or relationship stress, which may only make matters worse.

If you ejaculate quickly and before you and/or your partner prefers, it is called premature ejaculation and may be due to the following:

◆ A masturbatory habit of ejaculating as quickly as possible

◆ Anxiety or guilt around sexual issues

◆ Ambivalence about your partner or the relationship

Usually the treatment for premature ejaculation is a sort of retraining of your mind and sensitivity to stimuli. There are breathing techniques to help you postpone ejaculation, and learning to tune in to your responses can help you slow down as you get closer to orgasm and ejaculation. Medications and numbing creams and gels are usually not very satisfying remedies for premature ejaculation since they often diminish the pleasure of sexual activity.

If the causes are attitude or anxiety, cognitive therapies may help you sort out your responses so that you can relax and enjoy longer sexual interludes without such a quick climax.

Another ejaculatory disorder is retrograde ejaculation. This occurs when semen is ejected into the bladder instead of out the urethra during sexual climax. It is usually a result of medication side effect, prostate or urethral surgery, or nerve damage from medical conditions such as diabetes. The symptoms are a lack of ejaculate visible with orgasm and subsequent cloudy urine from semen in the bladder.

Retrograde ejaculation can cause infertility since semen is not deposited in the vagina. The treatment depends on the cause. Sometimes discontinuing medication can reverse the symptoms. But if it is caused by surgical scarring or nerve damage, it will probably not respond to treatment. It is not harmful to have semen in the bladder, and it will be excreted with urination. This disorder is not very common and is usually most distressing when men are interested in fathering more children.

When Sex Hurts—Pain Disorders

Sexual pain disorders can reduce sexual health and can lead to other sexual disorders—it's difficult to feel much enthusiasm for sex if it hurts. Pain with intercourse is much more common in women than in men, but it can occur for either.

Dyspareunia

Dyspareunia is the clinical term for pain with intercourse. In men, this can be caused by the following:

♦ Any infection of the urethra, testes, prostate, or epididymis, usually sexually transmitted

♦ A local or allergic reaction to spermicide or sexual lubricant

♦ Peyronie's disease, in which fibrous plaques disfigure the penis and cause painful bending of the penis during erection

♦ Arthritis

♦ Any inflammatory abdominal condition

Treatment and elimination of pain requires treatment of the underlying condition, pain medication, and/or experimentation with various sexual positions to reduce positional pain.

Try This! _____

If you are a man with arthritic changes in your back, you may experience less pain and therefore be more sexually responsive if you can find a position that relieves the pain. Instead of missionary position with man on top, try lying on your back with your partner on top and with a small pillow under your buttocks. You may find that this not only relieves your back pain but gives your partner some control over her own pleasure. Talk to your partner about what positions give you the most comfort.

Women experience dyspareunia from other sources such as the following:

♦ Not enough vaginal lubrication

♦ Vaginitis from sexually transmitted infections, yeast, or bacterial overgrowth

- Inflammation from allergy to condoms, spermicide, or lubricants

- A "fixed" uterus which has less mobility because of infection, inflammation, scarring, endometriosis, etc.

- Vaginal atrophy or thinning of the vaginal skin leading to a shorter and more fragile vagina. This results from less estrogen during and after menopause.

- Bladder problems

These causes of dyspareunia can be remedied by treating the vaginal infections, finding condoms and other lubricant products that you are not allergic to, using a different sexual position, and/or using a vaginal estrogen treatment.

Vaginismus

Vaginismus is a condition in which the vagina has spasms with penetration. It can be quite painful, and the spasms can close the vagina altogether, making penetrative sex difficult or impossible. Once any infectious reason for the pain has been ruled out, the spasms can usually be treated with a combination of behavioral therapy, pelvic floor exercises, and vaginal dilatation.

Treatment should occur with the support of a sex therapist or trained medical provider. A woman with vaginismus may be reacting to a previous traumatic sexual experience, so treatment must be sensitive to her needs and tolerances. If she has a partner, it is best to involve the partner when possible so that the couple can develop some shared sexual closeness and sensitivity in the process of reteaching her body to respond to sexual stimuli.

Vulvodynia and Vestibulitis

Two other conditions that cause pain during sex are vulvodynia and vulvar vestibulitis. These are both conditions of the female genitalia and can cause serious pain during sexual activities.

Vulvodynia is a pain in the female genital area that may be intermittent or constant and may last for a few hours or for weeks. It may feel like a general soreness, burning, itching, stinging, a "raw" feeling, or a throbbing. Sex almost always makes the pain worse. Sometimes even sitting is extremely uncomfortable.

It's not clear what causes vulvodynia, but it seems to be related to an irritation of the tissues surrounding the vagina. It may be due to an irritation of the nerves in the area, repeated vaginal infections, allergies, muscle spasms, or vaginal atrophy from low estrogen levels.

Treatment will depend on the most likely cause of the inflammation or pain but may include any of the following:

♦ Medications like tricyclic antidepressants for chronic pain, anti-inflammatory medications, antihistamines, and antiseizure medication for neurological pain

♦ Biofeedback and relaxation exercises to relax the area and lessen pain

♦ Local numbing agents to reduce pain during intercourse

♦ Vaginal estrogen

♦ Physical therapy or trigger point work to release muscle tension and allow for healing of the muscle fibers

Vulvodynia is difficult to understand and treat, but it can respond well to various approaches if they are used under the direction of someone familiar with treating these disorders.

Vulvar vestibulitis is another form of vulvodynia in which the vestibule or the vulvar skin just outside the introitus —or vaginal opening—is inflamed or reddened. Treatment may be any of the treatments previously mentioned, and in some cases of pain lasting over six months, laser treatment or surgical excision of this area may be recommended.

To diagnose vulvodynia or vestibulitis, your medical provider will want to do a thorough medical history, a physical exam, and tests to be sure that you do not have a sexually transmitted disease or fungal infection. Once those infections have been ruled out, other treatments can be tried. Psychological counseling may also be a good choice to help lower the pain associated with these conditions.

Other Sexual Disorders

There are other sexual disorders that are beyond the scope of this book. These disorders can certainly affect sexual health and fitness, but they require focused therapy and/or treatment to bring sufferers to a state of sexual health and balance. Some of these other disorders are as follows:

◆ Hypersexuality and sexual addiction, in which the preoccupation with sexual activity intrudes into every aspect of life, disrupts work performance and personal relationships, and may include high-risk sexual practices

◆ Paraphilias, which are attractions and sexual connections to someone or something other than a consenting adult partner

◆ Gender identity disorder, a disorder in a person of any age wherein they identify themselves with the opposite gender

Any of these uncommon sexual disorders can disrupt sexual health and fitness. When a person is drawn to sexual activity outside of cultural norms, it usually requires personal insight and professional support to find a sexual balance and expression that is both satisfying and healthy.

The Least You Need to Know

◆ Sexual dysfunctions are complicated and require an accurate diagnosis in order to be treated.

◆ Low libido can be a problem for both men and women and is treatable with therapy, hormones, and/or other medications.

◆ Although there are new treatments for arousal disorders, a careful diagnosis helps adjust the treatment to the cause.

◆ Problems with orgasm can be physical, psychological, or a side effect from medication.

◆ Pain disorders are extremely distressing and often take long-term treatment to resolve.

◆ Treatment is possible for most sexual disorders, and you can start by having open communication with your partner and by getting professional help when you don't see improvement.

Chapter 15

Medical Conditions That Cause Sexual Problems

In This Chapter

- How to minimize the sexual damage from heart disease, hypertension, and diabetes
- What to do when asthma leaves you breathless
- How to prevent pain from stealing your sexual momentum
- Hints for preserving your sexual health when coping with thyroid disease and cancer
- Medications that may be eroding your interest in sex or dampening your sexual performance

If you or your partner suffers from a chronic medical condition, your sexual health and fitness could be compromised. The condition itself—or the medications that treat it—may have a detrimental effect on your sexual performance, your level of desire, your self-esteem, and/or your attitude toward sex.

This chapter looks at some of the common medical conditions that damage sexual health and fitness and gives you hints for minimizing the damage and maximizing your sexual well-being.

Heart Disease: When Your Heart Is Broken

Heart disease is the leading cause of death in the United States for both men and women. The majority of people with any form of heart disease report some degree of sexual problems. Some of the problems are minor and go away with time, but some sexual problems associated with heart disease are life altering, can completely change a person's self-perception, and can damage his or her sexual health.

def•i•ni•tion

Heart disease, also called "cardiovascular disease," is any disorder of the heart and/or the blood vessels that supply the heart. It is actually a broad term for many individual conditions, including coronary artery disease (CAD), narrowing blood vessels (atherosclerosis), inflammation of the heart (myocarditis), rhythm abnormalities (arythmias), and others.

Because "heart disease" is such a general term, there are many factors that affect the sexual health and fitness of people who suffer from it. If you have been diagnosed with a cardiovascular disease or condition, you may want to consider these related aspects of sexual health:

◆ The same things that damage your heart damage your sex life. Poor circulation, narrow blood vessels, being overweight, and hormone changes can all contribute to both cardiovascular disease and sexual dysfunction.

◆ People with heart disease tend to be depressed. Whether it is physical changes or an emotional response, people with cardiovascular disease have a higher rate of depression, which can affect sexual health.

◆ People with heart disease may be fearful that sexual activity will cause a heart attack or stroke. This fear can prevent them from enjoying sex.

◆ Some of the medications that treat heart disease can interfere with sexual function.

◆ Some of the medications that treat heart disease can interfere with medications *that treat* sexual problems. (For example, Viagra and medications like it cannot be used if you are on a nitrite-based medication.)

◆ Either due to embarrassment or because they don't realize that sexual problems are related to their heart disease, many people are reluctant to bring up the issue with their physician.

Obviously, heart disease and sexual health have a complicated relationship. The physical changes, medications, and emotional issues that accompany heart disease combine to make it difficult to decide on the exact underlying issues that cause sexual dysfunction in people with heart disease.

Beyond the Basics

During sexual intercourse, heart rate and blood pressure rise for an average of 5 to 15 minutes. For most people, having sex is about the same level of activity as climbing two flights of stairs. Usually patients with heart disease can eventually resume normal sexual activity, even after a heart attack. If you (or your partner) are wondering whether it is safe to resume sexual activity, talk it over with your medical provider and make a plan that will help you get back on track. Oh, and don't stress yourself by expecting everything to be normal right away!

If you have a partner, talk to him or her about the sexual problems or side effects you are experiencing. Ask the person to support you in getting help from your medical provider. Even talking to your partner about the problem can help decrease your anxiety about it. Sexual problems are always a relationship issue, so engage your partner in the solution if it is at all possible.

If you are having sexual problems and are being treated for a cardiovascular disease, *talk to your medical provider about it.* These issues are very common—over 80 percent of people with cardiovascular disease report some sort of sexual issue since getting their diagnosis. You should not expect to solve sexual problems on your own when you are dealing with a cardiovascular condition. Physicians who treat patients with heart disease are usually familiar with the sexual health issues that arise and can probably offer suggestions and treatments that may help.

Hypertension: High Blood Pressure Takes a Toll

High blood pressure is a common medical condition that has many implications for sexual health. Both men and women who have high blood pressure are more likely than people with normal blood pressure to have sexual problems. It's not exactly clear why this is true, but there are several factors to consider.

First, there is the condition itself. For reasons that aren't entirely understood, people with high blood pressure have lower levels of nitric oxide in their systems. This chemical relaxes blood vessels, which is very important in sexual response because relaxing these vessels allows a penis or clitoris to fill with blood and therefore be erect. If levels of nitric oxide are low, genital blood flow is diminished as is sexual response. So if hypertension is accompanied by low levels of nitric oxide, that may explain, in part, why people with high blood pressure have sexual response problems.

Another sexual health issue associated with high blood pressure is the medication used to treat it. There are several types of medication prescribed to lower blood pressure, and many of them have sexual side effects. For some the side effect may be a decrease in sexual desire. For others it may be trouble getting or keeping an erection.

If you have high blood pressure, you may feel that you are in a sort of "damned if you do and damned if you don't" situation because sexual dysfunction may be associated with your hypertension, but treating hypertension may also cause sexual problems. What's a guy (or gal) to do?

First, don't despair. Many categories of medication treat hypertension. Drugs in the diuretic or beta blocker categories are most strongly associated with negative sexual side effects. Other types, called angiotensin receptor blockers (ARBs) or angiotensin-converting enzyme (ACE) inhibitors, seem to have fewer sexual side effects. If your medication is decreasing your ability to enjoy sexual activity, other choices may work as well without causing those side effects.

> **Beyond the Basics**
>
> There is some evidence that an ARB medication called losartan, used to treat high blood pressure, may actually improve erectile dysfunction. Drugs of this type seem to improve sexual function as well as mental attitude. The reasons for this are not understood, but for some people with hypertension these medications may be a good choice and may improve quality of life if sexual health has been an issue.

Lifestyle changes can also help you fight high blood pressure. Your body can reverse some of the changes that cause hypertension if you do the following:

♦ Eat a diet low in fat and high in vegetables.

♦ Exercise regularly.

♦ Stop smoking.

♦ Learn to manage stress and relax, with meditation or other techniques.

Untreated hypertension is dangerous and can lead to a heart attack or stroke. If your medications (or your partner's) are causing sexual side effects that bother you, don't stop taking them without talking to your medical provider. A change in treatment may help.

Diabetes: Silent Intruder

People with diabetes have high levels of glucose (sugar) in their blood. Over time, these high levels of glucose damage blood vessels and nerves, including those in the genital area. As a result, many people who have had diabetes for a long time develop problems with their sexual response.

For men, this usually takes the form of erectile dysfunction. In fact, sometimes erectile dysfunction is a symptom of undiagnosed diabetes. Men with diabetes may notice problems getting and/or keeping an erection, as well as reduced sensation in the genitals.

Several mechanisms may be at work in sexual problems for diabetic men. First, the damaged blood vessels do not deliver a good blood supply to the penis, even with stimulation to the area. Second, nerve damage can interfere with sexual response. Third, the muscle damage done by diabetes can affect the smooth muscle activity within the penis, which doesn't allow blood vessels to fill properly to cause an erection.

For women, the changes are similar. Sexual response is hampered if persistent high levels of glucose in the bloodstream damage blood vessels, nerves, and smooth muscles in the vagina and clitoris. Also, women with diabetes are more prone to yeast vaginitis and other vaginal infections, which can make intercourse painful.

Beyond the actual physical damage to tissues, people with diabetes have a higher incidence of depression, which can also cause problems with sexual response.

If you or your partner has diabetes, you can do the following to minimize the sexual side effects of the disease:

♦ Keep your blood glucose at normal levels by following your diabetic treatment plan faithfully and by monitoring your blood glucose as directed.

♦ Make lifestyle changes that support your body in managing blood glucose. These include getting regular exercise, eating a diet high in vegetables and fiber and low in fat, and drinking plenty of water.

♦ Drink little or no alcohol.

♦ Quit smoking.

♦ See your medical provider regularly to monitor your diabetic status and discuss your care.

♦ Talk to your medical provider at the first sign of sexual problems.

Treatment for the sexual side effects of diabetes can take several forms. The first priority is to manage your diabetic state so that the disease does not damage nerves and blood vessels. Once sexual side effects occur, men may be treated with medication injections to the penis, penile implants to "create" erections, PDE-5 inhibitor drugs like Viagra and Cialis, and/or vacuum devices to bring blood into the penis.

Women can be treated with some of the same PDE-5 inhibitor drugs, which may improve blood flow to the genital area.

Treatment for any underlying depression is also important since depression can cause low sexual desire and response. Monitoring your mental status as well as your blood glucose is an important part of a diabetic treatment plan.

Asthma: You Need to Breathe

Asthma is an inflammatory condition of the lungs that limits breathing capacity and lowers oxygen levels in the body. People with moderate to severe asthma may notice a marked decrease in their ability to enjoy sex. It's discouraging when you want to be breathing hard to find that you are hardly breathing.

When it is severe or poorly controlled, asthma limits activity, including sexual activity. One study found that the majority of moderate to severe asthma sufferers who visited an emergency room reported that asthma limited what they could do in bed. Those who were limited in their sexual activity were more likely to be depressed.

If you or your partner is asthmatic and you find that it limits your enjoyment or participation in a sexual relationship, here are some things to consider:

- **Try taking a more passive role in bed.** Talk to your partner about whether you could limit your exertion during sex. Find positions that allow for little pressure on the chest and require less movement on your part.

- **If your doctor has prescribed bronchodilators, try taking these medications about an hour before sexual activity.** This may provide better oxygen exchange while you and your partner are enjoying each other.

- **Change the time of day when you make love.** If possible, try planning sexual activities for late morning or early afternoon when lungs are functioning at their best.

- **Do a "trigger sweep" of your bedroom.** Go carefully through your bedroom and eliminate possible triggers like carpets, feather pillows, and anything that holds dust and allergens. Wash the bedding and wipe down the furniture. You will probably find that you breathe better during sleep as well as during sex.

♦ **Take the focus off genital sex and try just enjoying each other's bodies in ways that feel good.** Massage, touching, cuddling, kissing, and other nongenital activities can keep you close even when you can't manage genital sex.

♦ **If you or your partner smoke, it's time to stop.** Make your house and your lungs smoke-free zones. Talk to your partner about what it would take to quit smoking. Discuss it with your medical provider and use the nicotine patch if needed to break the hold that cigarettes have on you.

♦ **Keep your asthma as well controlled as possible.** The damage done by ongoing low levels of oxygen will keep you tired and without energy. Take asthma medications as prescribed and talk to your medical provider about fine-tuning your asthma treatment to give you the best lung function possible. Once the plan is made, follow it!

Back Pain: How to Cope

Back pain is very common. It is the leading reason for missed work hours in the United States, and 80 percent of adults will have some level of back pain at some point in their lives. When you are dealing with ongoing back pain, it requires energy just to get through a day. Sex may seem like a low priority when it hurts to tie your shoes or stand. But at some point you may realize that you miss the pleasure and closeness that sex offers.

First, of course, you need to find an approach to your back pain that makes life seem possible. Whether that means getting therapy or medication or doing an exercise program (or maybe all of the above), you can find ways to lessen the impact of the pain on your life. Frustration or even depression will result from untreated back pain that goes on for weeks or months.

Try This!

Have a playful attitude about sex, even if you are dealing with back pain. Take it slow, stay relaxed, and don't be afraid to laugh. You won't be any worse off for having tried, and you may find yourself enjoying each other in deeper, more caring ways. See sex as a way to get close, have fun, relieve the stress of your pain, and just be together—even when it isn't perfect.

Once your pain is at a level where you can think about enjoying sex, talk to your partner about what you want and need. Communication is essential so that both of you can enjoy sex with a minimal amount of discomfort and a maximum amount of satisfaction. The following lists provide some things to try if back pain is a problem.

Men whose pain is less when standing or bending slightly backward can try the following:

♦ Missionary position, supporting himself with his hands, arching back slightly

♦ Lying on his back with partner straddling him, placing a pillow under lower back

♦ Sitting in an armless chair with partner straddling him

Men who get relief from back pain by bending forward can try these:

♦ Getting behind his partner and entering from behind with both kneeling on the bed

♦ Having his partner kneel on the bed while he stands, bending slightly forward, and enters from behind

♦ Lying with his partner on their sides, spooning and entering from behind

Women with back pain can also adjust sexual position to accommodate their discomfort. As with the suggestions for men, try to find positions that reduce the strain on your back while allowing for penetration. For example, women who have less back pain when they are standing or leaning slightly backward may find the following positions easier on them:

- Lying face down with her upper body propped on a pillow, allowing her partner to enter from behind

- Straddling her partner as he sits in a chair

- Missionary position with a towel or pillow under her lower back, keeping legs straight or almost straight out

Women who find pain relief by bending slightly forward may have success with these adjustments:

- On the bottom in missionary position, with knees pulled up toward her chest

- On top and straddling her partner, bending forward and resting her chest on his

Keep a "love conversation" going during sex, telling your partner what feels good, better, or not-so-good all along the way. Enlist your partner in helping you find positions that work for both of you. Use pillows, towels, or any piece of furniture that seems to offer support for a comfortable position. The person with back pain usually takes a more passive role so that muscles in the back can be relaxed and to reduce the chance of spasm.

If genital sex is just too painful, refocus to other kinds of lovemaking and touching, including oral sex, massage, kissing, cuddling, stroking, and generally just feeling good with each other. Any pleasurable sexual contact will help reduce pain and will draw you closer to each other.

Arthritis: Working Around It

Like back pain, arthritis offers many challenges to your sexual health and fitness. You may feel less attractive or that your body is not appealing because of your condition. Joint pain can make sex seem daunting, or you may be self-conscious about your lack of flexibility. If you are depressed or frustrated because of your arthritis, that can dampen your sex life, too.

Here are some ideas for smoothing the way to satisfying sex if you suffer from arthritis:

- Plan sex for the time of day when you have the most energy and the least pain.

- Take medications so that they are at peak effectiveness when you will be having sex.

- Rest up on days when you will be having sex—save the house and yard work for another day.

- Take a warm bath or shower before having sex—have your partner join you and massage you during the bath if that is something he or she would enjoy.

- Do some gentle stretching and range-of-motion exercises before climbing into bed.

- Experiment with different positions to find the most comfortable ones.

- Use an electric blanket on the bed to keep you warm during sex.

- Include massage as foreplay to loosen your muscles up.

- Use pillows, towels, and other supports to ease joint pain and adjust your position for comfort.

- Take it slow; it saves your energy.

- Focus on pleasure, not climax—this is about being close to your partner *and* enjoying yourself.

 Try This!

If you have arthritis, talk to your partner about what you are worried about during sex and what would make it easier. With an ongoing condition like arthritis, you both need to be on the same page. Plan your sexual times like you would plan a date and have some fun talking it over—anticipation is part of the game!

Take your partner with you when you discuss arthritis pain with your medical provider. Not only is that supportive of you, but you will both learn ways to make sex enjoyable, and your medical provider will see that you *both* consider it an important aspect of your relationship.

Cancer: What Can Help?

Damage to your body image after surgery, fatigue, grief, pain, worry about recurrence, medications, hormone shifts, fertility issues—any one or all of these can have a significant effect on your sexual health and fitness if you have had a brush with cancer.

The most important element of preserving your sexual health in the face of a cancer diagnosis is to discuss frankly and ahead of time the impact that cancer is likely to have on your sexual function. Talk honestly about your fears and anxieties and encourage your partner to do the same. If possible, take your partner with you to medical appointments and discuss these things openly with your physicians. Get information and ask questions about the following:

- **The effect of chemotherapy on sexual function during and after treatment.** Will you need hormone replacement? Will it change your level of desire? Will there be changes in your genital tissues, such as vaginal dryness or blood flow to the penis?

- **The effects surgery will have on your genital function.** Are there nerve-sparing surgical techniques that will help you return to normal genital sensation after the surgery? Does your surgeon use those techniques?

- **Whether radiation will be used.** If yes, will that continue to have effects after the course is done, and what will they be?

- **Whether most people have problems with sex after similar treatment.** Ask your medical provider to give you specific information on the most likely sexual scenarios and where to get help following the treatment.

Depending on the type of cancer, your general health, your mental state, and your support system, here are some things to consider after a cancer diagnosis to help you recover your sexual well-being:

- Before, during, and after the treatment, focus on staying emotionally close to your partner, if you have one, so that you can find your way through this cancer event together. Sexual health is based on physical and emotional health, and cancer will challenge even the most solid relationships.

◆ Do as much homework as you can before you begin your treatment. Learn what you can about the effects of your cancer treatment, and make decisions about how you want to approach recovery *before* you are feeling exhausted and/or ill from the treatment.

◆ Continue to enjoy physical closeness and touch as much as is comfortable throughout treatment. Holding hands or a well-timed back rub will remind you that your body appreciates being touched.

◆ Once you have recovered your energy and begin to desire sexual closeness following treatment, make an appointment with your medical provider and/or mental health practitioner to discuss the best ways to recover your sexual self.

Beyond the Basics

There are "nerve-sparing" surgical techniques that can minimize the nerve damage from prostate surgery. Damage to the nerves that lie next to the prostate can affect the blood flow into the penis, or the muscle tissue around the urethra, making it difficult to get an erection or control urine. Although these techniques are still being studied, they show great promise for lowering the chances of incontinence and erectile problems after surgery.

The hormone shifts, bodily injury, fear of death, change in body image, anxiety about work and finances, and grief over losses of health and function all play an enormous part in how well you recover sexually from cancer. There are medications, medical devices, therapies, and counseling that can help you and your partner resume a satisfying sexual connection. Be as open and honest as you can with yourself, your partner, and your medical provider about what you want and how to get there.

Thyroid Disease

Your thyroid is a small gland in your neck that releases hormones. When it is overactive (hyperthyroid) or underactive (hypothyroid), it can have a tremendous impact on your body and sexual health. The following are some of the problems associated with thyroid disease that can affect your sexual health:

♦ Low libido

♦ Vaginal changes such as dryness or pain with sex

♦ Erectile problems

♦ Delayed or premature ejaculation

♦ Weight gain

♦ Irritability and depression

The most important first step to combat the sexual problems that come with thyroid disease is to get a good diagnosis and a proper course of treatment. Many of the sexual symptoms disappear once the thyroid problem is treated. If the sexual symptoms persist, you can address those separately. First get your thyroid back on track so that your body can respond, then discuss any remaining sexual side effect with your medical provider.

Are Your Medications the Problem?

Many medications that are excellent treatments for medical problems and diseases have sexual side effects. Sometimes people decide that the cure is worse than the disease and stop taking their medications. In the long run, this can do a lot of damage to your body. If you are experiencing sexual side effects from a medication, don't discontinue it without talking it over with your medical provider. There may be options that you are not aware of.

Antidepressants

Selective serotonin reuptake inhibitor (SSRI) medications are known for their sexual side effects. These medications may be very effective for depression, but patients are sometimes discouraged or frustrated by the side effects. The good news is that there are many choices of antidepressants, and a sexual side effect with one does not mean you will have sexual side effects with all of them.

Blood Pressure Medications

As discussed earlier in this chapter, high blood pressure can do a lot of damage to your sexual health over time. However, medications to treat hypertension also offer their own difficulties. If your blood pressure medication is giving you trouble in bed, discuss changing the medication with your medical provider because there are other choices. As with antidepressants, however, don't stop taking the medication on your own without talking it over with your doctor first.

Other Culprits

Many medications can cause subtle or dramatic sexual symptoms. Besides antidepressants and hypertension medications, you could have side effects from medicine that you take for acid reflux, mental health issues, high cholesterol, allergies, fungal infections, sleep problems, menopause symptoms, and birth control.

You may be having sexual side effects and not even realize it is from the medication you are taking. If you take any medicine regularly and are having sexual desire or function problems, check with your medical provider or pharmacist to see whether the problems you are having are related to medication.

Here is a chart listing some of the types of medication that can affect your sexual outlook and response:

Type of Medication	Why You Take It	Possible Sexual Side Effects
Antidepressants		
SSRI Like: Prozac, Zoloft, Celexa, Paxil	Depression	Delayed or absent orgasm; low desire; Erectile Dysfunction (ED); ejaculation problems
Tricyclic Like: Elavil, Norpramin, Aventil	Depression, pain management	Delayed or absent orgasm; low desire; ED; ejaculation problems

continues

continued

Type of Medication	Why You Take It	Possible Sexual Side Effects
MAO Inhibitor Like: Marplan, Nardil, Parnate	Depression, anxiety, Parkinson's disease, migraine prevention	Delayed or absent orgasm; low desire; ED; ejaculation problems
Antihypertensives		
ACE Inhibitor Like: Vasotec, Altace, Lotensin	High blood pressure, heart disease	ED; ejaculation problems
Alpha Blocker Like: Cardura, Minipress, Flomax	High blood pressure, enlarged prostate	ED
Beta Blocker Like: Inderal, Lopressor	High blood pressure, angina (chest pain), glaucoma	ED
Calcium Channel Blocker Like: Norvasc, Plendil	High blood pressure, angina (chest pain)	ED
Thiazide Diuretic Like: HCTZ	High blood pressure	ED
Clonidine	High blood pressure	ED; low desire; ejaculation problems
Methyldopa	High blood pressure	ED; low desire; ejaculation problems
Antipsychotics		
Phenothiazines Like: Thorazine, Haldol, Stelazine, Mellaril, Compozine	Psychotic illness	ED; low desire; ejaculation problems

Risperidone	Psychotic illness	ED; ejaculation problems

Anti-Seizure

Carbamazepine (Tegretal)	Seizures	ED

Other

Benzodiazapine Like: Valium, Xanax, Ativan, Halcion	Anxiety, sleep problems	Low desire
Acid Reducers Like: Cimetidine, Omeprazole	Acid Reflux, stomach ulcers	ED; low desire
Cyproterone acetate	Prostate cancer	ED; low desire; "dry" ejaculation
Disulfiram	Alcohol withdrawal	Low desire
Estrogen	Contraception, menopausal symptoms	Low desire
Finasteride	Enlarged prostate	ED; low desire; ejaculation problems; "dry" ejaculation
Antiemetics Like: Metoclopramide, Prochlorperazine	Nausea and vomiting	ED; low desire
Opioid painkillers Like: morphine, methodone	Severe pain	ED; low desire
Propantheline	Intestinal spasm	ED
Spironolactone	Heart failure, fluid retention	ED; low desire

You may be having sexual side effects and not even realize it is from the medication you are taking. If you take any medicine regularly, and are having sexual desire or function problems, check with your medical provider or pharmacist to see whether the problems you are having are related to medication.

The Least You Need to Know

- ◆ Cardiovascular disease can cause many sexual problems, so good treatment and careful monitoring is a must.

- ◆ Anticipating activity by using asthma medications ahead of time can help you breathe easier during sex.

- ◆ Using supports and timing your pain medications can reduce your pain during lovemaking.

- ◆ Proper medical treatment will go a long way toward minimizing sexual problems that come with thyroid disease.

- ◆ Sexual health following a cancer diagnosis depends on open communication with your partner and your medical provider, good information ahead of time, and a patient attitude.

- ◆ If you are on a regular medication and are having sexual problems, the medication could be a contributing factor.

Chapter 16

Other Challenges to Your Sex Life

In This Chapter

◆ Normal sexual changes as hormones diminish

◆ Medical conditions that men need to understand to protect their sexual health

◆ Medical conditions that women need to understand to protect their sexual health

◆ Sexually healthy and fit at *any* age—you're just getting started!

Men and women face various bumps in the sexual road as they approach 40 and beyond. Besides the aspects of sexual dysfunction and medical conditions covered earlier in this book, there are a few specific issues that can affect your sexual health and fitness. Some are typically male conditions, and some are common in women. Then there are a few that are equal opportunity hassles.

This chapter covers some of the gender-specific concerns and discusses ways to understand and overcome these puzzling or frustrating realities. The more you know, the more you can put your own situation into perspective and take steps to enjoy your life, including the sexual side of it.

When Hormones Fade

Anyone over the age of 30 is facing the reality of diminishing hormones. It is a biological fact that as you get along in the fertile years, your body begins to slowly turn down the hormone production. This isn't to say that you will notice symptoms on your 30th birthday, but no one stays 19 forever. However, there's a lot to be said for the judgment and perspective that come with years. And if diminishing hormones throw you some curves, at least you can say you saw them coming.

For Men: Slowing Down? That's Okay!

For men, there's a tendency to despair when hormones begin to wane since sexual virility and performance are so much a part of male identity. It's not unusual for men to quietly panic the first time they don't wake up with an erection or when they have a little performance glitch in bed. Some of this is completely normal, and before you send away for some mysterious hormone replacement pill or magical herb, at least understand that your body is doing what it was designed to do.

It's a given that older men have lower average testosterone levels than younger men. What this means to you and your particular set of biological characteristics is impossible to predict. It depends on inherited tendencies, lifestyle, health status, stress level, and perception. Some men are distressed if they can have sex only three times a week, while others would give their left arm to have it that often. Your level of concern is related to your experience and expectations.

Once you turn 40, your testosterone level drops at about the rate of 1 percent a year. Even though this drop is significant from age 45 to age 50, most men do not notice symptoms until later. Even men with clinically low levels of testosterone may not notice significant changes in their sex drive or performance.

Other men seem more affected by this diminishing testosterone and suffer more from symptoms. This corresponds to what some clinicians call *andropause*.

def•i•ni•tion

Andropause refers to the combination of low androgens and resulting symptoms experienced by some men between the ages of 45 and 60. Also called "male menopause" or "veripause," it is not as well studied or accepted clinically as female menopause. Men suffering from this hormonal drop may complain of decreased sexual desire and arousal, depression, irritability, inability to get an erection, poor concentration, increased body fat, and anxiety.

Determining what is normal for you will go a long way toward relieving the worry that you might have about waning virility. Some changes are very common and to be expected, while others might signal a need for medical help.

Normal changes in male sexual response include the following:

♦ Less frequent morning erection

♦ Longer time required to achieve an erection

♦ More manual stimulation needed to get an erection (thoughts and fantasy may not be enough)

♦ More manual stimulation required to reach orgasm

If any of these are happening for you, it is likely your body's normal response to a decrease in the available testosterone.

If you are still enjoying sex but everything takes a bit longer, it's probably your new normal. Men can take advantage of this slowdown to enjoy the touch and foreplay of sex more and can use this as an opportunity to tune in to their partner. Women take longer to respond and to lubricate, remember, so this may be your chance to bring her along while you accommodate your own new, toned-down sexual response. It may not be the same quick, intense response you think of as normal, but it can be deeply satisfying—for both of you.

For Women: Menopause and Sexual Response

Although sexual dysfunction already was discussed in Chapter 15, it's worth pointing out that women, too, have a shift in sexual response with menopause that is a normal easing off of sexual desire. This isn't to say that all women stop wanting sex, but it is to reassure you that if you are not as "hot to trot" as in your earlier days, it can be a normal adaptation to getting older.

The main thing to focus on for sexual health and fitness is this: is this change something that is okay with me, or does it take a bite out of my quality of life? If you are someone who has a lifestyle or identity that is dependent on high sex drive, this will be an unwelcome change. But if you have had moderate interest in sex, and this is congruent with your life and your partner's needs, then it is just a turn in your sexual road, not a barricade ending your journey.

If a lower libido doesn't alter your self-image or your enjoyment of life, it is not destroying your sexual health. On the other hand, if diminishing estrogen is creating physical problems with sex or if the difference in libido creates problems in your relationship with your partner, it is an obstacle to sexual health.

Life and hormones—together or separately—can have you on a roller coaster. This is true whether you are 30 or 60. Your ability to cope is the determiner of whether you need to intervene. You may want to consider getting medical or professional support if you notice any of the following:

◆ You are sad or distressed about the level of your libido.

◆ You still desire sexual activity, but it is painful.

◆ You and your partner argue about the differences in your sexual appetites.

◆ You don't enjoy life or sex as you used to.

◆ You can't achieve orgasm.

◆ Your clitoris is over- or undersensitive.

◆ Your irritability keeps you from getting close to your partner.

Any of these could be a sign that your hormone levels are part of the problem. Whether it is premenstrual swings or menopausal changes, there are hormone supplements, medications, stress-reduction techniques, and therapies that could help you cope with your body's ups and downs. Don't be afraid to reach out for professional help—start with your medical provider if you aren't sure where to turn.

Men, Watch Out for These

Besides the natural changes in testosterone levels that happen over time, there are some conditions that men may face that can affect their sexual function and/or self-image. Most are treatable, and all of them are worth recognizing and addressing in some way. Men are not always eager or willing to bring up their misgivings about their bodies, but knowing about these less common conditions can give you permission to follow up.

Peyronie's Disease

Peyronie's disease only occurs in about 1 percent of men, but it can be anxiety provoking or even alarming if they are not familiar with it.

Men who notice that their penises are "pointing in a new direction" are understandably anxious about it. Because they may be embarrassed or reluctant to see a doctor about this, it can progress and cause more discomfort or can even interfere with the ability to urinate.

Treatment of Peyronie's disease is most effective if it is started within six months of when you first notice the symptoms. The course of the disease is extremely variable, depending on what causes it, and it is different for each man who has it. The following are some of the variabilities:

def•i•ni•tion

Peyronie's disease is a condition of the penis known for the presence of firm or hardened tissue in the shaft of the penis, often causing distortion of the penile shape. It usually occurs in men between the ages of 45 and 60, but it can happen at earlier or later ages as well.

- Usually the fibrous tissue forms in the top of the penis shaft, making it point "up," but it can form in the bottom, too, making it point "down."

- Symptoms may occur rather suddenly or may happen subtly over time.

- Some cases of Peyronie's go away on their own without intervention.

- Some cases get progressively worse and do not respond to treatment.

- Some men experience pain with sex or when urinating; some men don't see any difference in comfort or function.

The causes of Peyronie's disease are not entirely known, but it is generally accepted that several things probably cause it. Scarring and the resulting distortion may be due to trauma to the penis, either from medical procedures like catheterization or from traumatic sexual activities. Peyronie's can also be caused by vitamin E deficiency or by an inherited tendency to develop this sort of hardened tissue.

Diagnosis is usually made by examining the penis and by getting a good history. Bringing in a digital or Polaroid picture of the erect penis to show your doctor how it is distorted by the fibrous tissue is a good idea. Sometimes an x-ray or ultrasound is ordered to see whether the fibrous tissue is calcified.

Beyond the Basics

If Peyronie's develops quickly or if the physical exam doesn't support the diagnosis of Peyronie's disease, your physician may perform a biopsy. Biopsy requires removing plaque cells for microscopic examination and is used to detect cancer.

Treatment for Peyronie's disease is aimed at reducing the pain and maintaining your sexual function. Early treatment may be medication and/or supplementing your diet with vitamin E. Sometimes injections of cortisone or calcium channel blockers are used to break down the connective tissue causing the problem. Surgery is a last resort since it may not be successful and may damage the tissue even more. Men with Peyronie's are usually encouraged to wait a year or two to see if nonsurgical treatment will work before opting for surgery.

Peyronie's disease may affect your sexual fitness if it interferes with sexual function. Mild cases either that go away on their own or that do not interfere with your sexual performance are more cosmetic issues than serious medical problems. Talk frankly with your partner about what is going on. More serious cases that interfere with sexual ability or urination need medical care and can have a permanent impact on your sexual function.

Prostatitis

Prostatitis is an inflammation of the prostate gland that can affect men at any age. As many as half of all men have this condition at some time during their lives. Prostatitis can cause pain with urination and ejaculation and can lead to serious complications if it is left untreated.

Acute bacterial prostatitis (ABP) usually occurs in men under 35 and is the most serious type of prostatitis. It must be treated promptly and can even be fatal if the bacteria get into the bloodstream and cause sepsis. ABP usually comes on suddenly and includes the following symptoms:

- Chills and fever
- Frequent urination
- Pain in joints, the lower back, and/or muscles
- Pain in the penis, testicles, and scrotum
- Pain with ejaculation
- Pain with urination
- Feeling an urgent need to urinate, sometimes accompanied with bladder spasm or pain
- Tender, swollen prostate
- Inability to empty bladder completely

Treatment is usually a course of IV antibiotics followed by a course of oral antibiotics. If either you or your partner has these symptoms, it is a medical emergency. Go to an emergency room or urgent care center or call your doctor right away. This is not an infection that can wait for business hours.

Chronic bacterial prostatitis (CBP) is an inflammation of the prostate and urinary tract that recurs. It is usually seen in men over the age of 40 but can occur at younger ages. The symptoms are similar to ABP but less severe. They include the following:

♦ Blood in semen

♦ Dull pain in the lower back

♦ Discomfort in the penis, testicles, and scrotum

♦ Pain with ejaculation

♦ Pain with urination

♦ Fever

♦ Frequent bladder infections

If you have these symptoms, have them checked to be sure you do not have CBP. Sometimes certain bladder conditions are misdiagnosed as chronic bacterial prostatitis, so if your symptoms do not disappear with treatment, see your doctor again.

Treatment for chronic bacterial prostatitis is usually an extended course of antibiotics, as long as 12 weeks for the initial course, and sometimes ongoing antibiotics if the infection does not go away with the first course. Surgery may be recommended to remove the infected or inflamed section of the prostate if no other treatments have an effect.

Nonbacterial prostatitis is inflammation of the prostate without infection, and *prostadynia* is pain in the prostate without inflammation or infection. These conditions can be quite uncomfortable and are often resistant to treatment. Management is with anti-inflammatory and pain medications.

def•i•ni•tion

Prostadynia is pain in the prostate that is not due to an infection. It is also called "chronic pelvic pain syndrome (CPPS)" and has the same symptoms as acute and chronic prostatitis but without inflammation or bacterial infection.

Avoiding sexually transmitted diseases will lower your chances of suffering prostatitis, so condom use is essential to minimize your chances of ABP.

Prostatitis is definitely a threat to your sexual health and fitness. If it is uncomfortable or painful to have sex, you will not be able to find a satisfying sexual balance. Keep your body healthy with diet and exercise, and see a physician if you have any symptoms of prostatitis.

Try This! _____

Because recurrent or chronic prostate conditions are difficult to treat, some men use other measures to control symptoms. If you have ongoing pain or discomfort from chronic prostate problems, you could try any of the following measures:

- Take warm baths to relax the pelvic muscles and bring circulation to the area.
- Use a split bicycle seat to relieve pressure on the prostate.
- Drink lots of water and urinate at regular intervals, not allowing your bladder to become overfull.
- Have regular sexual activity.
- Eat a healthy diet, limiting sugar, refined foods, spices, and caffeine.
- Avoid doing rigorous exercise with a full bladder.
- Try herbal remedies such as bearberry, flower pollen extract, pellitory of the wall, and saw palmetto.
- Take dietary supplements that support urinary health such as vitamin C, vitamin E, flaxseed meal, selenium, and zinc.

Inguinal Hernia

A hernia occurs when any part of an internal organ—usually the intestine—protrudes from a weak spot in the muscle or connective tissues (called *fascia*) holding the organ in place. Lifting, surgery, and anything that puts pressure on the weak area can cause the muscle to open, letting a portion of the intestine slide through.

An inguinal (groin) hernia appears as a bulge in the lower abdomen. Most of the time you can push

def•i•ni•tion _____

Fascia is the fibrous connective tissue that surrounds and/or separates muscles, organs, and other soft tissues in the body.

it back in, and it will stay. But if it cannot be pushed back in or if the muscle weakness or fascial defect gets larger and the hernia occurs repeatedly, it needs medical attention.

Beyond the Basics

Men are more prone to inguinal hernias because there is a natural opportunity for a weak section of abdominal muscle where the testes descend into the scrotal sac. The inguinal canal is a natural opening in the fascia of the lower abdomen that can widen and allow intestines to pass through. Lifting, straining during bowel movements, or a chronic cough can all increase your chances of developing an inguinal hernia.

If a section of the bowel becomes trapped outside the muscle wall, circulation can be blocked and that section of intestine will die. When this happens it is called "intestinal strangulation" and can be life threatening. If you have a hernia that you can't push back into place, see a doctor right away. If it's accompanied with severe lower abdominal pain, fever, or nausea and vomiting, get to an emergency room.

The treatment for hernia is a surgical repair. This is usually successful if you are careful to let the repair heal completely before resuming your regular activity.

An inguinal hernia can compromise your sexual health in a couple of ways. It can cause pain with sex, which will curtail your sexual activity and pleasure. Also, you may strain during sex in a way that worsens the tear in the muscle fascia and makes the hernia more serious. The best approach to an inguinal hernia is to get it repaired when it is small. Surgery is simpler then, and the tissue is in better shape to heal easily.

Pelvic Steal Syndrome

Pelvic steal syndrome is a frustrating condition wherein a man can get an erection, but when he begins to thrust during intercourse, the blood is shunted to the muscles in his pelvis and buttocks. This causes him to lose the erection before ejaculation.

While it is not a dangerous condition, it has a dramatic effect on sexual satisfaction since "all systems are go" until the blood in his penis takes a detour.

To remedy this situation, some men have good results by lying on the bed with their partner on top. This reduces the need for blood to flow down to the gluteal muscles, and allows him to maintain an erection longer. Sometimes a side-lying position works as well.

Common Problems for Women

Women also face some physical challenges to their sexual fitness. Some are more nuisance than actual threat, but these conditions can cause distress and can affect your willingness to engage in sexual activity and your enjoyment of it.

Urge Incontinence

The bladder is designed to hold a certain amount of urine—somewhere between 350 and 550 milliliters. Usually, you get an urge to urinate when you have about 200 milliliters of urine in your bladder, but your bladder continues to fill and you empty it when it is convenient, sometime before it is completely full.

With *urge incontinence,* the bladder doesn't seem to register the signals properly and empties at odd—and inopportune—moments. Emptying may be unrelated to the amount of urine in the bladder and may occur without warning. This can be embarrassing and discouraging to women.

The cause of urge incontinence may be hard to find. It can happen after a neurological injury such as a spinal cord injury or stroke, or it may be due to a bladder problem such as a bladder obstruction, inflammation, or infection.

> **def•i•ni•tion**
>
> **Urge incontinence** is the sudden, intense need to urinate followed by an involuntary bladder contraction, which pushes urine out of the bladder. Women with this type of incontinence feel out of control of their bladder function.

Diagnosis requires a medical exam to be sure this isn't caused by a bladder infection or other medical problem. Once the diagnosis is made, the usual approach is to begin bladder retraining.

> **Try This!**
> Bladder retraining is a program in which you "teach" your bladder to wait longer and longer periods of time before emptying, and it can be quite successful. If you are in a bladder retraining program, talk to your medical provider about adding one of these supportive treatments:
> - Biofeedback
> - Medications to relax the smooth muscle of the bladder
> - Pelvic floor exercises
>
> Avoiding chemical irritants such as bubble baths, soap, and "feminine hygiene" products will round out your bladder program and reduce irritants to the urethra. It is also very helpful to avoid bladder irritants in your diet. The three biggest offenders are caffeine, alcohol, and carbonation.

Urge incontinence does not usually have life-threatening complications, but a woman's quality of life is reduced if she doesn't control her bladder properly. Women report anxiety and depression if they have long-term incontinence. Sexually, it takes away opportunities for spontaneity, and women feel self-conscious about their unpredictable bladder.

If you struggle with urge incontinence, see a medical professional who specializes in these issues. Talk to your partner about what sorts of sexual activities you enjoy and what makes you anxious about your sex life and bladder control. Getting support from your partner will help reduce your self-consciousness and enable you to enjoy each other.

Cystitis

Cystitis is a bladder infection caused by bacteria that enter the bladder through the urethra. As women get older, and especially with the decrease in estrogen around menopause, the urethra and vagina lose elasticity. This makes it easier to injure the tissue, which creates an opportunity for bacteria to invade the urethra and then move into the bladder. Sexual activity can traumatize the area and can introduce bacteria into the urethra.

Women have such a short distance between the urethra and the bladder that they are much more prone to cystitis than men. Sexual intercourse creates friction and can force bacteria into the urethral opening.

Improper wiping technique (back to front) can also bring bacteria from the anal area forward, offering yet another way to establish bacteria in the urethra.

Symptoms of cystitis are urinary urgency (a sudden or continuous feeling that you have to urinate), frequent urination, blood in the urine, cloudy urine, lower abdominal fullness or pain, and odor to the urine.

The diagnosis of cystitis is done in a medical setting with a sample of your urine. Once the diagnosis made, treatment is a short course of antibiotics. Supportive measures include drinking large amounts of water while you have the infection and abstaining from sexual activity to give the urethra a chance to heal.

If you are prone to cystitis, there are things you can do to minimize your chance of getting a bladder infection:

♦ Drink eight to ten 8-ounce glasses of water a day.

♦ Wipe from front to back after using the toilet.

♦ Urinate every two to three hours during the day.

♦ Don't hold your urine beyond when you feel the urge to go.

♦ Urinate before and after sex.

♦ Use enough lubricant during sex to minimize friction to the urethra.

♦ Avoid scented bath products and "feminine hygiene" products.

♦ Be sure you and your partner's hands are clean before sex.

Proceed with Caution

Untreated cystitis can become a serious kidney infection. If you have symptoms of a bladder infection, get them checked. Treatment is usually simple and effective in the early stages, and treating it before it becomes a kidney infection is critical to maintain your health.

Cystitis can be caused by sexual activity, and it can make sex unpleasant or uncomfortable. Taking a few precautions and being aware that you are vulnerable can help you avoid bladder and urethral infections, thus maintaining your sexual health.

Vaginal Dryness

Having inadequate lubrication in your vagina will make sexual activity considerably less enjoyable for you and possibly even painful. There are many reasons why women might have vaginal dryness, including reduced estrogen at menopause, not enough time or foreplay to initiate lubrication, vaginal inflammation, reaction to douche solution or other products, or side effects from some medications.

Your sexual health and fitness are affected dramatically if your vagina is too dry to tolerate or enjoy sexual activity. Vaginal dryness also makes vaginal tissue open to bacterial and viral infections, which damages your sexual health.

If you notice itching or burning in the vaginal area (either during sex or in general), a feeling of pressure in the vulva, pain or spotting with sex, or urinary frequency or urgency, these are all signs that you may be experiencing vaginal dryness.

Your physician can confirm the diagnosis of vaginal dryness with a pelvic exam. Discuss treatment options with him or her since some of them require a prescription.

Treatment is usually multifaceted and can include the following:

- Vaginal estrogen if you are menopausal, perimenopausal, or breastfeeding. Vaginal estrogen works locally, in the area of the vagina, so it does not have the same risks as systemic estrogen.

- Use of lubricants during sex.

- Engaging in foreplay longer. Incorporate the use of lubricants and make it part of the fun.

- Vaginal moisturizers, which last longer than lubricants, can keep the area moister and healthier in general.

- More frequent sex! This can improve circulation to the area and can also keep your sexual response firing so that you are more easily aroused and will lubricate more readily.

- Avoid douching.

- Avoid other products with soaps and perfumes in the vaginal area.

◆ Phytoestrogen (plant estrogen) creams may be helpful, but results are mixed about their effectiveness.

Vaginal lubrication is a prime indicator of sexual health. If your body is sluggish in lubricating, help it out so that you can fully engage in the sexual activities you desire.

Getting Older Is Not a Disease

Whether you are 30 or 60, you get older every minute. There's no way around that little reality. But getting older is not the bad news, it's the good news. Every moment on the planet is one more chance to create the life, and the sexual life, that you want to live.

You Are as Good as You Feel

Aging is a fact. Feeling old is optional. We are always ready to see each other as "over the hill"—you will find this attitude at thirtieth birthday parties and sixtieth birthday parties. In both cases, it's only as true as the birthday boy or girl who feels it. In the 2004 AARP survey on sexuality, the strongest association for satisfaction with sex life was with health. Healthy people in all age categories were more likely to report sexual satisfaction. As your health goes, so goes your sex.

Staying Active—Sexually Active

The best insurance you can have for staying sexually active and satisfied is to stay active, period. Social interaction, physical exercise, and mental activity are all types of action that keep you ready for a rewarding and interesting sex life. If you are boring in your living room, you are probably boring in the bedroom.

Taking an interest in the world around you, and in people around you, keeps you vital and interesting. The more you engage in activities that stimulate your mind and spirit, the more stimulating a person you are to others. Sexual health is about more than a functioning body; it's also about connection with others. It reflects your ability to "reach out and touch someone." The more levels on which you can reach out, the more ways you have to connect. This only makes your sexual connections richer and more rewarding.

Sex Can Get Better and Better

You will never be 20 again. Get over it. But you can learn every day how to be a better lover. There are a million right ways to love people, including your partner, and you can improve on your attitude and perspective at every opportunity. If your hormones slow down or you find yourself in a sexual rut, there are unlimited ways to reach out and get closer to your partner or your own sexual self. Sex gets better with time, especially if you take the time to be present in the moment and appreciate the subtlety that comes with experience.

Sexual health and fitness are the means through which you participate in your sexual world. Sex is not an ultimate goal to which we all aspire (never mind what the commercials on television imply) but rather a way to enrich our lives and the lives of those with whom we share it. Staying healthy and fit enough to engage in our chosen sexual expressions is a gift to ourselves and a celebration of being human.

The Least You Need to Know

- ◆ Many symptoms of hormone decline are normal, but depression, loss of sexual function, anxiety, inability to concentrate, or hot flushes may mean that you need hormone supplementation.

- ◆ Peyronie's disease and inguinal hernias are not life threatening, but early treatment is highly recommended.

- ◆ Prostatitis can be life threatening and needs immediate attention.

- ◆ Urge incontinence and vaginal dryness can be treated, but it takes time and patience.

- ◆ Bladder infections require treatment right away to avoid a kidney infection.

- ◆ Sexual fitness makes it possible for your sex life to improve your quality of life at any age.

Appendix A

Glossary

aerobic exercise   Vigorous physical exercise that requires the heart and lungs to work harder to meet the body's increased oxygen demand, and results in the circulation of oxygen through the blood.

anaerobic exercise   Exercise done intensely for short periods of time, used primarily for building muscle strength. Also called *strength training*, *weight training*, or *resistance training*.

androgen   Male sex hormone responsible for development of male characteristics and thought to be largely responsible for sex drive in both men and women. This steroid hormone is produced in the testes of men and in small amounts in the ovaries of women.

andropause   The combination of low androgens and the resulting symptoms experienced by some men between the ages of 45 and 60. Also called *male menopause* or *veripause*, it is not as well studied or accepted clinically as female menopause.

androstadienone   A chemical compound that reportedly has strong pheromone-like activities in humans. Derived from testosterone, androstadienone has an odor of male sweat and is sold in male fragrances, professing to increase sexual attraction.

anorgasmia   A condition wherein a person is not able to achieve an orgasm, despite sufficient stimulation and sexual response.

aphrodisiac   Any substance used to enhance or improve sexual desire or performance.

autonomic nervous system (ANS)   The part of the nervous system that regulates involuntary functions like heartbeat, breathing, digestion, gland activity, and sexual arousal. It is divided into two subsystems with separate responsibilities: the sympathetic nervous system, which is responsible for initial stress response, and the parasympathetic nervous system, which is responsible for calming your body down when the immediate stress is over.

bacterial vaginosis (BV)   An overgrowth of several bacteria in the vagina. It occurs when the normal bacterial flora are disturbed by antibiotics or with a change in the pH of the vaginal environment. It can mimic other sexually transmitted infections and in some cases progress to PID.

balanitis   A condition in which the head and foreskin of the penis can become reddened and sore.

cantharides   Also called *blister beetles* and *Spanish flies,* they can be ground to a fine powder and then mixed with other substances to make medicines. This Spanish Fly is a famous aphrodisiac and a dangerous one.

chancre   An ulcer located at the first point of contact of a pathogen. A dull red, hard, painless sore that is the first sign of syphilis.

chancroid   A bacterial STD that causes painful sores on your mouth, throat, lips, genitals, and/or groin areas.

chlamydia   The most common bacterial sexually transmitted disease in the United States, caused by a bacteria called *Chlamydia trachomatis.* There are frequently no symptoms of chlamydia in either men or women.

circulatory system   The heart, blood vessels, and the blood that flows through them.

cognitive restructuring   Changing the way you think. It is a therapeutic technique useful with feelings of anxiety, anger, insecurity, fear, and sadness.

condom   A thin, pliable cover placed on the penis during sexual activity to prevent pregnancy or sexually transmitted disease. It can be made from latex, polyurethane, or animal skin. The female condom is a larger version placed inside the vagina, with an inner ring over the cervix and an outer ring over the vulva, also used to prevent the transmission of disease and/or pregnancy.

cortisol   A corticosteroid hormone produced in the adrenal cortex and released during stress response. Cortisol increases blood pressure and blood-sugar levels and suppresses the immune system. In pharmacology, it is referred to as hydrocortisone and is used to treat allergies and inflammation.

dopamine   A chemical messenger that increases endorphins and is essential to normal functioning of the central nervous system. A reduction in its concentration within the brain is associated with Parkinson's disease.

douche   A stream of water, often containing medicine or cleansing substances, that is used on a body part or cavity for sanitary or curative purposes.

dynamic fitness   Being able to move vigorously and with little effort. A combination of general strength, cardiovascular fitness, endurance, suppleness, balance, and speed.

dyspareunia   Painful intercourse, usually referring to women. It is a diagnosis that can have many causes, including infection, inflammation, depression, sexual abuse, and vaginal injury.

endocrine disruptor   *See* hormone disruptor.

endorphin   A naturally occurring pain reliever produced in the body. In addition to reducing the sensation of pain, endorphins can induce a state of calm well being.

epididymis   A narrow, tube, part of the spermatic duct system, that lies along the back of each testicle, connecting it to the vas deferens.

epididymitis   Painful inflammation in the testicles, specifically in the epididymis.

erectile dysfunction   Inability—either totally or in part—to get and maintain a penile erection. Previously called *impotence.*

estrogen   Any of several steroid hormones made by the body, particularly in the ovaries, that helps develop and maintain female sex characteristics and the growth of long bones. Artificial estrogens may be manufactured and are used, as are natural estrogens, to treat hormone imbalances and conditions associated with hormone imbalance. Estrogen is also a component of various birth control formulations delivered in various forms to women to suppress ovulation and prevent fertilization.

fallopian tube   Either of a pair of tubes conducting the egg from the ovary to the uterus.

fitness   Having a healthy body and/or being in good physical condition, usually as a result of adequate exercise and a nourishing diet.

ghrelin   A hormone produced in the stomach that is helps regulate appetite. Ghrelin accelerates appetite, while leptin decreases appetite.

glans   The rounded head of either the penis or clitoris.

glycemic index   A numerical index assigned to a carbohydrate-rich food and based on the average increase in blood glucose levels resulting from eating that food.

gonorrhea (GC)   A sexually transmitted disease caused by gonococcal bacteria. GC most often proliferates in the mucous membrane of the genital and urinary tracts and typically demonstrates a puslike discharge and painful or difficult urination, though women often have no symptoms.

hemoglobin   A protein molecule in red blood cells that is used to carry oxygen to each cell.

herpes simplex virus (HSV)   A double-stranded DNA virus causing disease marked by the outbreak of fluid-filled vesicles on the mouth, lips, face, or genitalia.

hormone   A molecule produced in one cell that acts as a messenger to particular target cells and whose purpose is to change the growth, function, or metabolism of those target cells.

hormone disruptor   Chemicals that, when absorbed into the body, change the way hormones function. Hormone disruptors may mimic or block hormones and can disturb the body's normal functions by altering normal hormone levels, stopping or stimulating the production of hormones, or by changing the way hormones travel through the body.

human immunodeficiency virus (HIV)   A retrovirus that causes AIDS by infecting helper T cells of the immune system.

human papilloma virus (HPV)   One of many viruses implicated in the formation of wart lesions in various locations on the body, including genitals, hands, feet, and others. The genital form of HPV is associated with cancer of the cervix, anus, and vulva. The virus may be sexually transmitted and may or may not result in noticeable symptoms or lesions.

hyponatremia   A low concentration of sodium in the blood outside of the normal range. Too little sodium can cause cells to malfunction, and extremely low sodium can be fatal.

Intermittent Explosive Disorder—a condition wherein a person has outbursts of uncontrolled violent and aggressive behavior, harming people or property, and where the response is out of proportion to the precipitating event. Classified by mental health clinicians as an "impulse control disorder."

Kegel exercise   Pelvic floor muscle training (PFMT). Exercises requiring controlled contraction and release of the muscles at the base of the pelvis, used particularly as a treatment for urinary incontinence.

leptin   A hormone produced in fat cells and having a role in appetite regulation and fat metabolism.

libido   The psychic and emotional energy of natural biological drives. Sexual desire.

limerence   An involuntary state of thought and feeling in which a person feels an intense romantic desire for another person (the limerent object). Unlike a crush, limerence is not short-lived and may persist for months, years, or even a lifetime. It is marked by intrusive thinking and minute attention to signs or situations that seem to demonstrate the intentions of the love object. A limerent person may be ecstatic or despairing, depending on whether or not the feelings are reciprocated.

metabolism   The chemical processes that occur in a living cell or organism necessary for the maintenance of life. In metabolism, some substances are broken down to yield energy for vital processes, whereas other substances, necessary for life, are synthesized.

molluscum contagiosum   A benign viral infection that is usually spread by skin-to-skin contact but can also be spread by using towels or sharing a bath with someone who is infected.

neurochemicals   Any organic substance that occurs in nerve cell activity.

neurotransmitter   A chemical that carries a message from a nerve cell to another cell. Neurotransmitters communicate from brain to motor cells to achieve movement and allow interpretation of sensory messages like pleasure and pain.

noradrenaline   A chemical hormone and neurotransmitter, produced by the adrenal medulla and by the nerve endings of the sympathetic nervous system which causes constriction of blood vessels and increases in heart rate, blood pressure, and the sugar level of the blood.

orchitis   Inflammation of the testis.

organic fitness   The condition of the tissues that make up your body. A baseline physical state, ideally one where organs are free of disease and are well nourished.

orgasm   The culmination of sexual arousal, accompanied by extreme pleasure and involuntary contractions of the muscles of the genitals. In men it is usually marked by the ejaculation of semen. Also called *climax*.

oxytocin   A chemical messenger that is released during orgasm and increases the endorphins in your system. It has been called the *trust hormone* for the feelings of well-being that it engenders.

paraphimosis   A condition of uncircumcised men in which the foreskin is pulled back and left too long behind the head of the penis. This can cause the penis to swell.

parasympathetic nervous system (PNS)   The part of the autonomic nervous system originating in the brain stem and the lower part of the spinal cord that counteracts the effects of the sympathetic nervous system, notably by restoring digestive secretions, slowing the heart, and dilating blood vessels.

pelvic inflammatory disease (PID) Inflammation of the female genital tract, particularly the fallopian tubes, caused by various microorganisms, chiefly chlamydia and gonococci, and characterized by fever, abdominal pain, vaginal discharge, and in some cases tissue damage that can result in sterility.

pH A measure of the acidity or alkalinity of a solution. Numerically equal to 7 for neutral solutions, it increases with increasing alkalinity and decreases with increasing acidity. The pH scale commonly in use ranges from 0 to 14.

pheromones Chemical messengers that trigger a natural behavioral response in another member of the same species.

phimosis Inability to pull the foreskin all the way back from the head of the penis.

probiotics Live microbial supplements that benefit the host animal by improving its intestinal microbial balance.

progesterone A steroid hormone, secreted by the corpus luteum of the ovary and by the placenta, that prepares the uterus for implantation of a fertilized ovum. Progesterone helps maintain pregnancy, and supports development of the mammary glands.

prolapse, pelvic or uterine Slippage or sagging of the uterus and/or bladder from its usual position, and its subsequent protrusion into the vagina or vulvar area.

prostadynia Pain in the prostate that is not due to an infection. It is also called *chronic pelvic pain syndrome* or *CPPS* and has the same symptoms as acute and chronic prostatitis but without inflammation or bacterial infection.

prostate gland A gland in men that surrounds the urethra at the base of the bladder and controls release of urine. The prostate secretes a fluid that is a major constituent of semen.

prostatitis An inflammation of the prostate gland.

scabies An intensely itchy skin condition caused by the mite *Sarcoptes scabiei*, and spread by contact with the skin or clothing of an infected individual.

seasonal affective disorder (SAD)   A depressed mood during the months of the year when sunshine is less available and characterized by any or all of the following: lethargy, difficulty concentrating, carbohydrate cravings, difficulty waking, sleep disturbance, social withdrawal, and irritability. SAD is probably caused by imbalance of serotonin and melatonin.

serotonin   An organic compound derived from tryptophan and found in body tissues, particularly the brain, blood, and gastric mucous membranes. It is a neurotransmitter and plays a role in vasoconstriction, stimulation of the smooth muscles, and regulation of cyclic body processes.

sexually transmitted disease (STD)   A sexually transmitted infection that has progressed to the point where there are symptoms or tissue damage from the infectious process of the organism.

sexually transmitted infection (STI)   An invasion of the body by a microorganism transmitted through sexual contact. An STI may or may not have symptoms.

smegma   The collection of skin cells and secretions that form a cheesy substance collecting under the foreskin of the penis in men and in the labial folds in women.

spermicide   A contraceptive chemical used to kill sperm, typically delivered via a foam, cream or gel.

spirochete   A spiral, motile bacteria of the order *Spirochaetales*. Most spirochetes are pathogenic, causing syphilis, relapsing fever, yaws, and other diseases.

SSRI medications   A selective serotonin reuptake inhibitor commonly prescribed as an antidepressant. SSRIs work by inhibiting the reuptake of serotonin, an action that allows more serotonin to be available to be taken up by other nerves. SSRIs have a number of side effects, including sexual dysfunction.

steroid or sex hormones   Any hormone affecting the development and growth of sex organs.

sympathetic nervous system (SNS)   The portion of the autonomic nervous system responsible for quickening of heart rate, constriction of blood vessels, and elevated blood pressure, which occurs when a threat is detected or during the "fight of flight" response to a stressful event.

syphilis A chronic infectious disease caused by the spirochete *Treponema pallidum*. It is transmitted either by direct contact, usually in sexual intercourse, or from mother to child in utero and progresses through three stages, first marked by local formation of chancres, then ulcerous skin eruptions, and finally, systemic infection leading to general paralysis.

testosterone An androgenic hormone produced in the male testes and in small amounts in the female ovaries. Testosterone is sometimes supplemented if a deficiency occurs in either men or women.

trichomoniasis A vaginal inflammation caused by a trichomonad (Trichomonas vaginalis) that results in a characteristic itchy discharge.

trimethylaminuria (TMA) An error in metabolism present at birth, this condition is characterized by a strong and offensive "rotten fish" body odor caused when trimethylamine is excreted in body fluids (urine, perspiration and saliva). When people with TMA eat foods containing tyramine (aged cheeses, avocados, dried fruit, and others) or use nasal sprays containing epinephrine, they may experience a very rapid heart rate and dangerously high blood pressure. Social rejection is common, and people with TMA may become clinically depressed and/or suicidal.

vaginismus A usually painful condition wherein the vagina has spasms with penetration.

vulva The female external genitalia, including the labia, clitoris, and vaginal entrance.

vulvodynia A chronic pain in the external genitals that may be related to irritation of nerve endings from constant inflammation of the area. This condition typically causes intense discomfort during sexual activity.

vulvovaginitis An inflammation in the vulva or vagina, often as a result of infection.

Appendix B

Further Reading and Resources

Aging and Sexual Health

Books

Butler, Robert N., and Myrna I. Lewis. *The New Love and Sex After 60*. New York, NY: Ballantine Books, 2002.

Price, Joan. *Better Than I Ever Expected: Straight Talk About Sex After Sixty*. Berkeley, CA: Seal Press, 2005.

Websites

Health Age and Life Expectancy: preventdisease.com/healthtools/articles/health_age.html

Live Expectancy Calculator: moneycentral.msn.com/investor/calcs/n_expect/main.asp

RealAge: www.realage.com/index.aspx

U.S. Department of Health and Human Services, Men's Sexual Health: www.4woman.gov/mens/sexual/

U.S. Department of Health and Human Services, Women's Sexual Health: www.4woman.gov/ow/sexuality/index.cfm?style=large

Organizations

AARP
601 E St. NW
Washington, DC 20049
1-888-687-2277
www.aarp.org

National Institute on Aging
Building 31, Room 5C27
31 Center Dr.,
MSC 2292
Bethesda, MD 20892
www.nia.nih.gov

Aphrodisiacs

Books

Hopkins, Martha, and Randall Lockridge. *The New InterCourses: An Aphrodisiac Cookbook, 10th Anniversary Edition*. Waco, TX: Terrace Publishing, 2007.

Lindberg, Marrena. *The Orgasmic Diet: A Revolutionary Plan to Lift Your Libido and Bring You to Orgasm*. New York: Crown, 2007.

Nickell, Nancy L. *Nature's Aphrodisiacs*. Berkeley, CA: Crossing Press, 1999.

Websites

FDA consumer article: www.fda.gov/fdac/features/196_love.html

WebMD article: www.webmd.com/webmddiet/news_articles/aphrodisi-acs.html

Cancer

Books

Katz, Anne. *Breaking the Silence on Cancer and Sexuality: A Handbook for Healthcare Providers.* Pittsburgh, PA: Oncology Nursing Society, 2007.

Websites

Sexuality for Women and Their Partners, American Cancer Society web page: www.cancer.org/docroot/mit/
mit_7_1x_sexualityforwomenandtheirpartners.asp

Sexuality for Men and Their Partners, American Cancer Society web page: www.cancer.org/docroot/MIT/
MIT_7_1x_SexualityforMenandTheirPartners.asp

Organizations

American Cancer Society
1-800-ACS-2345
1-866-228-4327 TTY
www.cancer.org

National Cancer Institute
NCI Public Inquiries Office
6116 Executive Blvd.
Room 3036A
Bethesda, MD 20892-8322
www.cancer.gov

Checkups and General Health

Books

Johns Hopkins. *The Johns Hopkins Medical Guide to Health After 50.* New York: Black Dog & Leventhal Publishers, 2006.

Komaroff, Anthony L., ed. *Harvard Medical School Family Health Guide by Harvard Medical School.* New York: Free Press, 2004.

Websites

Health maintenance visits: www.nlm.nih.gov/medlineplus/ency/article/002125.htm

Chronic Health Conditions

Books

Kaufman, Miriam, Cory Silverberg, and Fran Odette. *The Ultimate Guide to Sex and Disability: For All of Us Who Live with Disabilities, Chronic Pain, and Illness, Second Edition.* San Francisco: Cleis Press, 2007.

Kroll, Ken. *Enabling Romance: A Guide to Love, Sex and Relationships for People with Disabilities (and the People who Care About Them).* Horsham, PA: No Limits Communications, 2001.

Websites

Articles on chronic illness and sexuality from the American Academy of Family Physicians: www.aafp.org/afp/20030115/347.html familydoctor.org/online/famdocen/home/articles/768.printerview.html

Organizations

Arthritis Foundation
P.O. Box 7669
Atlanta, GA 30357-0669
1-800-283-7800
www.arthritis.org

Compulsive or Addictive Sex

Books

Carnes, Patrick. *Out of the Shadows: Understanding Sexual Addiction.* Center City, MN: Hazelden, 2001.

Forward, Susan. *Obsessive Love: When Passion Holds You Prisoner.* New York: Bantam Doubleday Dell, 2002.

Websites

Article from the American Psychological Society: www.apa.org/ monitor/oct03/compulsive.html

Overview of compulsive sexual behavior from the Mayo Clinic: www. mayoclinic.com/health/compulsive-sexual-behavior/DS00144

Organizations

American Association of Sexuality Educators, Counselors, and Therapists (AASECT)
P.O. Box 1960
Ashland, VA 23005-1960
Phone: 804-752-0026
www.aasect.org

American College of Sexologists (ACS)
P.O. Box 640405
San Francisco, CA 94164-0405
415-407-0354
www.AmericanCollegeofSexologists.org

National Council on Sexual Addiction and Compulsivity
www.ncsac.org

Sex Addicts Anonymous
P.O. Box 70949
Houston, TX 77270
www.sexaa.org

Contraception

Books

Boston Women's Health Book Collective. *Our Bodies, Ourselves: A New Edition for a New Era, Fourth edition.* New York: Touchstone, 2005.

Connell, Elizabeth. *The Contraception Sourcebook.* Columbus, OH: McGraw-Hill, 2001.

Websites

CIGNA birth control overview: www.cigna.com/healthinfo/hw237864.html

Medline contraception overview web page: U.S. Department of Health and Human Services, Women's Health contraception overview: www.4woman.gov/faq/birthcont.htm

Organizations

American College of Obstetricians and Gynecologists (ACOG)
409 12th St., SW
P.O. Box 96920
Washington, DC 20090-6920
202-638-5577
www.acog.org

Planned Parenthood Federation of America
434 W. 33rd St.
New York, NY 10001
Phone: 212-541-7800
Fax: 212-245-1845
www.plannedparenthood.org

Diet/Weight Management

Books

Gillespie, Larrian. *The Menopause Diet.* Beverly Hills, CA: Healthy Life Publications, 2003.

Oz, Mehmet C., and Michael F. Roizen. *You On a Diet: The Owner's Manual for Waist Management.* New York: Free Press, 2006.

Taubes, Gary. *Good Calories, Bad Calories.* New York: Knopf, 2007.

Websites

Heart healthy diet from the American Heart Association: www. americanheart.org/presenter.jhtml?identifier=353

Organizations

American Heart Association
National Center
7272 Greenville Ave.
Dallas, TX 75231
1-800-242-8721
www.americanheart.org

Exercise

Books

Franklin, Eric. *Pelvic Power: Mind/Body Exercises for Strength, Flexibility, Posture, and Balance for Men and Women.* Hightstown, NJ: Princeton Book Company, 2003.

Moffat, Marilyn, and Carole B. Lewis. *Age Defying Fitness: Making the Most of Your Body for the Rest of Your Life.* Atlanta: Peachtree Publishers, 2006.

National Institute on Aging. *Fitness Over Fifty: An Exercise Guide from the National Institute on Aging* (with DVD). Long Island, NY: Hatherleigh, 2006.

Tartell, Genie, and Ted Kavanau. *Get Fit in Bed: Tone Your Body and Calm Your Mind from the Comfort of Your Bed.* Oakland, CA: New Harbinger Publications, 2006.

Websites

Lower-back exercises: www.fda.gov/fdac/features/1998/298_exer.html

www.webmd.com/back-pain/features/
back-exercises-wow-them-coming-going?page=2

Pelvic floor exercises: kidney.niddk.nih.gov/kudiseases/pubs/
exercise_ez/

www.mayoclinic.com/health/kegel-exercises/WO00119

www.nafc.org/members/private/Professionals/OnlinePME.pdf

Grief/Loss

Books

Hartzler, Rachel Nafziger. *Grief and Sexuality: Life after Losing a Spouse.* Scottsdale, PA: Herald Press, 2006.

Websites

AARP overview of grief resources: www.aarp.org/families/grief_loss/

Positive Aging Resource Center: positiveaging.org/consumer/lc_grief. html

Hormones and Sexual Health

Books

Rako, Susan. *The Hormone of Desire: The Truth About Testosterone, Sexuality, and Menopause*. New York: Three Rivers Press, 1999.

Vliet, Elizabeth Lee. *The Savvy Woman's Guide to Hormone Headlines: What America Got Wrong About Estrogen (The Savvy Woman's Guide Series)*. Tucson, AZ: Her Place Press, 2008.

Love and Limerence

Books

Fisher, Helen. *Why We Love: The Nature and Chemistry of Romantic Love*. New York: Owl Books, 2004.

Lewis, Thomas, Fari Amini, and Richard Lannon. *A General Theory of Love*. New York: Random House, 2000.

Tennov, Dorothy. *Love and Limerence: The Experience of Being in Love*. Lanham, MD: Scarborough House 1999.

Wilson, Glenn D., and Chris McLaughlin. *The Science of Love*. London, UK: Fusion Press, 2001.

Mental Health

Books

Greenberger, Dennis, and Christine Padesky. *Mind Over Mood: Change How You Feel by Changing the Way You Think*. New York: The Guilford Press, 1995.

Ross, Julia. *The Mood Cure: The 4-Step Program to Rebalance Your Emotional Chemistry and Rediscover Your Natural Sense of Well-Being*. New York: Viking Press, 2002.

Websites

Medline overview of depression: www.nlm.nih.gov/medlineplus/depression.html

NAMI overview of cognitive-behavioral therapy: www.nami.org/Template.cfm?Section=About_Treatments_and_Supports&template=/ContentManagement/ContentDisplay.cfm&ContentID=7952

Optimism

Books

Seligman, Martin E. P. *Learned Optimism: How to Change Your Mind and Your Life*. New York: Vintage, 2006.

Websites

Seligman optimism website: www.authentichappiness.sas.upenn.edu/default.aspx

Revitalizing Sexual Relationships

Books

Berman, Jennifer, and Laura Berman with Elisabeth Bumiller. *For Women Only: A Revolutionary Guide to Reclaiming Your Sex Life.* New York: Henry Holt and Company, 2005.

Johanson, Sue. *Sex is Perfectly Natural, But Not Naturally Perfect.* New York: Viking, 1992.

Love, Patricia M.D., and Jo Robinson. *Hot Monogamy: Essential Steps to More Passionate, Intimate Lovemaking.* New York: Plume, 1995.

Macleod, Don, and Debra Macleod. *Lube Jobs: A Woman's Guide to Great Maintenance Sex.* New York: Penguin, 2007.

Winks, Cathy, and Anne Semans. *The Good Vibrations Guide to Sex.* San Francisco: Cleis Press, 1994.

Organizations

American Association of Sexuality Educators, Counselors, and Therapists (AASECT)
P.O. Box 1960
Ashland, VA 23005-1960
Phone: 804-752-0026
Fax: 804-752-0056
www.aasect.org

American Association for Marriage and Family Therapy (AAMFT)
112 South Alfred St.
Alexandria, VA 22314-3061
Phone: 703-838-9808
Fax: 703-838-9805
www.aamft.org

Sex Therapy

Books

Beck, Aaron T. *Love Is Never Enough: How Couples Can Overcome Misunderstandings, Resolve Conflicts, and Solve Relationship Problems Through Cognitive Therapy.* New York: Harper Paperbacks, 1989.

Green, Shelley K., ed., and Douglas G. Flemons. *Quickies: The Handbook of Brief Sex Therapy, Revised and Expanded Edition.* New York, NY: W. W. Norton, 2007.

Websites

Description of sex therapy: www.healthatoz.com/healthatoz/Atoz/common/standard/transform.jsp?requestURI=/healthatoz/Atoz/ency/sex_therapy.jsp

Hints for choosing a sex therapist: www.webmd.com/sex-relationships/features/searching-for-sex-therapy

Sex Toys

Books

Allison, Sadie. *Toygasms! The Insider's Guide to Sex Toys and Techniques.* San Francisco: Tickle Kitty Press, 2003.

Venning, Rachel, and Claire Cavanah. *Sex Toys 101: A Playfully Uninhibited Guide.* New York: Fireside, 2003.

Websites

Retail websites for sex toys, DVDs, and other sexual products: www.distinctivetoys.net, www.goodvibes.com, www.babeland.com

Sexual Dysfunction

Books

Bonnard, Marc. *The Viagra Alternative: The Complete Guide to Overcoming Erectile Dysfunction Naturally.* Rochester, VT: Healing Arts Press, 1999.

Jones, J. Stephen. *Overcoming Impotence: A Leading Urologist Tells You Everything You Need to Know.* Amhurst, NY: Prometheus Books, 2003.

Websites

American Urological Association patient information site: www.urologyhealth.org/index.cfm

Overview of erectile dysfunction from the Mayo Clinic: www.mayoclinic.com/health/erectile-dysfunction/DS00162

Overview of female sexual dysfunction from the Mayo Clinic: www.mayoclinic.com/health/female-sexual-dysfunction/DS00701/DSECTION=1

Organizations

American College of Obstetricians and Gynecologists (ACOG)
409 12th St. SW
P.O. Box 96920
Washington, DC 20090-6920
202-638-5577

American Urological Association
1000 Corporate Blvd.
Linthicum, MD 21090
Phone: 410-689-3700 or 1-866-746-4282 (U.S. only)
Fax: 410-689-3800
www.urologyhealth.org

The Kinsey Institute
Morrison Hall 302
1165 E. 3rd St.
Bloomington, IN 47405
Phone: 812-855-7686
Fax: 812-855-8277
www.indiana.edu/~kinsey

Sexual Medicine Society of North America, Inc. (SMSNA)
1100 E. Woodfield Rd., Suite 520
Schaumburg, IL 60173
Phone: 847-517-7225
Fax: 847-517-7229
www.smsna.org

Sexual Health and Fitness

Books

Hays, Scott. *Built for Sex, The Complete Fitness and Nutrition Program for Maximum Performance.* New York: Rodale, 2005.

Lamm, Steven, and Gerald Secor Couzens. *The Hardness Factor: How to Achieve Your Best Health and Fitness at Any Age.* New York: HarperCollins, 2005.

McCarthy, Barry, and Michael E. Metz. *Men's Sexual Health: Fitness for Satisfying Sex.* New York: Routledge, 2007.

Websites

Article "Boomer's Guide to Sexual Fitness": boomer-living.com/fitness/index.php?option=com_content&task=view&id=65

Exercises to improve your sexual health: health.discovery.com/centers/sex/exercise/exercise.html

Medline overview of sexual health: www.nlm.nih.gov/medlineplus/
sexualhealth.html

Sexual Health Center at Discovery Health: health.discovery.com/
centers/sex/sex.html

Smoking: Quitting

Books

Carr, Allen. *The Easy Way to Stop Smoking: Join the Millions Who Have
Become Nonsmokers Using the Easyway Method.* New York: Sterling,
2005.

Fisher, Edwin B. *American Lung Association 7 Steps to a Smoke-Free Life.*
Hoboken, NJ: Wiley, 1998.

Miller, Barbara. *How To Quit Smoking Even If You Don't Want To.*
Victoria, BC: Trafford Publishing, 2006.

Websites

The American Lung Association®
61 Broadway, 6th Floor
New York, NY 10006
1-800-586-4872
www.lungusa.org

National Cancer Institute
NCI Public Inquiries Office
6116 Executive Blvd.
Room 3036A
Bethesda, MD 20892-8322
1-800-784-8669
1-800-332-8615 (TTY)

U.S. Federal Government Quitting Resources
http://smokefree.gov

STDs/STIs

Books

Marr, Lisa. *Sexually Transmitted Diseases: A Physician Tells You What You Need to Know, Second Edition (A Johns Hopkins Press Health Book)*. Baltimore: The Johns Hopkins University Press, 2007.

Websites

CDC STD overview page: www.cdc.gov/std/

FDA listing of home test kits for HIV: www.fda.gov/cber/products/testkits.htm

Medline STD overview page: www.nlm.nih.gov/medlineplus/sexuallytransmitteddiseases.html

U.S. Department of Health and Human Services, Women's Health STD web page: www.4woman.gov/faq/stdsgen.htm

Centers for Disease Control and Prevention
1600 Clifton Rd.
Atlanta, GA 30333
Public Inquiries: 404-498-1515 or 1-800-311-3435
www.cdc.gov/std

Supplements and Herbals

Books

Kilham, Chris. *Hot Plants: Nature's Proven Sex Boosters for Men and Women*. New York: St. Martin's Griffin, 2004.

Meletis, Chris, Susan M. Fitzgerald. *Better Sex Naturally: A Consumer's Guide to Herbs and Other Natural Supplements That Can Jump Start Your Sex Life*. New York: HarperCollins Publishers, 2000.

Websites

Medline overview of complementary and alternative medicine: www.nlm.nih.gov/medlineplus/complementaryandalternativemedicine.html

Medline overview of drugs, herbs, and supplements: www.nlm.nih.gov/medlineplus/druginformation.html

National Center for Complementary and Alternative Medicine
NCCAM, National Institutes of Health
9000 Rockville Pike
Bethesda, MD 20892
nccam.nih.gov

Stress Management

Books

Talbott, Shawn. *The Cortisol Connection: Why Stress Makes You Fat and Ruins Your Health—And What You Can Do About It, Second Edition.* Alameda, CA: Hunter House, 2007.

Luskin, Frederic, and Ken Pelletier. *Stress Free for Good: 10 Scientifically Proven Life Skills for Health and Happiness.* New York: HarperOne, 2005.

Websites

Common signs and symptoms of stress from AIS: www.stress.org/topic-effects.htm

Overview of stress from the Mayo Clinic: www.mayoclinic.com/health/stress/SR99999

Overview of stress management from Medline: www.nlm.nih.gov/medlineplus/stress.html

Toxins and Hormone Disruptors

Books

Baillie-Hamilton, Paula. *Toxic Overload: A Doctor's Plan for Combating the Illnesses Caused by Chemicals in Our Foods, Our Homes, and Our Medicine Cabinets.* New York: Penguin Group, 2005.

Rapp, Doris. *Our Toxic World: A Wake Up Call.* Annapolis, MD: Environmental Research Foundation, 2003.

Schapiro, Mark. *Exposed: The Toxic Chemistry of Everyday Products and What's at Stake for American Power.* White River Junction, VT: Chelsea Green Publishing, 2007.

Websites

Environmental Working Group
1436 U St. NW, Suite 100
Washington, DC 20009
202-667-6982
www.ewg.org

Children's Health Environmental Coalition
12300 Wilshire Blvd., Suite 320
Los Angeles, CA 90025
Phone: 310-820-2030
Fax: 310-820-2070
www.checnet.org/about_main.asp
or
healthychild.org

Index

C

toxins, 67-70
water recommendations, 66-67
disorders
  sexual dysfunctions
    arousal disorders, 217-220
    desire disorders, 214-217
    ejaculatory disorders, 223
    gender identity disorder, 227
    hypersexuality, 227
    orgasm disorders, 220-222
    pain disorders, 224-226
    paraphilias, 227
  sleep disorders, 78-79
douching, 115-116
dynamic fitness, 54
dysfunctions (sexual
  dysfunctions), 213-227
  arousal disorders, 217
    erectile dysfunction, 217-219
    FSAD (female sexual arousal
    disorder), 219-220
    PSAS (persistent sexual
    arousal syndrome), 220
  desire disorders
    aversion disorder, 216
    low libido, 214-216
    treatments, 216-217
  gender identity disorder, 227
  hypersexuality, 227
  orgasm disorders, 220-223
    absent orgasms, 221
    delayed orgasms, 221-222
    ejaculatory disorders, 223
  pain disorders
    dyspareunia, 224-225
    vaginismus, 225
    vulvar vestibulitis, 225-226
    vulvodynia, 225-226
  paraphilias, 227
dyspareunia, 224-225

E

ejaculatory disorders, 223

emotional health
  feelings and sex connection
    bad feelings, 34-40
    good feelings, 32-33
    managing negative feelings,
    40-43
    trust issues, 33-34
  mind/body connection
    attitude concerns, 138-140
    exercise and mood, 135-137
    minimizing stress, 132-135
    overview, 126-127
    physiology and thought,
    127-128
    role of optimism, 137-138
    stress response, 128-130
    training your mind, 130-132
  sexual health and, 6-7
energy, body and sexual health
  connection, 50-51
erectile dysfunction, 217-219
erotica versus pornography,
  152-153
estrogen, 59-61
exercises
  impact on mood, 135-137
    depression, 136
    walking in the sunshine,
    136-137
  maintaining sexual fitness
    abdominals, 95-96
    aerobic exercises, 85
    amount recommendations,
    89
    anaerobic exercises, 85-86
    back and lower body, 94-95
    daily exercises, 84
    including exercise in daily
    routines, 88
    Kegels, 92-93
    men versus women, 90-91
    stretching exercises, 86-88
    upper body, 93-94

tips for improving sexual
health, 72-74
aerobic, 73
balance, 74
resistance training, 73
stretching, 73-74

F

fantasy play, 152-153
fats, diet tips, 65-66
feelings (sex and feelings
connection)
bad feelings, 34-40
good feelings, 32-33
managing negative feelings,
40-43
trust issues, 33-34
female sexual arousal disorder.
See FSAD, 219-220
feminine hygiene, 114-115
fertility awareness, 198-199
fitness (sexual fitness)
annual physicals
importance of, 96-97
lab tests, 98-99
screening tests, 97-98
warning signs, 100
weight checks, 99-100
dynamic fitness, 54
exercises
abdominals, 95-96
back and lower body, 94-95
Kegels, 92-93
upper body, 93-94
feelings and sex connection
bad feelings, 34-40
good feelings, 32-33
managing negative feelings,
40-43
trust issues, 33-34
maintaining
aerobic exercises, 85
anaerobic exercises, 85-86

daily exercises, 84
exercise recommendations,
89
including exercise in daily
routines, 88
men versus women, 90-91
stretching exercises, 86-88
organic fitness, 52-54
overview, 7-11
lifestyle and, 8-9
maintaining, 9-11
stamina, 54-55
flexibility, 51-52
foods
aphrodisiacs, 21
sexy foods, 70-71
FSAD (female sexual arousal
disorder), 219-220
fungal infections
tinea, 187
yeast infections, 185-187

G

gender identity disorder, 227
gonorrhea, 176-178
good feelings
sex and feelings connection,
32-33
"good sex," defining, 19-20
grief, 37-40

H

health (sexual health)
body connection
flexibility, 51-52
hormone issues, 58-61
posture and strength, 48-50
roles of cells, 55-58
sexual energy, 50-51
improvement tips
alcohol consumption and, 81
diets, 64-72

N